T0266780

Acquiring Card Payments

Acquiring Card Payments

Ilya Dubinsky

CRC Press
Taylor & Francis Group
Boca Raton London New York

CRC Press is an imprint of the
Taylor & Francis Group, an **informa** business
AN AUERBACH BOOK

CRC Press
Taylor & Francis Group
6000 Broken Sound Parkway NW, Suite 300
Boca Raton, FL 33487-2742

© 2019 by Taylor & Francis Group, LLC
CRC Press is an imprint of Taylor & Francis Group, an Informa business

No claim to original U.S. Government works

Printed on acid-free paper

International Standard Book Number-13: 978-0-3673-4284-5 (Hardback)

Visit the Taylor & Francis Web site at
http://www.taylorandfrancis.com

and the CRC Press Web site at
http://www.crcpress.com

To my father.

Contents

Preface

At some point, I had a few card scheme manuals printed and bound. Slamming about three thousand pages on a desk in front of a newly-hired payment systems engineer seemed to leave a long-lasting impression and get them in the right mood. And those pages weren't even nearly all the documents they would have to be familiar with and skillfully navigate.

Few people who interviewed for open positions on my team had any practical experience or were taught relevant knowledge in college. Any pre-packaged trainings on the market were very narrowly focused, overly expensive and inconveniently scheduled.

And there wasn't a book, not even several books, that would cover the needed areas without nosediving into too many details way too early.

Except that now there is.

It is not meant as a replacement to any of the technical standards mentioned in it, or an alternative to up-to-date card-scheme manuals. Many details were purposefully left as an exercise to the reader who, should the job so require, would, hopefully, be able to read and comprehend in-depth information in existing technical standards after making sense of them with the help of this book.

Finally, the book is dedicated to card acquiring only, and thus only mentions any issuer-side features or standards insomuch as they are required for the sake of completeness.

Thus, for example, protocols such as EMV 3-D Secure are not covered to the last exhaustive detail. Instead, this book provides an overview, justification and logic behind each message of the protocol, leaving the task of listing all fields and their formats to the standard document itself.

The longer chapter on EMV contact transactions is more comprehensive out of necessity. In case there is no immediate need to know the minutia of the protocol, a reader can keep to the overview. However, EMV contactless cannot be properly understood without the foundation of the full EMV protocol.

I humbly hope the reader will find this book useful.

Preface

PAYMENT CARDS AND PROTOCOLS

I

1

PAYMENT CARDS AND PROTOCOLS

Chapter 1

Overview of Card Payments Industry

CONTENTS

1.1 The First Supper

Throughout the entire history of currency, the payments evolved alongside our understanding of money. As people began to realize that money is an idea, the expectations for simplicity of payment grew accordingly.

Between a business and a consumer, consumers expect their payment means to always be at their disposal, be convenient to use and safe to carry. Merchants, on the other hand, expect to have their payment guaranteed. Both would like the transaction cost to be as low as possible and would prefer to to deal with instantaneous transactions. Both would like the payment means to be fraud-safe. Government, another unseen but important player in the field, would like to track purchases to collect taxes and prevent fraud and money laundering.

Hard cash does not rank particularly high with almost all of these metrics. People run out of cash in most at the most inappropriate moment or leave their purses and wallets at home. People get pickpocketed and mugged for the cash. Coins as well as notes have been forged since times immemorial. Finally, cash-only transactions are difficult to trace and tax, and so governments tend to frown on high-volume cash deals.

In a sense, banknotes, cheques and traveller's cheques were supposed to address at least some of these challenges in search for speed and convenience of payments.

Take cheques, for instance. A cheque contains some indication of the drawee or obligor (the organization that produced it), identification of the account from which the amount is to be deduced, counterfeit measures (which, obviously, grew more sophisticated with time), and a signature to verify authenticity of the account holder.

A client paying by cheque in a store would fill out the amount, date, payee of the cheque, sign it and give it over to the merchant. Then the merchant would need to take the cheque to the payee bank and either deposit or cash it. After that, the bank would take the cheque to a clearinghouse where the drawee bank would reimburse the payee bank. If the merchant and the client were both customers of the same bank, then the bank would simply check the balance of the client account and save the clearing step.

Technological advances allowed enhancing cheques with machine-readable data that greatly simplified their processing and routing. Clearinghouses and store cashiers grew more sophisticated as well, and nowadays it is sufficient to snap a picture of the cheque with your smartphone using a bank-provided application to deposit it to your account almost instantly, keeping the actual cheque as a receipt.

Of course, cheque payments used to be much clumsier in the 1950s. However, even despite very recent technological improvements, paying by cheque requires much more time and effort than paying in cash. The cheque still needs to be properly filled and signed, cheque books are quite bulky to carry around and tend to run out of cheques—so while being a relatively convenient payment method, it was still far from addressing all of the aforementioned requirements.

A revolutionary event occured in New York in 1949. A businessman called Frank McNamara was entertaining his guests in a restaurant, and when the dinner was over, reached out to foot the bill only to discover that his wallet had been left in his other suit. He called his wife, she brought the wallet over and the bill was settled.

That could have been the end of the story if not for Mr. McNamara's entrepreneurial spirit and the fact that he was rather annoyed at the inconvenience. Presumably, he wondered why a businessman of his standing was not free to spend as much money as he could afford, having to limit his cash spending to the amount of cash currently available in his pocket.

Mr. McNamara and his lawyer, Frank Schneider, worked out a scheme: they created a club whose members, the diners, were able to sign for their suppers at restaurants and settle their bills at a later date.

In February 1950, a few months after the original incident, the two sat down in the same restaurant and became the first diners to say "charge it". The event, also known as the "First Supper", was the beginning of the card payments industry; the arrangement became Diners Club®, the world's first card scheme.

The invention took off immediately. By the end of the same year, Diners had 20,000 card members, whose number doubled in 1951, and within two years of its inception, established presence in Canada, Cuba and France. The card became so successful that it even managed to reach beyond the Iron Curtain—in 1961, Diners cards began to be accepted in Czechoslovakia (nowadays Czech Republic and Slovak Republic) and in 1969, in the Soviet Union.

Very quickly, other organizations followed both in the United States and abroad. In 1958, American Express® began issuing cards for T&E (travel and entertainment). In 1959, Bank of America made its first attempt to issue a "revolving credit" card which, in addition to serving as a charge card, also did not require pay-off of the entire bill every month. Later the card later grew to become the global brand of Visa®.

In 1961, Japan Credit Bureau and Osaka Credit Bureau were founded in Japan. In 1965, Eurocard International was established in Brussels. In 1967, the same year when France launched its first spacecraft, Cartes Bancaire, association of 6 French banks, handles its first payment transaction. In the same year in California, four banks established a competitor to Bank of America's BankAmericard program. It was called Master Charge: The Interbank Card, which in the late 1970s became MasterCard®.

Local markets grew and went global; card schemes went out of business, merged or were acquired by other players.

In Europe, Eurocard International became Europay International and in 1992 launched a joint venture with MasterCard, which was called Maestro. Ten years later, Europay was acquired by MasterCard.

In Japan, Japan Credit Bureau merged with Osaka Credit Bureau to become the dominant Japanese payment card brand.

In the United States, Sears, then the biggest national retailer, made a foray into the financial market and launched its own brand of payment cards known as Discover®. Later the oldest card scheme Diners was acquired by Discover.

Emerging markets lagged behind, but began to catch up rapidly with mature European, Asia Pacific and North American card schemes in the 21st century. In 2002, following the rapid growth of Chinese economy, China Union Pay™(later rebranded as UnionPay) was founded. It began as a Chinese domestic scheme but soon outgrew the mainland China to become a global player, becoming on par or even surpassing transactions processed through Visa and Mastercard networks in terms of volume.

In 2012, RuPay, a domestic card scheme, was launched in India.

In 2014 after imposing of Western sanctions on several Russian banks, NSPK—a domestic card scheme and a UnionPay wannabe with global ambitions—was kicked off in Russia. Perhaps, it is the only domestic card scheme that was deployed out of spite. The card scheme was later marketed under the Mir brand name.

At the turn of the 21st century, internet followed by mobile technology advances had revolutionized the retail industry. Although bigger and incumbent players were naturally less agile than new entrees to the market, the payment industry as a whole had quickly filled the void in those newly-appearing areas with such prominent players as PayPal and AliPay and a multitude of service providers, independent sales organizations, technology vendors, alternative payment means, digital and mobile wallets, marketplaces, crowdfunding platforms and even new electronic currencies (cue Bitcoin) coming into being.

Ubiquity of payment and interbank networks (the latter connecting ATMs and banks into an interoperable network transparent to consumers) had caused governments around the world to increasingly see payments as a public infrastructure. Governments around the world act to improve availability and quality of service while driving down transaction costs by enforcing standardization, simplifying licensing of new entrees and by directly regulating prices.

Major areas of card industry technology and protocols are governed by ISO/IEC standards, and big networks support interoperability to a significant degree. Security for the payment card industry is governed by the PCI Security Standards Council through various standards, and magnetic stripe formats are based on ISO/IEC. A body called EMVCo (Europay, MasterCard, Visa) has been set up to standardize the chip and contactless technology, and although it is a long time since Europay was acquired by MasterCard and Visa, MasterCard, American Express, Discover, JCB and UnionPay are among the actual members of the body, the US trademark of EMV is reserved for their Integrated Circuit Card (ICC) technology.

1.2   Industry Actors

The industry keeps evolving with the times, with veterans adjusting to new trends and new and sometimes disruptive players entering the game. This ecosystem might be perplexing as certain terms are sometimes used interchangingly or mean slightly different things depending on the context. Therefore, it is important to understand who is participating in the industry, what roles and functions are critical to facilitate payments and how they are distributed between various actors.

The two framing actors of the market are customers and businesses. In a typical transaction, a customer (also referred to as *cardholder* or *card member*) pays money in exchange for goods or services provided by a business (a *merchant*) or is refunded by the business in case of cancellation, mistake or dispute. Certainly, a business can be a cardholder—it can hold a corporate card and use it for corporate procurement. Similarly, a merchant can actually be a municipal or a government entity. Finally, a merchant can be a physical person, subject to local fiscal regulation and legal framework of their jurisdiction. However, regardless of whether it is a legal or a physical entity, there is a *payer* and a *payee* and the goal of the entire industry is to facilitate the payment.

It can be done either by using a payment card or by utilizing alternative payment means—such as a digital wallet, a variety of mobile solutions or a cryptocurrency.

Payment cards and networks which are linked to them, including but not limited to technical infrastructure, membership governance, risk and compliance management, brand rules, insurance and remittance guarantees are called *card schemes*. Examples of card schemes include Visa, MasterCard, American Express, Discover, Diners, JCB, UnionPay. A card scheme can be managed by a consortium of banks, by a for-profit company (such as Visa Inc. or Master-Card), or by a government-owned company (such as NSPK). A single company might own multiple card schemes—for example, Discover is also the owner of Diners Club card scheme—or several companies might control a card scheme—as in case of Maestro when it was jointly managed by Europay and Master-Card.

Depending on the card scheme specifics, additional institutions may participate in the payment cycles. An entity that issues cards for its customers is called the *issuer* (sometimes, imprecisely, the *issuer bank*), while an entity that services merchants and facilitates acceptance of cards is the *acquirer* (or, likewise, the *acquirer bank*).

The issuer institution manages relationships with cardholders. It issues cards according to card scheme brand guidelines, tracks cardholder balance or allowed credit (open-to-pay amount) and pays out transactions that are presented to it by acquirers. It also manages card fraud risks, provides credit to its consumers, collects card bill payments and manages disputes of fraudulent or invalid transactions on behalf of the cardholder.

The acquirer institution is responsible for relationships with merchants. Some acquirers provide merchants with terminals for acceptance of cards (a common practice in Russia, Israel and some other markets) while others delegate this function to other market participants or let the merchants bring their own devices (as it is done in United States, Japan or Europe). The acquirer is responsible to process transactions according to card scheme guidelines, presenting authorized transactions to issuers for clearing, remitting the funds to merchants and managing disputes on behalf of the merchant.

The issuer and acquirer roles can be borne by the same entity, which is, in fact, quite common.

Both issuer and acquirer may or may not also operate as a retail or a commercial bank, servicing the respective party. For instance, an issuer that is a retail bank can maintain the checking account of the card holder, deducting outstanding card payments from it directly or validating the open-to-pay amount versus

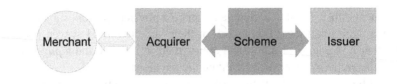

Figure 1.1: Skeleton ecosystem of four-party card scheme

account balance, while an issuer that is not a retail bank requires deposits and issues bills to the cardholder. Similarly, an acquirer that is also a commercial bank directly credits accounts of its merchants as opposed to issuing wire transfers through a correspondent bank.

The skeleton ecosystem (see figure 1.1) of merchant, card scheme (issuer/acquirer) and cardholder is complemented with providers of additional services.

A typical merchant would like to accept as a large a variety of card brands as possible and commercially feasible, to provide its customers with the widest choice of payment means possible. However, that would require very high technical skills on behalf of the merchant. In addition to necessary integration and certification processes, the merchant is supposed keep their systems up to date and properly secure. The task is quite hard for a large retail chain, while for a small shop it is unrealistic and impossible.

Parties that bridge this gap are called *Payment Services Providers* or *PSPs*. PSPs provide a uniform interface to all supported card schemes and manage relationships and technical connections with card schemes and acquirer banks. Many PSPs provide value-added services, such as additional risk management abilities or alternative payment methods. A PSP that also onboards merchants on behalf of the acquirer and disburses funds to them is a *Payment Facilitator* (PF) or *Merchant Aggregator*. The niché occupied by PSPs or PFs is shown in figure 1.2.

Similarly to any business process or technology, a large market including software and hardware vendors, processing systems and business processes outsourcing has developed in the field. Almost any function of the payments industry can be performed by the in-house team, or using an on-premises system of the institution, or by outsourcing and relying on specialized services providers.

An acquirer, issuer or PSP can outsource their processing to a third-party processor, focusing on business processes instead. Acquirers and PSPs can employ services of an *agent* or an *ISO* (which in this context stands for Independent Sales Organization) to find and onboard new customers.

A payment facilitator that also provides a unified marketplace for very small submerchants is, in turn, frequently referred to as a *marketplace*.

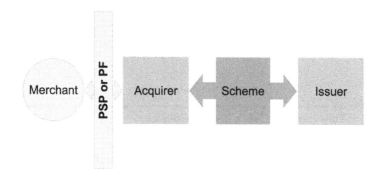

Figure 1.2: PSP/PF niche in the ecosystem

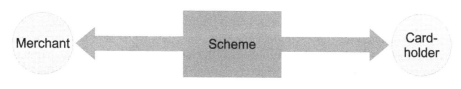

Figure 1.3: Three-party (or "closed") scheme model

1.3 Three-party and Four-party Schemes

There are two major types of card schemes, **closed** and **open** (or *three-party scheme* and *four-party scheme*) ones.

In a three-party model (see figure 1.3, the card scheme itself acquires transactions and is responsible for financial settlement with merchants, as well as issues cards and bills the cardholders.

A three-party model allows the card scheme to retain the fullest degree of control over customer experience. The roll-out of changes as well as new products and solutions is also somewhat simpler due to the lesser numbers of parties involved. Also, there is no in-brand competition: the scheme controls the experience and only competes with other schemes. In fact, the three-party model is a mixed blessing as, on the one hand, it allows for a better governance and, on the other, opportunities for growth and innovation are sometimes overlooked.

Expansion into new markets such as new geographical areas requires establishing strong local presence, which is not always economically feasible or possible for a three-party scheme. Hence, three-party card schemes frequently rely on franchises and partnerships to maintain global presence. Such schemes include, for example, American Express, Diners Club or Discover.

In a four-party model (see figure 1.4), the card scheme acts both as a rule setter and a facilitator, but delegates the issuing and the acquiring to other institutions.

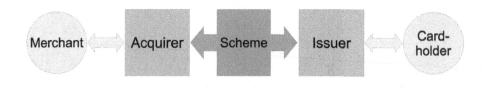

Figure 1.4: Four-party (or "open") scheme model

Although the four-party or "open" card scheme model provides card schemes with less control over the customer experience and requires additional effort to coordinate the roll-out of services across all participant institutions, it allows for a much faster growth of the customer base, since makes it possible to partner with local incumbents rather than expand card-scheme-owned presence.

Examples of four-party schemes are Visa, MasterCard and UnionPay.

With franchises representing three-party schemes while also serving as acquirers and issuers of four-party schemes, the landscape of card scheme partners and participants may be somewhat confusing. However, another key difference between three-party and four-party schemes is the lack or presence of the *interchange fees* as primary means for mutual fee settlement of acquiring and issuing entities.

1.4   Payment Online and at the Store

Payment card processing can be divided into a smaller obvious part and a much larger behind-the-scenes part.

A cardholder begins the payment process initiating the purchase. The card may or may not be physically present at the point of sale; furthermore, the point of sale itself can be a fully virtual shop. The cardholder may or may not use their card number as sometimes the merchant can keep the card on file. The cardholder may verify their identity by entering a personal identification number (the PIN), or by entering several passwords, fixed and/or generated for the purpose of this particular transaction, or may tap their card at a transit terminal without any identity verification. All of these conditions and methods are valid and are described further in more details. However, regardless of these specifics, there are several major steps which are common for all payment transactions.

To illustrate both the commonalities and the differences of payment flows, consider the side-by-side description of transaction steps in card-present, (i.e., physical store and physical card environment) and card-not-present (i.e. online) scenarios, as shown in Table 1.1.

For now, it is assumed that the terminal or the online e-commerce shop is connected directly to a payment network. Additional intermediaries that are typically present in the real world do not affect the payment logic.

Table 1.1: Major steps of a payment

Card-present scenario	Card-not-present scenario
An EMV chip online PIN transaction in a retail store.	A 3D Secure transaction in an online e-commerce shop.
Step 1. Card account identification.	
Cardholder inserts the card into a chip-reading device. The integrated chip on the card interacts with the terminal and communicates the account number or numbers linked to the card and other related details.	Cardholder types in the card number and other additional identification fields into an online form on the e-commerce website.
Step 2. Card verification.	
A cryptographically protected exchange occurs between the terminal and the card. If either the card or the terminal has failed the verification, the transaction is cancelled. The chip produces values which are captured by the terminal to be used to verify authenticity of the card by the payment network or the issuer.	The cardholder enters an additional security value (CVV2 or CVC2) that is captured by the e-commerce software to be later used to verify authenticity of the card by the payment network or the issuer.
Step 3. Cardholder verification.	
Upon negotiating with the terminal, the card requests PIN to be entered. The PIN is encrypted by the terminal and to be later used to verify cardholder identity by the payment network or the issuer.	The e-commerce software plug-in redirects the cardholder to their issuer's page. The issuer confirms cardholder identity using a static password or, more commonly, with a one-time password that is texted to the cardholder's phone. Once the identity is confirmed, the issuer generates cryptographic evidence to be later used to confirm the transaction once it is submitted to the network.

Step 4. Request message.	
The card generates a cryptographic signature for details of the transaction, including amount, currency, date/time and other fields. The terminal generates a payment message, incorporating business environment details (terminal ID, date and time), transaction details (amount, currency), encrypted PIN and the chip data. Then the payment message is forwarded to the payment network.	The e-commerce software generates a payment message, incorporating business environment details (terminal ID, website details), transaction details (amount, currency), issuer authentication result and card security number. Then the payment message is forwarded to the payment network.
Step 5. Response.	
The network relays the request to the issuer or handles it on the issuer's behalf. Chip-generated cryptogram and the PIN code are validated, and a decision to approve or decline the transaction is made. The result is sent back to the merchant point of sale and is displayed on the terminal.	The network relays the request to the issuer or handles it on the issuer's behalf. The cryptographic evidence and the card check value are validated and a decision to approve or decline the transaction is made. The result is sent back to the e-commerce shop and is displayed to the cardholder.

Chapter 2

Payment Flow and Basics of Technology

CONTENTS

2.1 Card Shape

The physical characteristics of a plastic payment card are governed by a family of standards, including ISO/IEC 7813, 7816 and 14443 as the most prominent ones. Additional standards are referred to by these key standards, as required.

The ISO 7813 standard defines the card size and shape and the magnetic stripe location (if the card has it). The ISO 7816 standard defines the physical characteristics of a smart card—a card with an integrated circuit chip embedded into it. Finally, contactless cards (cards with an embedded antenna in addition to the chip) are governed by the ISO 14443 standard. Consider the card image given

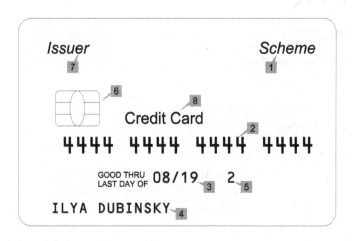

Figure 2.1: Annotated credit card image

in figure 2.1. On the front side of the card, one can see the following elements:

1. *Card scheme branding* Card schemes prescribe the logo location and size of their logo as well as the other aspects of the card design.

2. *PAN* or the card number. PAN stands for the Primary Account Number and its format will be discussed shortly. The embossment of the characters is defined in ISO/IEC 7811 international standard. The PAN is also encoded on the magnetic stripe and on the chip, if present.

3. *Card expiry date.* The format is typically two digits of a month over two digits of a year. It is also encoded both on the mag stripe and the chip.

4. *Cardholder name.* The name is limited to 26 characters. It is human-readable on the card itself and is also contained on it in machine-readable format.

5. *Card sequence number* or *CSN*. If an account by a particular issuer is extended beyond the original expiry date, the issuer can decide on not changing the original PAN number. In order to distinguish between the old and new cards which share the same PAN number but have different expiry dates and other security characteristics, the card sequence number is increased by one on each card renewal.

6. *Integrated chip*, sometimes also referred to as the EMV™ chip.

7. *Issuer logo* which indicates the bank that issued the card. Information on the issuer is also part of the PAN.

8. *Card product.* Within the brand, there are multiple types of card products with varying terms of settlement, fees and available balances. The indication of the card product is visible on the card. Besides card branding rules, there are also regulatory requirements for display of card type (for instance, EU regulation 2015/751).

With certain card schemes, such as, for instance, American Express, the card front side contains an additional functional element (not shown in figure 2.1). In the specific case of AmEx, it is called the *CID* or *4DBC* and is a variation of CVV code (see section 2.5).

Before the introduction of EMV™ technology, card schemes relied on a hologram that was embedded into the plastic. As it was not easy to be forged, verifying a valid hologram was a requirement for POS attendants as an additional way to confirm card authenticity.

2.2 Card Number (PAN)

The PAN or the primary account number can consist of between 13 to 19 decimal digits. It uniquely identifies the card account and the cardholder with the issuing institution. Obviously, multiplicity of institutions and card schemes required standardization and a degree of centralized allocation of numbers or number ranges. Hence, the PANs are governed by ISO/IEC 7812 standard and have a well-defined structure, as can be seen in figure 2.2. The card number consists of

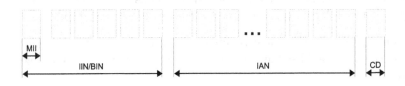

Figure 2.2: PAN structure

the following major parts: *IIN/BIN*, *IAN* and the check digit (marked as CD in figure 2.2.

The check digit is there to ensure that there is no typo or mistake in the account number. It is a simple parity checksum, calculated using the *Luhn algorithm* (see section 10.1 for details).

The BIN is an important component of the PAN. Its first digit is called MII or Major Industry Identifier which identifies, at a very high level, the industry of the card issuer. Some of the MIIs are shown in table 2.1.

It is not advisable to rely solely on the MII to determine card scheme and brand since some MIIs are shared by multiple card schemes. Also, ranges of

Table 2.1: Major industry indentifiers

MII	Description	Notes
2	Airlines, financial and other future industry assignments	MasterCard began utilizing this MII for its BIN ranges. Parts of the range are used by Diners.
3	Travel and entertainment	This MII is used by Diners, American Express and JCB.
4	Banking and financial	This MII is used by Visa
5	Banking and financial	This MII is used by MasterCard and Diners.
6	Merchandising and banking/ financial	This MII is used by MasterCard for Maestro cards as well as by Discover and UnionPay.

IIN numbers are known to have change hands due to the string of mergers and acquisitions in the industry.

In order to understand the role of the card BIN better, let us consider the matter of an electronically captured transaction. A standard web-based UI prompts a consumer for little more than the card number, only sometimes asking to specify the card brand as well.

Having a PAN in hand, the software of the PSP that services an online store is to decide whether it is a supported card brand, apply relevant processing rules based on that card brand (for example, purchase amount or currency can be limited with a particular card) and then route the transaction to the proper card scheme network connection. In some cases it is also important to identify the card type to process the transactions properly (more on card types below).

To facilitate proper routing and handling of various card types, card schemes distribute BIN table information to their member institutions and affiliates[1].

The BIN tables contain definitions of some or all of the following:

■ beginning and end of a PAN range (may cover an entire BIN or be its subrange)

■ card brand

■ full length of the PAN (13 to 19, with 16 being the most common one)

■ issuer member ID (may or may not be identical to the BIN depending on card scheme and institution structure)

■ card type and product indicators (more on card types below)

Typically, three-party schemes do not provide elaborate BIN tables since the technical effort that is required to generate and distribute accurate and up-to-date data is not worth the benefit for it's consumers—the scheme controls routing and business rules around different card products.

With four-party schemes, however, the tables are provided to eligible members routinely in form of full and incremental updates and in great detail and as part of routine file exchange operations.

2.3   Card Types and Products

Cards are divided into several major classes. First and foremost, there is a division between *consumer cards* and *corporate cards*, the former are issued to a person while the latter are issued to companies.

Cards also differ depending on *usage* or pattern of reconciliation with cardholders. The card usage types include *charge cards* (also known as *delayed debit*

---

[1]Free public database of BIN table entries is available at http://www.binlist.net/

cards), *credit cards*, *debit cards* and *prepaid cards* (sometimes also called *stored-value cards*).

Charge cards, the earliest type of payment card, allow the cardholder to make purchases paid for by the issuer, and the cardholder became indebted to the issuer. The cardholder must settle the outstanding debt in full by the end of the agreed period (for example, by the end of a calendar month). This type of card is also sometimes called "delayed debit" card.

Credit cards are the type of cards when, similar to charge cards, the issuer pays for the purchase and the cardholder becomes indebted to the issuer. However, unlike default behavior of the charge card, as far as credit cards are concerned, the cardholder can settle a portion of the outstanding amount with the issuer, maintaining revolving credit with it (and perhaps accruing a huge debt in process).

Despite the formal distinction between these two types of cards, the lines are somewhat blurred in practice. It is, of course, possible (and sometimes advisable) to always pay the outstanding credit card debt in full. On the other hand, many charge card issuers enable their cardholders to pay for a purchase in installments, capping the monthly charge and offering additional credit products.

With *debit cards*, the cardholder either deposits the amount with the issuer or allows direct access to cardholder's checking account at a bank. Rather than paying with issuer's money and then settling with the issuer, the cardholder is only allowed to make purchases based on their balance of the deposit or checking account. The funds are deducted from the account immediately rather than by end of a funding cycle.

Prepaid or stored-value cards are similar to debit cards in the sense of the open-to-buy amount limited by the balance associated with the card account. The differences between prepaid and debit cards vary between markets—in markets where a debit card is typically linked to a checking account, a prepaid card stands out by having a dedicated account of its own maintained by the issuer. Prepaid cards are also often sold and used anonymously or used as means to shop online while retaining a certain degree of financial control.

All possible combinations of credit/debit and corporate/consumer card types were in existence at some point. Consumer credit cards and consumer debit cards as well as corporate credit and debit cards are certainly among them.

However, simply classifying a card as a "consumer credit card" is not enough to describe various options and conditions that issuers package and market to their customers since a much greater variety of detailed terms and conditions exist. For example, issuers often market cards for premium and VIP segments or offer special conditions for college students. Such offerings vary between markets and issuers but conform to global brand marketing guidelines. These definitions of individual issuer terms and conditions sets, conforming to card scheme rules, are called *card products*.

Four-party card schemes usually publish card product information alongside BIN ranges and subranges. Hence, a BIN table can contain multiple entries that belong to the same BIN or the same institution but with different product identifiers. Visa product codes typically have one or rarely two capital Latin characters, while MasterCard product codes consist of three capital Latin letters.

However, it is important to note that these values only indicate the card product which was chosen for this particular account when it was first created. In many countries issuers support a feature called *account-level management* allowing promotion of an account to a different product (usually to a premium-class product that corresponds to the basis product) based on one's monthly or annual spending. In other words, in the case of some issuers an account with a PAN that belongs to a range of basic cards can actually be a different card product altogether.

2.4   The Magnetic Stripe

The back side of a credit card typically contains three major functional areas: signature strip, magnetic stripe and a card security code (CSC). However, perhaps except for the signature strip, both the magnetic stripe and the CSC value can in some cases be found on the front side of the card.

The *signature strip* is an area that is supposed to be filled by hand. For transactions requiring the cardholder's signature, the card is not considered valid until it is signed by them. In this case, an attendant processing the payment is supposed to compare the signature on the sales draft with the one provided on the signature strip, flagging the transaction as suspicious or even cancelling it if circumstances so require. Like many other solutions that depend on method and procedure, this one grew unreliable once card payments really scaled.

The *card security code* value is usually found at the back side of the card, except some cases where two separate codes are displayed on the front and back side of the card.

The *magnetic stripe* (often abbreviated as *magstripe*) is a band of magnetic material containing iron-based particles capable of storing data. The data is read when the card is swiped i.e. when the magnetic stripe is read by a magnetic head. Physical-level details of the data-storing method are descibed in the ISO/IEC 7811 standard.

The original magnetic stripe card relied on a method pioneered by Forrest Parry, an IBM engineer back in 1960s, who attached the magnetic stripe to plastic using a heating process. As the story goes, Parry came back home from a very frustrating day at the office where he had made numerous attempts to reliably glue a magnetic stripe to a plastic card and failed to do that. In the end, he sought counsel from his wife, Dorothea Parry, who was ironing clothes at that moment, and tried the thermal method to affix a magnetic stripe to plastic. Her husband found the method effective and successful. That contributed greatly to the proliferation of magnetic stripes as the main method for storing and retrieving card data.

Although currently the standard is universal, parallel development of card processing technology in Japan has led to creation of a similar but competing standard of JIS-U (with ISO-compatible magstripe referred to as JIS-T). Besides differences in the logical structure of data that is stored on a JIS-U magnetic stripe, it is located on the front rather than on the back side of a payment card. To comply with global branding standards and preserve technical compatibility with existing card-reading devices, Japanese issuers produce cards containing an invisible magnetic stripe on the front side and a visible one on the back side. Japanese magnetic stripe readers, in turn, are equipped with dual magnetic reading heads allowing them to read magnetic stripe data both of ISO and JIS-U cards successfully.

The ISO magstripe has three tracks called *Track 1*, *Track 2* and *Track 3*. Formats of Track 1 and Track 2 are described in ISO/IEC 7813, while Track 3 is detailed in ISO/IEC 4909. Alphanumeric data on the magnetic stripe is encoded using ANSI/ISO ALPHA Data Format, while numeric data on the magnetic stripe is encoded using ANSI/ISO BCD Data Format.

While Track 1 and Track 2 tracks are read-only, the Track 3 data can be updated by a terminal. It is worth noting that Track 3 abilities have been unused by the issuers, especially since the introduction of integrated chip circuits and the related EMV standards-based technology.

Tracks 1 and 2 contain data regarding the PAN, its expiration date, the cardholder and the so-called *discretionary data*, which differ between issuers but can contain largely same types of discretional values encoded at varying offsets. The discretionary data typically contains a cryptographic signature of some track fields which is sent to the payment network and is usually validated by the issuer. This signature is called *CVV* or *CVC* and serves as means to validate card authenticity by relying on an open algorithm with a secret key known only to issuer.

2.4.1 Track 1

Maximum length of Track 1 is 79 alphanumeric characters. Its structure, if read verbatim from the magnetic stripe, is as follows:

SS—start sentinel. Always contains the % character.

FC—format code. In case of a standard international payment card, contains the B character.

PAN—primary account number, up to 19 digits length.

FS—field separator. Always contains the ^ character.

NM—cardholder name. It contains between 2 and 26 characters, including separating / (slash) character between first name and surname, as appropriate.

In case the cardholder name is not applicable, two blanks separated by a / character are populated in the field.

FS—field separator. Always contains the ˆ character.

ED—expiry date. Two digits of the year followed by two digits of the month of the card expiry date.

SC—service code. Possible values of the service code are described below (see 2.4.4).

DD—discretionary data. It can contain one or more of the following details:

> **PVKI**—*PIN verification key indicator.*
>
> **PVV**—*PIN verification value.* Computation and validation of the value is described below (see section 2.8.3).
>
> **CVV/CVC**—*card verification value* or card verification code. Computation and validation of the value is described in section 2.5.

ES—end sentinel. Always contains the % character.

LRC—*longitudinal redundancy check*, the checksum to confirm validity of magstripe read (also see section 10.2).

2.4.2 Track 2

Maximum length of Track 2 is 40 characters. Except for the sentinels and the field separators and unlike Track 1, all data contained in Track 2 is numeric only. The structure of track 2 is as follows:

SS—start sentinel. Always contains the ; character.

PAN—primary account number, up to 19 digits length.

FS—field separator. Always contains the = character.

ED—expiry date. Two digits of the year followed by two digits of the month of the card expiry date.

SC—service code. Same value as the SC element of Track 1 (section 2.4.1) and described in details in section 2.4.4.

DD—discretionary data. The data follows the same rules as DD field in Track 1 does, containing one or more subelements of PVKI, PVV, CVV and other values at issuer's discretion. However, the field is not identical to the same element in Track 1 due to length limitations (Track 2 is shorter).

ES—end sentinel. Always contains the ? character

LRC—longitudinal redundancy check value. See also section 10.2.

2.4.3 Track 3

Maximum length of Track 3 is 107 characters. Except for the sentinels and the field separators, all data in Track 2 is numeric only. Track 3 was originally designed to be overwritten and it contains parameters that control cardholder's spending within a period of time. However, and especially since the introduction of integrated chip circuits, this ability had fallen out of use and currently is not utilized by all major card schemes. Certain cards even contain narrower magnetic tape strip and have no physical room for Track 3.

However, for the sake of completeness, here are the contents of Track 3:

SS—start sentinel—contains the ; character.

FC—format code, consists of two digits.

PAN—primary account number, up to 19 digits.

FS—field separator, contains the = character. In case an optional field is omitted after the first occurrence of FS, the FS character should appear in its stead.

Additional data of Track 3 includes the following fields—refer to ISO/IEC 4909 for details.

Country code (optional)—3 characters.

Currency code—3 characters.

Currency exponent—1 character. As a rule, amounts are always transmitted as integers with a predefined exponent. The currency exponent usually means the number of times the amount should be *divided* by 10 to receive the major currency unit (thus an amount of 123 euros and exponent of 2 means €1.23). However, with Track 3 the logic is reversed—the exponent denotes the number of times the amount should be *multiplied* by 10 and with the above values, corresponds to €12,300.

Amount authorized per cycle.

Amount remaining this cycle—this value is supposed to be dynamically updated with each transaction, alongside with cycle begin date. The idea behind these fields is to track the account spending without the need to query issuer.

Cycle begin (validity date)—4 characters.

Cycle length—2 characters.

Retry count—1 character.

PIN control parameters (optional)—6 characters.

Interchange controls—1 character.

PAN service restrictions—2 characters.

SAN-1 service restrictions—2 characters.

SAN-2 service restrictions—2 characters. *SAN* stands for "Subsidiary account number" and is tied to the first and second subsidiary account numbers below. In theory the mechanism allows linking up to two additional subsidiary accounts to the PAN and, in case when the primary account balance is insufficient to perform a transaction, to debit the subsidiary account instead or in addition to the primary one.

Expiration date (optional)—4 characters.

Card sequence number—1 character.

Card security number (optional)—9 characters

First subsidiary account number (optional).

Second subsidiary account number (optional).

Relay marker—indicates whether data can be stripped from Track 3 in transit

CCD or cryptographic check digits (optional)—6 characters.

Discretionary data —same as in Track 2.

ES—end sentinel. Contains the ? character.

LRC—longitudinal redundancy check value. See also 10.2.

As well as in the case of Track 1 and Track 2 data, the CCD field contains a cryptographic signature. However, since Track 3 is designed to be overwritten at the terminal, protecting it cryptographically required the exchange of cryptographic material between acquirers and the issuer. That significantly limited interoperability of cards that can possibly utilize this feature and, consequently, restrained its uptake.

2.4.4 Service Code

The service code defines geography, specifics of the authorization process and the range of services that should be allowed with the card at ATMs and point-of-sale terminals reading the magnetic stripe.

Each digit of the service code has a different meaning (see figure 2.3).

The first digit specifies the permitted type of interchange—international, national or limited to bilateral agreements between institutions. In addition, the first digit specifies whether the ICC should be used if available. Some valid values of the first digit are given in table 2.2.

Figure 2.3: Service code structure

In the context of the permitted service codes, limitation of processing to a bilateral agreement means that a terminal is not expected to handle this particular card unless explicitly programmed to do so following a special agreement between the acquirer and the issuer.

The second digit specifies the authorization mode for the card. Some possible values for the second digit of the legacy mag-stripe service code are shown in table 2.3.

This service code value was supplanted by chip-based EMV technology, where the integrated chip and the terminal engage in a dialogue and rely on a set of elaborate rules to determine the authorization mode.

The third digit limits the range of services that is available to the card and the cardholder, including the cardholder verification method (see also section 2.7). Some possible values for the digit are listed in table 2.4.

As with the authorization mode, EMV technology provided a more flexible and elaborate technique replacing the range of services and cardholder verification method digit of the service code.

Some common values of service codes include 101 (no restrictions, international transactions are allowed), 201 (prefer chip, international transactions are allowed, no further restrictions), 106 (prefer PIN if feasible, international

Table 2.2: First digit of the service code

Value	Description
1	International interchange is allowed
2	International interchange is allowed, use of IC chip is required when feasible. If an attendant or the cardholder swipes a chip-enabled card through the magnetic stripe reader of a chip-capable terminal, the terminal prompts to use the chip reader instead.
5	National interchange only—international interchange is not allowed, but exception is made for bilateral agreements.
6	Same as above, but use of IC chip is required when feasible.
7	Bilateral agreement only.

Table 2.3: Second digit of the service code

Value	Description
1	All types of authorizations allowed
2	Online authorizations only—transactions must be authorized by contacting the issuer
7	Online authorizations except when governed by a bilateral agreement

Table 2.4: Third digit of the service code

Value	Description
0	No restrictions, PIN validation is mandatory
1	No restrictions whatsoever
2	Goods and services only, cash not allowed
3	ATM only, PIN required
4	Cash only
5	Goods and services only, cash not allowed, PIN required
6	No restrictions, prefer to use PIN
7	Goods and services only, prefer to use PIN

transactions are allowed) and 206 (prefer PIN if feasible, international transactions are allowed, prefer integrated chip if feasible). For debit cards, value of 226 (prefer chip, prefer PIN, always authorize online) is also quite common. A chip-containing card's first digit of the service code would typically be 2, directing the terminal to prefer chip if a supporting reader is available.

2.5 Card Verification Values

Let us consider a fraud scenario when a criminal steals the card number and account expiry date and produces a counterfeit card. This can be done, for instance, by intercepting a mail order or by copying the details from a card sales draft. The details could later be used to shop by mail or telephone order or to create a new magnetic stripe card and use it in physical stores.

Alternatively, a fraudster could replicate an actual card and modify its service code, which, in the world of magnetic stripes (i.e., without integrated chip circuits) could cause devices not to validate the transactions online or not require a PIN code. To prevent this type of attack, a cryptographic method for card integrity protection has been devised. A special check value, known as the Card Security Code (CSC), Card Identification Number (CID), Card Validation Code (CVC), Card Verification Value (CVV) or Card Validation Number (CVN), is calculated by the issuer and is stored on the magnetic stripe, printed on the card, stored on the integrated circuit chip or calculated dynamically per each transaction. For the sake of simplicity, we are to refer to it as CVV from now on.

There are four types of CVV values:

CVV (or CVV1)—stored on magnetic stripe and used to validate its authenticity.

CVV2—printed on the card and used to validate card authenticity in card-not-present transactions (mail order, telephone order, electronic commerce).

iCVV—stored on the ICC. Although EMV technology provides a much more reliable way to validate card authenticity, the method was devised to simplify transition and allow for interoperability with systems that do not yet support transmission and handling of chip data.

dCVV—the dynamic CVV is calculated by the integrated chip based on card transaction counter and an external unpredictable number. This value is used to secure contactless magstripe transactions.

2.5.1   CVV Calculation Algorithm

The CVV is a one-way hash function of certain data elements. Except for the dynamic CVV, all of the aforementioned types of card verification values are calculated using similar principles, but utilizing a different set of original data.

The dynamic CVV relies on unique derived keys and hard-to-predict data that changes with every transaction. All other CVV types rely on a CVK (Card Verification Key) that is kept as a guarded secret by the issuer.

The algorithm has three steps:

1. Data vector preparation

2. Data vector 3-DES-based encryption

3. Decimalization of the result

The data vector typically contains PAN, expiry date and the service code. To pack the data, the last 16 digits of the PAN are used. If the PAN length is less than 16 digits, it is padded with zeroes from the left. Then, the expiry date is concatenated with the PAN, the service code and the overall result is padded with zeroes to the total length of 128 bits, while all of the above values are numeric only and are packed into nibbles as hexadecimal digits.

Thus, for example, the PAN number of 90123456789012 (14 digits long), expiry date of October 2018 and service code of 101 will be translated into two 64-bit blocks, as shown in figure 2.4

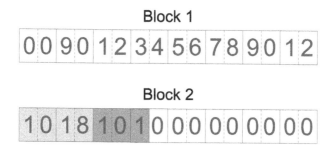

Figure 2.4: CVV calculation block 1 and 2

The CVK or Card Verification Key, being a 3-DES key, consists of two 64-bit parts, K_A and K_B. The following steps are then performed with Block 1 (further denoted as B_1) and Block 2 (B_2):

1. B_1 is encrypted using K_A to obtain the intermediary value R_1.

2. The result of step 1, R_1, is XOR-ed with B_2 to obtain an intermediary value R_2.

3. The value of R_2 is then encrypted using 3-DES encryption (see section 12.2) with K_A and K_B, meaning that the value of R_2 is sequentially:

   (a) encrypted with K_A

   (b) decrypted with K_B

   (c) encrypted with K_A

For the sake of the example, let K_A be 0123456789ABCDEF and K_B FEDCBA9876543210. Then, R_1 would be CECFBC9F0529CAB5. After XOR-ing it with B_2, the intermediary value R_2 is DED7AC8F0529CAB5. Finally, after encrypting it with 3-DES encryption, the outcome is 37BAE5346B2D2C52.

For step 1 of the algorithm, some schemes may rely on 3-DES encryption of the data instead of a single-DES encryption. This aligns algorithm to a standard CBC computation of HMAC with initialization vector set to 0 (see also section 12.4).

The result is a 64-bit vector that contains a binary value which at this stage should be decimalized. The algorithm for decimalization is as follows:

1. All decimal digits, left to right, are extracted from the value.

2. All remaining hexadecimal digits are taken modulo 10 and appended to the value from step 1.

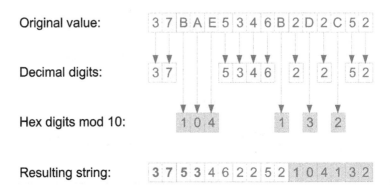

Figure 2.5: CVV decimalization

3. Necessary number of decimal places (3 or 4) is then taken from the result to obtain the necessary CVV.

An example of decimalization can be found in figure 2.5. The result of the calculation would be 3,753.

By repeating the calculation, the issuer is able to verify the authenticity of the submitted card data, depending on the transaction processing scenario and transaction conditions. Obviously, compromise of the CVK renders the entire mechanism unreliable. Due to the sensitivity of Card Verification Keys, they are typically stored in HSMs (hardware security modules), to which the function of CVV validation is also delegated.

As card schemes provide services for stand-in processing, handling incoming authorization requests on behalf of the issuer in certain cases, the CVK and PVK values, alongside their specific locations in the discretionary data part of magnetic tracks, are either shared with card schemes or provided by card schemes. In the former case, the keys are generated by the issuer, and in the latter they are generated and securely delivered by the card scheme.

2.5.2 CVV1

The CVV1 value is stored as part of discretionary data on Track 1 or Track 2 of the magnetic stripe. The purpose of CVV1 is ensuring the card authenticity and preventing fraud cases when fraudsters might obtain the PAN and expiry date and use them to create a duplicate magnetic stripe card.

In addition, the presence of the CVV1 value makes it impossible to bypass limitations imposed by the issuer in the service code. Consider the scenario when a certain card is prohibited for international use and always requires online validation by the issuer and a PIN check, carrying the service code value of 520.

In some cases, setting the value to 101 might allow using the card after crossing a country border and at a terminal that does not authorize the transaction online immediately. However, the value is also signed by CVV1, rendering this bypass impossible as well.

The length and location of the CVV value as part of discretionary data that is stored on Track 1 and 2 is usually prescribed by the card scheme. Due to high sensitivity of the field, neither the CVV1 vlaue nor the entire value of Track 1 and 2 should be stored by any entity involved in the transaction according to PCI DSS standards (see section 8.1 (PCI DSS)).

2.5.3 CVV2

The CVV2 value is used to validate card authenticity in card-not-present trans-actions, such as telephony orders or electronic commerce. The cardholder is re-quired to enter the value or spell it to the phone representative to prove that the actual card is in his possession. The value is typically printed on the back side of the card and contains three digits. However, on American Express cards an additional CVV2 value (4DBC) has 4 digits and is located on the front side of the card.

The algorithm used to calculate the value is identical to that of CVV1. How-ever, service code limitations are useless and do not apply to card-not-present transactions, and, therefore, a value of three zeroes (000) is used in its stead.

The issuer can choose to use a separate set of CVKs for CVV1 and CVV2, or rely on the same set of keys for both values.

2.5.4 iCVV

A full-grade EMV implementation, when the terminal, the acquirer system, the network and the issuer all support necessary EMV fields relies on methods far more sophisticated and stronger than CVV for card authentication. However, since the introduction of the EMV technology to various markets requires a tran-sitional period, certain provisions have been made to support part-grade EMV, i.e., in particular scenarios when the terminal and the integrated chip on the card engage in an EMV dialogue, but the terminal then relies on its legacy protocol to transmit card data to the acquirer host.

In this case, the payment message contains magnetic stripe data only. The data is stored on the integrated chip and returned to the terminal by the chip. That raises a concern that the Track 2 data can be skimmed from the chip and used to create a magstripe-only card with identical magnetic track contents.

To counter the aforementioned type of fraud, the chip stores a static CVV value that differs from CVV1 and CVV2. The value is called iCVV and is calcu-lated using exactly the same algorithm only with service code set to 999. Having a separate verification value for chip cards in a part-grade environment provides the issuer with an additional distinction between cases when the card is read by the chip reader (and, therefore, the discretionary data contains its iCVV) and when the card is read by the magstripe reader (with CVV1 value embedded in the discretionary data).

The issuer can opt to calculate the iCVV properly according to the verification algorithm, or simply place an invalid CVV value that, if used as part of a skimmed magnetic stripe card, causes the existing validation mechanism to fail.

2.5.5 Dynamic CVV

In the Contactless EMV environment, many card schemes support a so-called "Magstripe" mode for part-grade environments to rip some benefits of the advanced technology while relying on legacy infrastructure. In some implementations (see chapter 6 for details) the POS subroutine (a Kernel) is capable of operating in a special dedicated mode when either using a dedicated set of commands (see section 5.3.2.2 for description of commands) or by relying on additional data elements, the Kernel generates Track 1 and Track 2 data based on the values returned by the card.

The Kernel typically provides a random value ("unpredictable number") to the card, which generates a one-time verification value based on it. Then the number and the verification value are embedded into Track 1 and/or Track 2 fields in their Discretionary Data part. This verification value is called *dynamic CVV* or *dCVV*, as it is similar to other card verification value types in its format and embedding. The value is also sometimes referred to as CVV3.

2.6   Overview of Card-Present Technology

Typically, several major technologies are used in card-present/cardholder-present environments.

They are:

Magnetic stripe—there, of course, is the magnetic stripe that is being gradually phased out globally due to its numerous limitations and vulnerabilities.

EMV chip—EMV technology having contact readers and integrated chip circuits embedded into cads, where the card is to be inserted into a compatible reader and the chip on the card engages in a dialogue with the terminal.

EMV contactless—is also an ICC-based technology, having an antenna is embedded in the card in addition to the chip. When placed near a compatible reader, the chip on the card is powered by electromagnetic induction of the reader's magnetic field. Then the chip engages in a dialogue with the reader.

EMV tokenization—a technology that combines security benefits of tokenized cards with those of an EMV chip, allowing in-store payment using a token. Instead of the actual PAN, the token identification is transmitted to the terminal instead. That technology is behind such payment methods as Apple Pay®, Android Pay®, Samsung Pay®, etc.

Implementations of both chip and contactless technologies are still underway, and the magnetic stripe cards and readers have not been completely phased out. As there is still a considerable number of magstripe-only cards in use as well as locations where such cards are still issued, terminals are expected to continue supporting magnetic stripes for years to come. Besides compatibility with magnetic cards, that provides an additional benefit of being able to fall back to a magnetic stripe transaction in case there is a problem with the card reader or the chip itself.

End-to-end implementation of EMV technology is also sometimes called *full-grade* EMV. In a full-grade EMV implementation the card and the terminal rely on EMV protocols for the exchange of payment data. The payment message, containing all the additional values generated by card and terminal (these are carried in ISO field 55), is sent through to the acquirer host to the payment network and to the issuer.

However, host systems' and networks' upgrades to support the extra data takes time and requires considerable effort. Hence, the EMV standards allow a *part-grade* EMV implementation, meant as a transitional state of a payment solution that utilizes some but not all of the EMV features.

In case of both contact and contactless EMV, while the dialogue between the terminal and the card is performed according to EMV protocol, the message that is sent further down the line conforms to a magstripe transaction format. In other words, instead of a full-grade cryptographic signature of the transaction data, a limited and simpler method, utilizing the discretionary data subfields of Track 1 and Track 2 magnetic stripe values, is used. In particular, that means that instead of an ARQC, the issuer relies on iCVV or dynamic CVV to confirm the card authenticity. More details on those abilities and conditions can be found in section 2.10. See also sections 2.5.4, 2.5.5.

The description of full-grade EMV, chip technology and protocols is given in detail in chapter 5.

2.7   Cardholder Verification Methods

The card is typically identified by its PAN (and sequence number, if multiple cards were issued for the account) and authenticated by one of the cryptographic methods mentioned elsewhere in this book.

Once the authenticity of the card is confirmed by the terminal and data for further authentication by the issuer is gathered, cardholder verification usually takes place.

In a card-not-present environment which increasingly converges with card-present on mobile devices, additional means of authentication such as 3D Secure (Verified by Visa/SecureCode or others), its successor EMV 3DS 2.0 or a digital wallet (Visa Checkout®, MasterPass®, AmEx Express CheckOut®) are frequently applied. In these cases, the cardholder's identity is verified by one or more of the following means:

Static password which is defined by the cardholder on a digital wallet or the issuer bank website according to issuer's or wallet provider's password security policy. The method is used in digital wallet applications and sometimes with 3D Secure-based applications (see section 4.3).

One-time password which is generated by the issuer or wallet provider and is communicated to the cardholder via an independent verified channel. Most frequently, the one-time password is sent to the cardholder as an SMS message. The method is used for web-based commerce, since the access to a mobile phone is ubiquitous. A significantly more secure method for one-time password generation involves a mobile app tied to a specific mobile device that, upon entering a passcode, generates a one-time password that expires within short timeframe, typically one minute. This method is rarely used for mass end-user authentication.

Mobile authentication is exclusively used with mobile commerce to authenticate the cardholder, confirming that mobile device or application user is indeed the owner of the account. Multiple methods can be used for that type of authentication, with passcodes, passwords, swipe patterns, and fingerprints being used most frequently. These methods are growing more sophisticated with further development of mobile device technology and some experimental authentication approaches include enhanced swipe pattern recognition that takes into account the speed and angle of the pattern swipe, gesture recognition method relying on accelerometers, as well as voice and facial biometric recognition. It is worth noting that it is important to distinguish between a numeric passcode used to unlock mobile devices or authenticate mobile applications, and the card-related Personal Identification Number or PIN. The former is typically shared and used by the smartphone user, the mobile application and the device while the latter has strict entry device requirements, security guidelines and audit processes ensuring its security. This passcode is sometimes referred to as mPIN, to distinguish it from PIN and PIN-based cardholder verification methods (see Offline PIN and Online PIN below).

In the card-present environment, there is a closed well-defined list of Cardholder Verification Methods that is codified as part of the EMV standard. Some of these methods are performed by a terminal attendant, some can be executed by the chip on card and the others require the issuer's involvement. These methods are as follows:

Failed CVM—is a technical CVM method that is mentioned here for the sake of completeness. It is primarily used in exceptional scenarios and indicates that the card has decided to purposely fail all CVM checks. For example, an issuer may decide to put "failed CVM" as the last cardholder verification rule in the CVM list on the card, to make sure that if no other rule is applied, the cardholder verification is to be considered failed.

No CVM is the "zero hypothesis" of cardholder verification methods. During the interaction between a terminal and a chip card, or due to limitations predefined on the terminal, authorization may be attempted or performed with no additional cardholder verification. Usually that method is applied in unattended terminals such as vending machines, offline terminals and on public transit, where a PIN code or other verification method leads to unreasonable congestion and passenger traffic build-up.

Signature—is the legacy method of cardholder verification during which the terminal, if equipped with a printer, prints a sales draft. Then the attendant asks the customer to sign the slip and, at least according to regulations, is supposed to compare the signature on the slip with the one on the signature stripe on the card. The method has obvious deficiencies as besides relative ease of forging the signature that is already present on the card, shop attendants often skip the signature comparison step[2]. Obviously, the method does not depend on EMV technology and can be used with a magnetic stripe card as well.

Offline PIN—is part of the EMV specification; this method is further subdivided into *plaintext offline PIN* and *enciphered offline PIN*. In both cases, the integrated chip circuit on the card is the entity that confirms PIN validity and thus verifies the cardholder identity. As for the cleartext offline PIN, the value of the PIN entered is transmitted to the card unencrypted and in the case of the enciphered one exactly as the name implies. Terminals that are equipped with a PIN pad (certified and EMV-compliant PIN entry device) are typically able to support both methods, and the choice between plaintext and enciphered offline PIN validation is left to the issuer and limited by the integrated chip capacity (with enciphered PIN, obviously, placing higher computational demands on the chip). The process itself is described in more details in section 5.3.10.5. The ISO/IEC 9564 standard governs encoding of PIN data that is exchanged between the integrated chip and the PIN pad (see also description of format 2 in Chapter 13).

---

[2] As of April 2018, shops that accept EMV cards are no longer required to keep cardholder signatures.

Online PIN—is packaged into an encrypted PIN block (referred to as EPB) and is sent to the issuer for validation alongside other transaction details. There are several formats of the EPB as defined by ISO/IEC 9564 (see description of formats 0, 1, 3 and 4 in chapter 13). The PIN block is encrypted by the terminal using 3-DES. Then the encrypted PIN block undergoes several "PIN translations" by a terminal management system, acquiring host and the payment networks, during which the EPB is decrypted and re-encrypted again using the symmetric secret key shared between subsequent entities in the connection chain. That verification method also does not depend on EMV technology and can also be used with magnetic stripe cards.

The methods and the format of cardholder verification rules are described in more details in section 5.3.10.2.

2.7.1 Strong Customer Authentication

Cardholder verification serves as a step to ensure that the payment is performed by its rightful owner. While these methods were initially deployed, with varying degree of market penetration, as a way for market players to better secure their transactions and combat fraud, since September 2019 the so-called "Strong Customer Authentication" has been mandated by law in the European Union, albeit with some specific exemptions.

The Strong Customer Authentication, or SCA, requires a combination of at least two dynamically linked factors of "something you are", "something you have" and "something you know" types to authenticate the payment account owner (in the card world, the cardholder) prior to performing a payment transaction.

While in the card-present environment one factor of authentication is the card itself (something the cardholder has), and various PIN-based methods adequately meet the requirements of the law, in the card-not-present environment only mandatory 3D Secure-based cardholder authentication has provided the necessary level of compliance with the SCA rule, and that only if the actual authentication is correctly implemented by the card issuer.

2.8 PIN Handling

2.8.1 PIN Verification

There are two possible PIN verification methods depending on the decision of the issuer. It is possible to either store the PIN in the database in encrypted form, delegating its validation to an HSM, or to rely on PVV—the PIN code verification value—that is handled and utilized in a manner similar to that of CVV (see section 2.5), when only the verification key is kept secret and the validation value arrives alongside the enciphered PIN value.

2.8.2 Storing Encrypted PIN

If the issuer decides on storing the PIN value itself, the PIN values are encrypted in a secure way inside an HSM and then the result of the encryption is then stored in a database on the issuer host, alongside either the index of the encrypting key or the KEK-encrypted key itself (see also section 8.3.2). The issuer stores the ethalon PIN encrypted under PEK (PIN encryption key), an index of the PEK or the value of the PEK itself under KEK (PEK_{KEK}). The issuer receives an encrypted PIN block as part of the payment message and hands it over to the HSM with the ethalon PIN and the necessary key information to validate the PIN. Then the issuer host system receives an indication from the HSM regarding whether the PIN that was received as part of the payment message is valid.

2.8.3 Relying on PIN Verification Value (PVV)

Another method of PIN verification is utilizing PIN verification keys (PVK) and PIN verification values (PVV).

The PVV is calculated in a manner very similar to the CVV values and is encoded as part of discretionary data on magnetic stripe tracks 1 and 2. Its precise location (i.e., specific character positions holding the value as part of the DD vector) is kept secret as well as the PVK that is only shared with the relevant card scheme.

The issuer stores the KEK-encrypted PVKs in a database. Upon receiving a payment message, the issuer sends the incoming encrypted PIN block, the incoming PVK and the necessary key data to the HSM which then securely validates the PVK value.

Regardless of the method the issuer prefers the PVV value is still in use for stand-in processing, during which card schemes authorize requests on behalf of the issuers.

2.9 Transaction types

Various transaction types can be performed at a terminal, physical or virtual. These can be divided into three categories—retail-related transactions, cash withdrawals and deposits and payment transactions.

2.9.1 Retail transactions

Purchase is the most frequent and basic type of a cardholder transaction. During a purchase, the desired amount is typically authorized online by sending an authorization request. The acquirer host either receives an indication that the transaction is to be presented for clearing or clears the transaction by default. Card schemes impose limitations on the time interval between authorization and clearing of the transaction, and encourage timely clearing (usually within three calendar days).

Certain card schemes explicitly distinguish between basic purchases and purchases in the gambling industry, since the latter bear higher risk of fraud and money laundering. Gambling transactions are sometimes called *unique* or *quasi-cash* to further the distinction.

Pre-authorization is a type of authorization request when the transaction is unlikely to be presented for clearing immediately. Pre-authorizations are used when the final amount of the transaction is not known or the delivery of goods or services comes at a much later date. This is particularly so with the rental and lodging industry or with retailers whose goods take significant time to ship. Consider such examples as the use-case of a hotel pre-authorizing a security amount from a guest's card or a custom furniture shop performing the transaction for an order to be delivered next month— both would use a pre-authorization followed by some sort of finalization for the transaction upon delivery of goods or services.

Account validation is a type of authorization request when there is no immediate purchase intent and no actual transaction is performed, but rather the card number and other account details are being validated for the purpose of future use. The request is typically made as a pre-authorization with zero amount and in many solutions, issuers reply to it with a response code of 85 ("No reason to decline") in addition to the widely used 00 ("Success"). (See also section 3.3.4).

A worse alternative to the dedicated account validation operation is card pre-authorization for a minimal amount of money (such as $ 0.01).

Completion or capture is a type of transaction following a pre-authorization. Consider the aforementioned scenario of a custom furniture shop. In that case, the amount of the payment is pre-authorized once the order is placed, but once the goods are shipped, the merchant can perform a completion operation to finalize the transaction and execute payment.

Refund transaction s an operation of crediting funds to a card account due to returned products, cancelled services or price adjustments related to a prior purchase. A refund can be made for the full or partial amount of the original purchase, and multiple refunds for the same purchase can be made.

Card scheme rules limit the amount of refund to the full amount of the original purchase to limit fraud and money-laundering risks. However, it is possible that a valid and compliant bigger refund for the original purchase might be made in case different currencies are used and the currency rate changes accordingly.

Reversal, either full or partial, is an operation of original transaction cancellation. Reversals can be caused by technical reasons and be sent automatically. Unlike refunds, which credit funds after a purchase, reversal is a universal operation applied to additional transaction types besides purchases. For example, it is possible to reverse a pre-authorization, a payment transaction (see below) or a refund. In addition to financial implications on the cardholder and the merchant, reversals help recoup some of the fees that are applicable to the acquirer. Thus a reversal of a balance inquiry (see below) is also a valid practical scenario.

Perhaps the simplest way to comprehend the difference between a reversal and a refund is assuming the cardholder billing statement perspective. A purchase followed by a refund, would show up in the cardholder statement as two separate transactions. A purchase followed by a timely reversal does not appear in the statement at all. There are rules and limitations for timing of reversal transactions: schemes limit the time window during which the reversal might be performed, or require that a reversal is only sent while the transaction has not been cleared yet.

Balance inquiry is an operation during which an inquiry is sent to the issuer and the issuer responds to it with balances of one or more accounts that are associated with the card. Balance inquiries are used in ATMs but also are useful in POS environments with prepaid cards. Upon identifying a prepaid card, the merchant can send a balance inquiry message to the issuer manually or automatically to check the available card balance. That helps avoiding unnecessary authorization declines as the merchant can notify the customer about insufficient balance and advise them to regard split tender. An alternative to balance inquiry is partial authorization - in which issuer responds to a regular purchase authorization message with a special decline code, indicating the allowed partial amount in the response message. Them the merchant's POS system can ask the cardholder for another pay mean for the remainder of the full amount.

Purchase with Cashback is an operation during which a certain amount of cash is provided to the cardholder alongside the purchased goods or services.

The cardholder can request to receive an amount in cash alongside the purchase. The cash is withdrawn from the cardholder's account and handed to the cardholder at the point of sale. That is a convenient way to combine a purchase with cash withdrawal without accesssing an ATM or authorizing the withdrawal separately. This transaction type is applicable mostly to debit cards.

An arrangement or a promotional offer,in which the issuing institution shares a small percentage of the cardholder's net expenditures (purchases minus refunds) with the cardholder in form of loyalty points, purchase discount or by mailing an actual cheque, is also referred to as a purchase with cashback. However, in this case the cashback arrangement is between the issuer and the cardholder. It is transparent to the merchant and the card acceptor and these transactions are technically basic purchases and are indistinguishable from transactions on cards without cashback.

2.9.2   Cash Withdrawals and Deposits

Withdrawal is a removal of funds from an account in cash. That type of transaction is performed at a teller machine equipped with a cash dispenser or manually by a cashier equipped with a terminal. During a withdrawal, the cardholder can choose the account type associated with this particular card, from which the withdrawal is going to be performed. Not all acquirers or issues support this operation. This operation is immediate.

It differs from a *cash advance* or cash disbursement transaction, when cash is handed over to the cardholder as an advance on credit card balance and can be repaid as a lump sum or in instalments at a later date. Emergency cash advance on a lost card is not considered a withdrawal.

Withdrawals and especially cash advances usually bear higher risks of fraud and money laundering than other transaction types.

Deposit transaction is a deposit of funds at a card-associated account, typically performed at an ATM. Like any other cash-related transaction, it bears a high risk of money laundering or fraud.

2.9.3   Payment Transactions

Payment transaction, also referred to as *original credit* or *credit fund transfer*, is a money transfer transaction during which funds are sent to the designated recipient by the merchant or from one cardholder to another. There are two types of payment transactions: business-to-cardholder and cardholder-to-cardholder.

Payment transactions from business to a cardholder, also called *fund disbursements*, are directed from merchants or government institutions to primarily consumer card holders. Merchants can use these transactions to issue rebates or deliver gambling payouts. Government institutions and companies can use fund disbursements to deliver salaries or pensions directly to a cardholder account. Financial institutions can use payment transactions to pay insurances or deliver loans to card holders.

Although from point of view of direction of funds both refunds and fund disbursements such as rebates are debiting the merchant and crediting a cardholder, there are significant differences as to when and how they are supposed to be used. That depends on card scheme rules. Also, card scheme and interchange fees for these transaction types differ. Fund disbursement transactions are usually accompanied by extra details such as full name and address of the receiver of the funds.

Payment transactions or *money transfers* between cardholders transmit funds from one card account to another. Unlike transferring funds from a merchant to a cardholder, money transfer transaction includes two parts. First, the sender transfers the funds to the merchant that facilitates the operation in a *funding transaction*. Once completed, the merchant then transfers the funds to one or more recipient accounts with separate payment transactions.

There are strict legal and regulatory limitations on money transfers due to their potential for fraud, money laundering and other illicit use. A payment transaction can be maliciously used to launder or integrate illegal funds. It can be used as a concealed gambling payout in a jurisdiction where gambling is prohibited, or even utilized to defraud the acquirer bank itself. Consequently, card schemes requre significant additional details about actors involved in payment transactions. These details are used in fraud prevention mechanisms. In addition, limitations on target countries and maximum transfer amounts vary greatly between areas and jurisdictions.

2.10   Point-of-Sale Types, Conditions and Entry Modes

Capabilities of the terminal and the card, the technology in use to transfer data between the two and conditions of a particular transaction all affect the ways in which the transaction is then processed by acquirers, card schemes and issuers.

A terminal can be attended or unattended, reside on or off card acceptor premises, or have differing display capabilities. A terminal may or may not be able of capturing the card. A terminal can work properly or its pin entry device (PED) may malfunction at the moment. At the same time, a card may or may not be present at the terminal, and so may the cardholder. The card itself can contain magnetic stripe, an embedded chip and a contactless NFC transmitter, or a mobile device might be used instead of a card. Furthermore, read of the chip or magstripe may not be fully reliable.

Some or all of the aforementioned terminal characteristics, pay mean and transaction can be transmitted as optional or mandatory fields as part of every transaction. Specifics of values in use depend on a particular implementation.

To navigate that essentially multi-dimensional complexity, it is easier to move from more common and significant POS characteristics to less common ones. Unless explicitly specified otherwise, all mentions of "card" in this section refer to a card as well as a mobile device capable of the specific technology.

2.10.1 Data Transfer Methods

Data transfer method is the means by which data is transferred or exchanged between the card and the terminal, as supported by the terminal. The data can be transferred as a result of physical contact between the card and the device ("contact") or by proximity ("contactless")[3]. In the former case, the terminal will be equipped with a chip reader, a magnetic stripe reader, or both. In the latter case, the terminal will contain a proximity reader only.

The card can, in turn, contain a chip, a magnetic stripe and an NFC module.

2.10.2 Data Formats

Data format describes a high-level set of data representation requirements. The acceptable terminology relies on technologies that first introduced the requirements, which creates some confusion. The data can be represented as "Magstripe" or "EMV", with the latter referring to full-grade EMV. Combined with the above options of data transfer methods, this yields four possible major options for a card-present transaction: "EMV contact", "EMV contactless", "Magstripe contact" and "Magstripe contactless":

EMV contact. The option is not supported by mobile devices. In case of an EMV contact transaction, the card is being inserted into a chip reader. The option can also be referred to as a "chip and dip" or simply "EMV chip" transaction, with the latter as a common but an imprecise term. An EMV contact transaction condition implies a card equipped with a chip to be inserted into the reader. Full cryptographic EMV exchange takes place and an outgoing message contains ICC data in data element 55 (ICC data) and Track 2 data in data element 35 (Track 2 data).

EMV contactless. The option is supported by NFC-capable mobile devices, the architecture of which allows for a secure element to which the issuer-provided cryptographic data can be loaded. The option is also sometimes referred to as simply "contactless". An EMV contactless transaction condition implies that a card equipped with a contactless antenna and an integrated chip is placed in front of the contactless reader (or tapped on it) and a successful message exchange between the chip and the reader takes

---

[3]Certainly, the data may not be exchanged at all if card is unable to communicate with the device. In that case, attended terminals with keypads may allow manual key-in of some card details.

place over radio waves. In that case, the authorization message contains ICC data in data element 55 (ICC data).

Magstripe contact. The option is not supported by mobile devices. It is sometimes referred to as "magstripe". In case of a magnetic stripe contact transaction, the card is swiped through the reader and the data recorded on its magnetic stripe is read by the reading head[4]. The authorization message contains data in data element 35 (Track 2 data), data element 45 (Track 1 data) or both.

Magstripe contactless. The option is supported by NFC-capable mobile devices. A magstripe contactless transaction condition implies that a card with a contactless antenna or a mobile device is placed in front of the contactless reader ("tapped") and a successful message exchange between the card or device and the reader takes place. In this case, though, the solution emulates magstripe read, generating and transmitting track 2 data with additional dynamic cryptographic elements embedded into the discrete data portion of the track. The authorization message contains data in data element 35 (Track 2 data) and, optionally, data element 45 (Track 1 data).

2.10.2.1 Terminal Capabilities and Conditions

Devices used to accept payment transactions vary greatly in configuration, architecture and abilities. Certain features of these devices and solutions involving them are governed by PCI security standards (for instance, PIN entry devices or PEDs should be secure enough to prevent PIN code theft), some others are controlled by card scheme brand rules (prescribing, among others, design features such as location and prominence of the card scheme logo).

Card schemes usually have a specific set of terminal capabilities which have to be properly communicated both during the terminal certification process (see section 2.10.3) and every authorization request. Furthermore, besides permanent capabilities, a terminal might have certain temporary conditions (for instance, terminal's PIN pad may malfunction and prevent cardholder verification using a PIN).

Although specific condition and rules vary greatly between schemes, the following set covers the most common cases the schemes would care about.

PAN and PIN Entry Capabilities

Core terminal capabilities include those related to card data transfer methods, supported data formats and ability for PIN entry.

---

[4]A "contact magstripe" read can also occur in a part-grade EMV environment, where the chip and the terminal are both capable of a full chip-based contact transaction, but the network isn't. As this is a transitional state, for the sake of clarity it is not extensively covered here.

From purely technical point of view, a terminal may have some or all of the following core capabilities for PAN entry:

Key entry is the ability to enter PAN and expiry data into the terminal using a keyboard. Note that this does not imply the ability to support PIN codes, as PIN entry devices have stricter security requirements. Therefore, a terminal can support key entry without being able to capture PINs securely.

Magnetic stripe is the ability to enter card data by reading track data from the magnetic stripe on the card.

Chip reader is the ability to enter card data by interacting with the integrated circuit on it with contact data transfer technology, i.e. the ability to support "EMV contact" transactions (see section 2.10.2).

Contactless reader is the ability to enter card data by interacting with the integrated chip on the card or a compatible mobile device, using with contactless data transfer technology, i.e. the ability to support "EMV contactless" transactions (see section 2.10.2).

Contactless magnetic stripe - ability to enter card data with contactless data transfer technology but without chip data - i.e. ability to support "Magstripe contactless" transactions. This terminal capability is specified here separately because some schemes have a separate set of data values or flags to indicate it. Some of the schemes mandate contactless magstripe support for all contactless terminals.

A terminal may also have or not have the capability for PIN entry. In case a terminal does have such a capability, some schemes would require specifying the maximum length of the PIN supported (up to 12 characters), as older terminals may limit maximum PIN length to 4 or 6 characters.

Other Interface Capabilities

A terminal can have some of the following additional capabilities that might be made known to card schemes:

Card capture is the ability of the terminal to perform card retention or physically capture the payment card in case a fraud rule or a response by the payment scheme or the issuer instructs to do it. The ability is always present in ATMs where the card can be not returned back to the terminal's user.

Card data output is the ability of the terminal to output data to the card. All EMV-compliant chip devices have the ability to send issuer-originated instructions to the chip on the card which can translate into data being updated on the ICC storage. Some card schemes also support indication of magstripe write capability (used to update Track 3, see section 2.4.3).

Terminal output is the ability of the terminal to output data to the user/attendant. The ability includes a display, a printer or both. One can see the potential use of the indicator for fraud detection: obviously, a terminal without printing capabilities should never report signature as a cardholder verification method.

Terminal Location and Attendance

A terminal can be considered "attended" or "unattended" (also sometimes referred to as "cardholder-activated terminal" or CAT). In the former case, there is an attendant employee that operates the terminal for or together with the cardholder, while in the latter case, the cardholder operates the terminal with no assistance from an attendant.

A terminal can be owned by the merchant, the card acceptor or the cardholder (the latter is a rare case in the age of modern electronic and mobile commerce).

A card acceptor-owned terminal can be located on or off card acceptor premises.

To illustrate possible business scenarios, consider the following combinations 20 of terminal location and attendance (it is assumed to be owned by the merchant or the card acceptor):

Attended, on acceptor premises—this is the basic scenario of a terminal that is located in a store and is operated by a store attendant.

Attended, off acceptor premises—in this scenario the terminal is owned by the merchant and is activated by their representative but is not located inside the store, for instance, a field technician or a travelling salesman, equipped with a POS device.

Unattended, on acceptor premises—in this scenario a terminal such as a parking lot machine or a vending machine is located on card acceptor premises, but is activated by the cardholder.

Unattended, off acceptor premises—in this scenario, a terminal is located outside the card acceptor facilities. A good example is a network of vending machines that is deployed in various locations outside the merchant's main facility.

Terminal Categories

In addition to the aforementioned specific capabilities of terminals, schemes often define terminal categories. A terminal belonging to such a category has a predefined set of certain capabilities and has transaction acceptance rules associated with its category.

For instance, it is common to defined mobile POS or mPOS as a separate category. An mPOS consists of a mobile phone or tablet with a supporting application and a PED (an external PIN pad) usually containing necessary chip/contactless/magstripe readers.

Card schemes usually define airline on-board purchase terminals as a separate terminal category for in-flight commerce. Even though a terminal of this kind can support any data format or transfer method, due to very limited connectivity on board a plane in flight, all transactions are authorized offline by the terminal and are later transferred to schemes for clearing.

Unattended terminals are classified based on the availability of a PIN pad, with unattended transactions on terminals without a PIN pad being limited to a maximum amount.

Automated fuel dispensers, toll booths and mass transit terminals are also divided into different categories due to specifics of transaction processing on these types of devices. Fuel dispensers require an initial authorization of the payment card while the full amount of the purchase depends on the volume of pumped gasoline which is initially unknown.

Toll booths and mass transit terminals have very strict requirements for time it should take to authorize a transaction and perform a sort of delayed authorization with card issuers via scheme networks. A card might become blacklisted and not accepted on a terminal of this category any longer if the initial payment is later declined by the issuer and the cardholder had a free ride. However, this calculated risk is considered preferable to a big queue building up, should each transaction actually be authorized online.

Transient Transaction Conditions

As mentioned previously, besides permanent characteristics of a terminal it may be in a transient condition. Also, the environment in which the actual transaction takes place may sometimes be reflected in data elements that are sent as part of authorization request.

At the time of the transaction, the card and the cardholder may both be either present or absent at the physical terminal. Although most of card-not-present transactions are handled as mail, telephony, e-commerce, standing order or recurring payments, it is still possible to, say, perform a refund in the cardholder's presence when they do not have their actual physical card on them.

In certain solutions, in cases when the shop attendant suspects fraud but cannot retain the payment card in a safe manner, there are means to indicate the suspicion to the payment network and the issuer, i.e., the transaction can be marked as "suspected fraud".

The PIN pad can be present at the terminal but not function at the particular moment when the transaction is processed. This condition is indicated separately from terminal permanent capability to process PIN codes, so that there is a clear distinction between a terminal that is not capable of handling PIN entry at all and a terminal that is not capable of handling PIN entry at this particular moment as an exceptional condition.

Besides the terminal conditions, transient conditions apply to the process of card data transfer. For instance, the chip read might be completed but is not reliable or contactless data transfer is not successfully completed. The terminal might decide to allow processing of the magnetic stripe instead of the integrated chip, due to inability to communicate with the chip or a malfunction. The magnetic stripe itself may not be reliable, but Track 2 data can still be retrieved from it, etc.

Entry Modes

The data transfer mechanism and the related transient conditions of the terminal and the card that applied at the time of interaction are otherwise referred to as "POS entry mode". The set of valid values and associated business rules vary between implementations, however, common values and groupings can be found in the description of Data Element 22—see section 3.3.4.

2.10.3   Terminal Certification Process

A POS device must conform to several standards, depending on jurisdiction in which it operates and depending on the POS type.

For example, if the device is capable of PIN entry, card schemes will require a PCI PTS (Pin Transaction Security) certification of the device to be performed. A device sold or deployed in Europe certainly requires a CE marking, to declare its conformance with European health, safety and environmental requirements. A device with wireless capabilities intended for sale in the US needs an FCC test, and so on.

Beyond the list of standalone certifications attesting to terminal compliance with a plethora of laws and standards, prior to device deployment for actual processing in a live environment, it has to undergo a sort of end-to-end integration test usually referred to as "card scheme certification".

The goal of the process is to certify the device for correct processing of card transactions in the specific environment, including connectivity to the acquiring host and, through it, to a card scheme. A change in host system or a new terminal device usually mandates a re-certification of the solution.

Such a certification process involves utilization of test cards, available from card schemes or from third-party vendors. The test cards are used to execute tests which are prescribed by each scheme separately. The host system can be connected to a simulator or plugged into a test environment of the card scheme.

Depending on the business environment, the certification can be performed at the initiative of a PSP that wishes to deploy their terminal as part of an integrative solution provided to brick-and-mortar stores, or by a manufacturer that wishes to sell POS devices directly to merchants.

As part of the process, once the tests on the POS device are executed, the logs generated during testing are submitted to card schemes for verification. In some cases, a live test performed by a card scheme engineer may be part of the scheme requirements.

2.11   Card-Not-Present Point-of-Sale Types, Conditions and Entry Modes

In the "card-not-present" environment POS is a virtual concept as there is usually no physical device that is utilized to interact with the card. As it is possible to process transactions without the card on physical devices, too, the card-not-present environment refers to processing of transactions when the card cannot be present by definition, rather than physically absent for a minority of transactions.

The card-not-present virtual POS environments can be divided into the following categories:

Mail/fax order—referring to use cases when PAN numbers and expiry dates are sent by the customer via mail or fax[5]. For instance, a direct mail order when the customer is mailing back the order form is considered a mail order.

Telephony order—when the PAN is communicated by the cardholder to a phone representative or via an IVR/ARU solution, either by pressing phone buttons or using voice recognition technology. For instance, dialing in to book a movie ticket when the card number is communicated with DTMF signals or dictating the card number to an operator are considered telephony orders.

These two modes are jointly referred to as *MOTO* (Mail Order/Telephony Order) and are not always treated separately by card scheme protocols.

e-commerce—when the PAN is communicated by the cardholder electronically over the Internet. As many processors offer merchants electronic remote interfaces, including browser-based ones, to type in MOTO orders, it is important to emphasize that e-commerce condition only applies in case card data is communicated by the cardholder directly to card acceptor systems.

Merchant-initiated transactions—is a common term for the following three environments, in which a particular transaction is not initiated by the cardholder but rather by a merchant system.

Standing authorization—refers to conditions when cardholder information is kept on file by the merchant, acquirer or processor and can be used to perform ad-hoc or non-periodic charges. For example, an online store can

---

[5]Mail orders had received an obvious boost with the ascent of payment cards in the late 1950s and pre-date electronic terminals.

associate a stored card number with a customer account, then allow easier checkout and payment by enabling the customer to use a stored card. This type of condition is also referred to as "card on file". Not every scheme handles it as a separate transaction condition—some of them still define the aforementioned example as an e-commerce transaction.

Recurring transaction—refers to a case when the card is stored on file and there is a periodic billing such as a membership fee or other regularly scheduled charge invoked.

Installment transaction—refers to a type of recurring transaction when the specific payment is a part of a larger transaction, for instance, when a large purchase is made. Depending on the funding arrangement, installments can be provided by the merchant, the acquirer or the issuer[6]. Not every solution is able to distinguishe between recurring and installment transactions.

---

[6]In certain regions there are custom and special installment schemes in widespread use. For instance, in Japan it is customary to break payments for large purchases into installments that are tied to two traditional semi-annual bonuses paid to Japanese employees.

Chapter 3

Payment Services and Protocols

CONTENTS

3.1 Introduction

Despite the variety of payment means and methods, there is basically a single family of closely related and very similar technical protocols at the backbone of the payment industry. Essentially, there are three mandatory phases and one optional phase in processing of a payment. They are authorization, clearing, settlement and dispute (the latter is an exception case, but a frequent one).

The authorization and clearing of payment transactions are performed using two principal methods—with a single payment message or with two payment messages. The former method is sometimes and will be herein be referred to as SMS (Single Message Service) with the latter being referred to as DMS (Dual Message Service).

In case of the SMS, a single payment message requests authorization of a certain amount and presents the authorization for clearing. The method is widely used in ATMs, where a cash disbursement is irreversible. It has advantages over the DMS, which is more historical, in several aspects. The SMS response message typically carries information that aids acquirers in reconciliation of their accounts, including precise interchange fees and currency conversion rates, if applicable. Such a method of payment has the functional benefits of being atomic (one message, one payment transaction) and having a single technical protocol instead of multiple ones (since the clearing part of DMS varies between card schemes).

In case of the DMS, a payment message requests authorization of a purchase but does not present it for clearing. The clearing part of the transaction is done with either a separate online message, or, more frequently, by transmitting presentments of transactions in a batch file.

While online authorizations are typically performed with messages that conform to a shared standard[1] (a dialect of ISO 8583 protocol), batch clearing files can vary in their format significantly between card schemes. To present transactions for clearing, an institution typically submits one or more clearing files to card schemes before certain cut-off deadline. The timing of file submission affects the business day on which its contents are considered presented—this date is sometimes also called the "Processing Day" or "Central Processing Date".

Naturally, the cut-off time differs per card scheme, but in addition a card scheme can provide multiple settlement services.

The settlement phase of the process involves bank transfers and the exchange of accompanying reports. Card scheme settlement rules vary greatly: a scheme can settle the entire amount of a daily submission in five or even seven business days or decide to settle intra-country, intra-region and inter-regional transactions at different speeds. For instance, domestic settlement in Iceland (transactions that are performed by Icelandic cardholders at Iceland-incorporated stores) is on the same day, while a payment performed by, for instance, an American cardholder could be settled within three business days.

The cardholder or the issuing institution can decide that a certain transaction was presented in error or, worse, is not a legitimate request of funds. The former can happen if due to a technical glitch, such as the acquirer's system had submitted the same transaction twice, while the latter is possible when a card has indeed been skimmed or the merchant has not supplied the goods but yet attempts to collect the payment. As, quite literally, the dispute process means a dispute between the cardholder and the merchant, handled and/or initiated by the respective banks or entities, it usually allows for a well-defined exchange of documentation and mutual claims with an ability to appeal to the card scheme for the dispute's final resolution. It is worth noting that in locations like Japan, as long as domestic

---

[1] With notable exception of the legacy CAFIS protocol in Japan.

transaction interchanges stay off the grid of global card schemes, parties prefer to discuss the disputed transaction directly (by, for instance, a representative of the issuing bank calling the acquirer or vice versa) instead of embarrassing themselves with a formal card-scheme mediated dispute.

3.2   Authorization Service Messages

As was already implied beforehand, the transaction authorization by the issuer bank or by the card scheme does not necessarily constitute its approval. In case of a Dual-Message Service, an authorized transaction means that it can be presented for clearing which can be honored or rejected.

The majority of card schemes worldwide rely on payment authorization protocols which are dialects (customized versions) of a protocol governed by ISO 8583 standard. These protocols' messages can be grouped into two categories: cardholder and network messages[2].

Acquirers, interchange network services and issuers use network messages to establish or tear down sessions, to exchange keys, test the counterpart's responsiveness or communicate file updates (the latter feature is used for stand-in processing by payment networks).

Cardholder messages can be used to perform purchases, pre-authorizations, withdrawals, deposits, refunds, reversals, balance inquiries, payments and inter-account transfers.

3.3   ISO 8583 Message Structure

Card schemes utilize custom modifications of the standard ISO 8583 protocol. Such modifications are also called *ISO dialects*. In this chapter, some variations of the ISO 8583 standards alongside the standard structure are discussed. For the sake of brevity, the ISO 8583 protocol will be referred to simply as ISO.

An ISO message consists of:

header carrying meta information regarding the message.

message type indicator (or *message type identifier*), abbreviated as MTI or MTID, which describes class, type and source of the message.

bitmap indicating which data fields to expect in the rest of the message.

data fields (or data elements) encapsulating message data.

---

[2]Technically, file management messages should be a separate category, but an acquirer does not encounter them

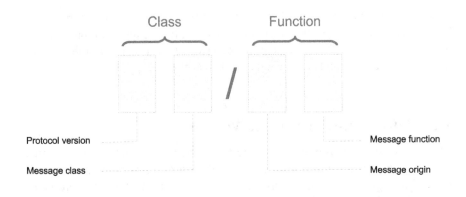

Figure 3.1: MTID structure

3.3.1 Message Header

Each ISO message contains a header. The header can be trivial, containing only the full byte length of the message, or non-trivial, carrying multiple additional data fields with routing and protocol details.

Non-trivial ISO message headers usually contain routing information in form of station or institution identifiers, a separate field for header and body lengths and a special field for *reject code*. In cases when the message is poorly formatted but its header is at least legible, some card schemes can respond by mirroring back the offending message but populating the reject code that indicates the field that is in error or points at conflicting values found in several fields. In such cases card scheme manuals contain tables listing reject codes and their meanings. Other card scheme protocols mandate response with a full valid response message, allocating special data field or fields to elaborate on the error.

3.3.2 Message Type Indicator

Each ISO message necessarily contains a message type indicator or MTID. The MTID is a four-digit code transmitted as a binary-coded decimal, specifying the version of the ISO protocol, message class, function and origin. Although in later versions of the ISO protocol all four digits have special meaning as well as a well-defined set of values and can also vary between messages, from practical point of view it is easier to think of MTID as a concatenation of two two-digit values: the message class and the message function (see Figure 3.1). MTID's first digit specifies the version of the protocol. The three most common values of the first digit correspond to revisions of ISO 8583 which are shown in table 3.1: The 1978 revision of the ISO protocol is the most common one in the industry. For the sake of simplicity, it is assumed for all the future examples of ISO messages.

Table 3.1: First digit of MTID and ISO 8583 revisions

Value	Description
0	1978 revision
1	1993 revision
2	2003 revision

MTID second specifies the message class. Some of the values for the message class include:

1 authorization. This message class contains authorization-related messages and is mainly used in dual-message protocols. Purchase, pre-authorization, refund or a payment transaction can all result in one or several authorization messages in the payment network. An authorization message is only part of a payment transaction and a single exchange of messages of this class does not suffice for the actual payment or fund transfer[3].

2 financial. This message class contains full financial messages and a message exchange of this class can cause an actual movement of funds if approved. This message class is used in single-message protocols.

4 reversal. This message class contains messages that reverse messages from other classes, in particular, authorization and financial messages. This message class is utilized in both single- and dual-message protocols.

8 network management. This message class contains messages that facilitate the session establishment and teardown, protocol-level keepalive messages and is also used for key exchange in some dialects.

MTID third digit specifies a message function. Common values of the digit are:

0 request

1 request response

2 advice

3 advice response

The difference between a request and advice is best described as the difference between asking and telling. In the former case, a party requests authorization of an operation. In the latter case, a party advises that an operation has been

---

[3]Although, since most processors and schemes charge per message, such an exchange still incurs fees and costs.

performed. Consider an example of a cardholder's pre-authorization performed at a hotel. Since the approximate amount has already been pre-authorized by the issuer, it is possible that the actual payment is sent as an advice message.

MTID fourth specifies the message origin. There are multiple valid values for the digit in various editions of the ISO 8583 protocol. We only consider 0 acquirer-originated message and 1 acquirer repeat out of them. The former indicates an original message, and the latter indicates that an attempt is being made to resend the previous message to which the response has not been received.

Consider various combinations of message classes and functions (assuming ISO 8583 1978 edition) as listed in table 3.2.

Table 3.2: Examples of message class and function

	Class	*Function*	
Authorization	01	00	Request
Financial	02	01	Repeat
Reversal	40	10	Response
Network management	80	20	Advice
Network management	80	30	Advice response

Some possible scenarios including messages involved are listed below. The scenarios are provided for illustration only and specific card scheme protocols will probably differ in some of these cases.

Session setup and teardown

An acquirer, setting up a session with a card scheme, sends a 0800 message to its network—"Network management request". Then the card scheme responds with a 0810 message—"Network management response", indicating successful sign-on to the network. Upon shutdown of the connection, the acquirer sends a 0800 message and receive a 0810 message in response.

Purchase

A DMS acquirer sends a 0100 (authorization request) to the network which in turn forwards it to the issuer asking to authorize the amount of the purchase. The issuer responds with a 0110 (authorization response) that, in turn, is forwarded to the acquirer.

Pre-authorization and completion

A DMS acquirer would send a 0100 (authorization request) message to pre-authorise a purchase. The message would get forwarded to the card issuer and prompt a 0110 (authorization response) message in return. In case the original request is authorised by the issuer successfully, the acquirer—at a later stage—sends a 0220 (financial advice) message to indicate the completion of the purchase. The 0220 message is forwarded to the issuer that responds to it with a 0230 (financial advice response), acknowledging the receival of the advice.

Purchase cancellation

An acquirer first sends an 0100 (authorization request) message to perform a purchase, to which the issuer responds with a 0110 (authorization response). Then, the merchant that is serviced by the acquirer could decide on cancelling the transaction if, for instance, it was erroneously sent due to a software bug in the merchant's e-commerce platform. Then the acquirer sends a 0400 (reversal request) message and receives a 0410 (reversal response) in return.

3.3.3 Bitmap

The data fields (or data elements) presence in a ISO message can vary greatly between different message types. As such, the data elements presence or absence is defined by a bitmap. An ISO message can contain one, two or three bitmaps, called primary, secondary and tertiary or extended bitmap.

Most major card schemes use up to two bitmaps in their messages, and the primary bitmap must be always present.

A single bitmap consists of 8 bytes, in which bits are numbered from left to right, starting from 1. Thus, a primary bitmap contains bits 1 through 64, a secondary bitmap contains bits 65 to 128 and an extended bitmap, correspondingly, covers data elements 129 to 192.

The first bit of primary and secondary bitmaps (bits 1 and 65) do not correspond to a data element but indicate the presence of a subsequent bitmap.

Consider the following sample bitmap: 82 20 00 00 0A 00 00 00. It corresponds to the following string of bits:

```
10000010 00100000 00000000 00000000 00001010 00000000 00000000 00000000
1        9        17       25       33       41       49       57
```

The bitmap has bits 1, 7, 11, 37, 39 set. Since bit 1 is set, a secondary bitmap is present in the message and the application processing the message should read subsequent 8 bytes from the input stream and interpret them as a bitmap. This particular message does not contain data element 2 (where the PAN is stored, see below), and is therefore likely to be a network management message not linked to a particular cardholder account. Furthermore, judging by presence of data element 39 (the result code) this bitmap likely belongs to a response message.

3.3.4 Data Elements

An ISO message's data elements can carry a very diverse set of data types encoded in several different ways. Some data elements are defined by the ISO standard, others are considered proprietary and card schemes set their own format and usage for the fields. Proprietary fields can have a fixed pre-defined set of subfields, or a sort of tag-length-value (TLV) subformat where the subfield ID (tag) is followed by the data length and then by value. On certain occasions, schemes use proprietary bitmaps to indicate which optional subfields are present in a proprietary data element. Last but not least, it is not unusual for an ISO dialect message to contain data in both ASCII and EBCDIC encodings simultaneously.

Formats

As mentioned, there are several data encoding formats for ISO data elements. The standard notation includes the following definitions of valid values for the elements:

a—denotes alphabetic characters—both upper and lower case letters of the Latin alphabet. Although these can be encoded in both ASCII and EBCDIC, depending on the field and dialect, national characters are not used in online authorization messages.

n—denotes decimal digits.

s—denotes "special characters" which are printable characters of the ASCII table other than alphabetic or numeric. Quite often, the *s* notation comes with additional limitations or requirements for a particular field. [4]

b—denotes binary data. It is worth mentioning that EMV data, transmitted in field 55, is denoted as *b* and further has an additional set of rules on how to interpret the binary contents (see section 11.6).

z—denotes special formats of Track1 and Track2 data (see section 2.4).

The definitions can be combined when it makes sense: for example, there are fields denoted as an or ans ("alphanumeric" and "alphanumeric and special characters", correspondingly), but, obviously, *b* and *z* cannot be combined with other notations.

Length

ISO message fields can vary in length. Some of them allow fixed-length values which must be always filled with meaningful characters (for instance, field 14, the card expiration date, is numeric and has a fixed length of 4 symbols), others have a fixed length and require values to be padded with spaces (e.g., field 38,

---

[4]For example, a field with the *s* notation may allow spaces but cannot be all blanks.

approval code—alphanumeric, has a fixed length of 6 but can contain less mean-ingful characters and can be space-padded), yet some others have a variable data length. A variable length can be specified either in bytes or in other units, such as nibbles (half-bytes) or bits, in which case, there are padding rules for field values. Some common length notations are:

-digit(s)—fixed length notation. For instance, the aforementioned expiry date field can be described as n-4 (numeric-only datafield with fixed length of 4).

..digit(s) or ...digit(s)—variable-length notation with maximum length speci-fied. Depending on specifics of a particular field, the standard and the dialects contain rules determining the length or describing padding.

LLVAR or HLVAR—variable-length fields which contain two sub-elements: LL (single-byte length of the field) and VAR (the data). The length is BCD-encoded and, therefore, an LLVAR field can contain up to 99 data units.

LLLVAR or HLLVAR—variable-length fields which contain two sub-elements, LLL (double-byte length of the field) and VAR (the data). The length is BCD coded and contains three meaningful digits. It follows that an LLL-VAR field can contain up to 999 data units and the value in its LLL portion is zero-padded from the left. For example, a 125 byte long field 55 (binary) has its length encoded as 0x0125.

Padding

Padding of variable-length fields can differ, but there is a rule of thumb that applies to most dialects. It is as follows: if a value is alphanumeric or special (any of *as*, *ans*, *ns* fields), it is considered a string and is padded with spaces from the right. If the value is numeric-only, it is considered a number and is padded with zeroes from the left.

Thus, a value of "ABC" when populated in an alphanumeric field with total fixed length of 4, is represented as ABC⌃ (⌃being the space character) in a charac-ter encoding (see below), while a numeric value of 123, when encoded as a BCD value, is transmitted as 01 23.

Encoding

Several data-encoding methods can be highlighted in the ISO 8583 realm. First and foremost, there are the character encodings: ASCII and EBCDIC. Numeric data is also represented as BCD (binary-coded decimals). Finally, as part of a later addition for full-grade EMV transactions, there is the BER-TLV X.690 for-mat, set by ITU-T.

ASCII stands for "American Standard Code for Information Interchange"[5]. Originally developed as a 7-bit format, the encoding has been widely superseded

---

[5]More details on ASCII can be found in section 11.3.

by UTF-8 which is backward-compatible to it. Although it was extended to an 8-bit code which has seen multiple national code pages, the original 7-bit table is predominantly used in most payment applications.

Space character in ASCII is encoded as 0x20 (32 decimal), while decimal digits are mapped to codes 0x30 to 0x39. Thus, abundance of 0x20 values in an ISO message usually hint at a space-padded field while byte sequences like 31 39 36 33 indicate ASCII-encoded numeric sequences.

EBCDIC stands for Enhanced Binary Coded Decimal Interchange Code[6]. Originally developed as a 8-bit proprietary format of IBM's System/360, it had to be compatible with existing arrays of input/output devices and was designed as an incremental extension of existing punch card encodings. It is still being used in payment industry. Sometimes card scheme requires using EBCDIC for all text fields, in other cases the requirement covers proprietary fields (which routinely yields ISO messages in which some data elements are encoded in ASCII and some in EBCDIC).

A space character in EBCDIC is encoded as 0x40 (64 decimal) and decimal digits are encoded in range 0xF0 to 0xF9. Uppercase Latin letters occupy ranges 0xC1 to 0xC9, 0xD1 to 0xD9 and 0xE2 to 0xE9. The presence of byte sequences in which the first nibble is C,D, E or F and the second nibble is always between 0 and 9 hints at a possible EBCDIC-encoded character sequence.

BCD stands for "Binary Coded Decimal" and is a simple encoding in which numerical values, instead of being represented as a binary number, are encoded by allocating a fixed number of bits to each digit. In ISO 8583 messages the so-called packed BCD format is used: as four bits are sufficient to represent numbers from 0 to 9, each 4-bit nibble is used to contain a single digit.

To illustrate the three aforementioned encodings, consider the following example.

The decimal number of 17471, represented base 16, equals to $443F_{16}$. If transmitted on the wire, and, therefore, represented in big-endian or network byte order, the binary value occupies two bytes exactly as can be seen above, 44 3F. If encoded in packed BCD format, the value occupies three bytes and is represented as 01 74 71[7]. In EBCDIC and ASCII, the decimal value is encoded as F1 F7 F4 F7 F1 and 31 37 34 37 31, accordingly. Consider some other examples in the table 3.3.

Table 3.3: Examples of value encodings

Value	Format	Byte 1	Byte 2	Byte 3	Byte 4	Byte 5
12905	Binary	32	69			
12905	BCD	01	29	05		
12905	ASCII	31	32	39	30	35

---

[6]More details on EBCDIC can be found in section 11.4

[7]Note the left-padding with 0.

12905	EBCDIC	F1	F2	F9	F0	F5
7376	Binary	1C	D0			
7376	BCD	73	76			
7376	ASCII	37	33	37	36	
7376	EBCDIC	F7	F3	F7	F6	

BER-TLV or simply TLV encoding stands for "Basic Encoding Rules—Tag/Length/Value" encoding and is a means to represent a data structure in a serialized form suitable for data transfer. The BER-TLV format used in payments industry adheres to X.609 standard by ITU-T.

The encoding is called "tag-length-value" since each element of the data structure is represented by an identifier (or tag) followed by value length and then followed by the value itself. This allows packing of an arbitrary set of elements in arbitrary order into a single data element.

The EMV standard defines a set of tag values that should be used for data exchange between parties involved in an EMV transaction. For example, tag 5F34 corresponding to PAN sequence number, is defined as having numeric value and a nibble length of 2 (byte length of 1). This means that a sequence number of 2 is represented as 5F 34 01 02, with first two octets are the tag (0x5F34), third octet represents length in bytes (0x01) and the fourth and final octet is the value (0x02).

More details on BER-TLV format can be found in section 11.6.

Key Data Elements

The ISO standard defines a core set of data elements with specific semantics and formatting rules but also allows for a significant number of national and implementation-specific data elements. Furthermore, even the same definition of the data element in the standard is interpreted differently between dialects. The following section lists common fields and formats which do not differ much in their interpretation by card schemes.

Data Element 1—Bitmap The data element is always present in an ISO message, as it is required to parse the rest of the message. Details on the bitmap can be found in section 3.3.3.

Data Element 2—PAN The element is present in most ISO transactions, excluding some administrative/network management messages. The field format is LLVAR, and it contains a BCD-encoded PAN number. The length is specified in digits, rather than in bytes, and is also BCD-encoded. In case the PAN contains an odd number of digits, it is padded from the left with zeroes but the padding does not count towards the length. As the maximum length of a PAN is 19 digits, the maximum length of the data element is 11 bytes (1 byte of length and

10 bytes for the longest possible value). Consider examples of PANs and their ISO 8583 encodings in table 3.4. In the representation, length values are in *italics* and the zero padding is in **bold**.

Table 3.4: Examples of PAN formatting and padding

PAN	Length	Representation
3000 0000 0000 007	15	*15* **03** 00 00 00 00 00 00 07
4000 0000 0000 0002	16	*16* 40 00 00 00 00 00 00 02
5000 0000 0000 0000 005	19	*19* **05** 00 00 00 00 00 00 00 00 05

Data Element 3—Processing Code The processing code data element indicates the type of financial service requested and the type of source and target accounts affected by it. The format of the field is n - 6, i.e. it is always a 6-digit BCD-encoded numeric value.

The data element has three subelements and each of them has a length of 2 digits. Subelement 1 corresponds to the transaction type, subelement 2 indicates the source account type and subelement 3 indicates the target account type.

Actual values of processing codes that are in active use vary between implementations in different card schemes. Values of 00, 20 and 30 for subelement 1 indicate basic POS purchase, refund and balance inquiry, correspondingly, and values of all zeroes are the most common for subelements 2 and 3. In other words, an implementation should probably expect to use values of 000000, 200000 and 300000 for those operations. However, that may vary per card scheme and per geography.

Data Elements 4, 5 and 6—Amounts Data elements 4, 5 and 6 are defined as "amount, transaction", "amount, settlement" and "amount, cardholder billing" correspondingly.

These fields share a common format: they are all n - 12 BCD fields, left-padded with zeroes. Values in these fields are unsigned integers representing amounts in a currency that is either transmitted in another data element (for instance, transaction currency) or is implied as part of message context (for example, the cardholder's billing currency).

The decimal place in the amount fields is implied by currency exponent which is governed by ISO 4217 standard. A currency exponent expresses the number of digits after the decimal dot or the power of 10 by which the integer value should be divided to obtain the exact amount. Most currencies have an exponent of 2 (for example, US dollars, euro, British pounds or yuan renminbi); there are some currencies, mostly Middle Eastern ones, that have the exponent of 3 (Omani rials or Kuwaiti dinars to name two). Finally, in cases when the minor currency unit does not exist or is not in use, the exponent is 0 (for example, Japanese yen).

Table 3.5 displays some examples of encoding money amounts in different currencies.

Table 3.5: Examples of amount encodings

Amount	Currency	Exponent	Representation
32.15	US dollars	2	00 00 00 00 32 15
45.902	Kuwaiti dinar	3	00 00 00 04 59 02
2520	Japanese yen	0	00 00 00 00 25 20

Fields 4, 5 and 6 differ in their usage. Field 4, "amount, transaction", is the most frequently used field. It contains the POS or ATM transaction amount and is initially populated on the acquirer side. Field 6, "amount, cardholder billing", contains the amount which the cardholder should be billed and is usually populated by the payment network before the transaction reaches the issuer. Field 5, "amount, settlement", contains the amount of funds to be transferred between the issue and the acquirer (or vice versa, depending on the transaction type). If in use, it is typically populated by the payment network.

Data Element 7—Transmission Date and Time The field contains the timestamp of transmission and not the date and/or time when the actual transaction was performed. It is possible that, due to offline processing or other reason, the transaction was performed in the past and is transmitted at a different moment.

The format of the field is n - 10 BCD, and it contains the timestamp in MMD-Dhhmmss format, meaning that two digits of the month are followed by two digits of the day, 24-based hours, two digits of minutes and two digits of seconds.

For example, a transaction that was transmitted on March 4th, two minutes and 13 seconds after noon, has the timestamp value of 03 04 12 02 13 in the ISO message.

Timezone of the timestamp differs between card schemes and implementations.

Data Elements 9 and 10—Conversion rates Data Elements 9 and 10 are defined as "Conversion rate, settlement" and "Conversion rate, cardholder billing", correspondingly. These elements accompany data elements 5 and 6 in cases when they are present and when the currency of settlement or billing differs from the transaction currency. In other words, some issuers might see data element 10, but data element 9 is quite rare.

The format of these elements is n - 8, BCD. The first digit of the field contains "displacement" or "decimal indicator", a number from 0 to 7 indicating the position of the decimal point from the right. The remaining 7 digits contain the actual rate. Consider the example rate of 23.12032. The decimal dot is located at position 5 from the right, hence on the wire the value is represented as 52 31 20 32.

Data Element 11—System Trace Audit Number or STAN This field's format varies between implementations and ISO 8583 protocol revisions. In the older ISO 8583 standard it is n - 6 while later versions allow alphanumeric and special characters to be put in this field.

It is set by the transaction originator to uniquely identify a cardholder transaction and all messages that comprise it. For instance, an authorization, its response message and further reversal and reversal response messages (if a reversal event occurs) should all contain the same STAN value.

When the STAN is numeric, it cannot be all zeroes. The STAN, combined with DE 7 (transmission date and time) should uniquely identify transactions sent on the same day. However, if the daily volume of a particular institution is over 1 million transactions for a particular card scheme and an older ISO 8583 revision is in use with the payment network, the same values in the field can be repeated by the transaction originator.

Data Elements 12 and 13—Time and Date of Local Transaction In most cases data element 12 is n - 6 BCD and contains time in hhmmss 24-hour format, while data element 13 is n - 4 BCD and contains date in MMDD format. However, certain implementations utilize data element 12 as n - 12 and require a full timestamp to be populated in that field.

This data element contains the date and time of the card acceptor location. In the card-present environment, this means the date and time at the store when the actual transaction was performed, set in the *local timezone* of the card acceptor (as opposed to data element 7 which is sent in a scheme-defined timezone).

Consider the example of a transaction that happens in a store in the EST timezone at exactly 1:15 pm on May 18th, 2012. Assuming both data element 12 and 13 are utilized, data element 12 should be set to 13 15 00, and data element 13 should be set to 05 18.

However, message data element 7 according to the hypothetical card scheme rules should be set in UTC. That means that the hour part of the data element 7 transmission timestamp is be 18 and not 13 due to the +5 hours timezone difference. In addition to that, it is possible that the transaction was sent to the acquirer host a few microseconds before the end of the exact second and by the time the host has prepared the transaction for transmission to the network, the time of the host server is 18:15:01 and that also will be the value that will be sent in data element 7 (05 18 18 15 01).

Furthermore, it is possible that the transaction will be transmitted after a minute has flipped (for example, transaction captured at 13:15:59.999 but by the time it is sent to a scheme it is 13:16:00), or after a day or a month had changed.

In the card-not-present environment this field should be populated by the server that captures the transaction—in a proper, compliant implementation an e-commerce application that handles customer payment should transmit its server date and time in its local time zone.

Data Element 14—Date, Expiration This data element holds the card expiration date, as stored on the magnetic stripe, reported by card integrated chip circuit or entered manually. This field is n - 4, BCD and the expiry date is transmitted in YYMM format.

The card expiry date is defined as the last day of the month. I.e., if the card expires in May, 2015, it is valid through the 31st of May and is considered expired on June 1st.

Card schemes typically do not require their processors to decline transactions based on expiry date of the card. However, since the vast majority of card authorizations will be declined past the expiry date, most processors decline transactions on expired cards at the front-end, without sending them to payment networks.

Data Element 18—Merchant Type In most implementations, this field contains the so-called MCC (Merchant Category Code)—a 4-digit industry code that is assigned to the merchant when it's account is open with an acquirer. Its definition is n - 4.

The list of MCC codes partially coincides with the list of 4-digit SIC codes (Standard Industrial Classification codes)[8], in particular, in services and retail code groups. In 2004, the Internal Revenue Service had advised taxpayers to rely on merchant category codes in order to identify reportable payment card transactions.

However, while SIC allocates code per industry, covering industries such as mining and manufacturing, in the payment card industry codes were allocated to major airlines (3000-3299), car rental companies (3351-3441) and hotel chains and resorts (3501-3790). In SIC these ranges are assigned to manufacturing industries like rubber/leather/concrete/electronics and the likes.

Thus, certain generic MCCs co-exist with specific ones, as there also are generic codes for airlines (4511), car rentals (7512) and hotels (7011).

While the MCC table is in general shared across card schemes, rules under which they are assigned may differ. It follows that some merchants might have several different MCCs assigned according to rules of different card schemes.

---

[8]Standard Industrial Classification codes were introduced in the United States in 1937. Although a newer 6-digit classification had came since into being, 4-digit SIC codes are still in use by US authorities such as the US Department of Labor Occupation Safety and Health Administration.

Furthermore, in some cases the same outlet or terminal can utilize different MCCs based on the type of operation performed. For example, an automated teller machine is typically assigned MCC of 6011 (automatic cash disburse) but it can send transactions with MCC of 4829 (money transfers) provided that it supports that functionality.

Data Element 22—POS Entry Mode The data element varies in length between implementations. In most cases it is fully numeric, up to 4 positions in length and contains 2 or 3 meaningful digits. However, there are dialects with significantly different definitions of the field.

The POS entry mode describes the method used to enter the PAN and the card expiry date at the point-of-service. In some cases when an electronic terminal is used, the field can also contain an indication regarding terminal PIN input capability.

POS entry modes in use by different schemes can be largely grouped as follows[9]:

Unknown/no terminal used—is the value corresponding to transactions when the PAN/expiry date capture method is unknown or when the transaction was a paper-based one. In either case, it is either a rare method or a very bad default value, since other PAN entry modes are more appropriate for overwhelming majority of transactions. A common value for this entry mode is 00.

Manual/key entry—in the card-not-present environments, this value should be used whenever the PAN is manually entered by an operator after having been transmitted to the merchant by cardholder—in other words, in mail order/telephone order (MOTO) transactions. In the card-present environments, this value is used when the sales attendant types in the PAN number manually into the POS—usually after attempts to have the card read electronically fail. A common value for this entry mode is 01.

Magnetic stripe read/magstripe fallback—several possible conditions can lead to choosing the magnetic stripe read as a PAN entry method for a payment card. It is possible that a terminal is only equipped with a magnetic stripe reader, or, alternatively, a terminal is EMV-capable but the card has no chip embedded into it. In some cases, the conditions of the magnetic stripe read are distinguished further as reliable and partial. Such a "basic" magstripe read is typically indicated with values of 02 or, more commonly, 90.

Another possible condition is the **magstripe fallback**, when an attempt to read a chip-capable card on a chip-capable terminal has been made but failed. This condition is usually denoted by the value of 80.

---

[9]The codes listed in line are the ones used in the industry most frequently. As mentioned, in the case of a specific implementation values may vary significantly.

Payment networks and issuers expect full Track 1 and/or Track 2 data in case the PAN is entered using a magnetic stripe read.

Integrated circuit card read—this condition indicates that a contact chip read has been performed at the terminal to enter the card PAN and expiry date. Like with a magnetic stripe, unreliable ICC reads are often distinguished from reliable ones by a separate code value. This condition is usually denoted by the value of 05.

Electronic commerce—this condition is often defined as "PAN auto-entry using electronic commerce" but is used to indicate such conditions when the PAN is manually entered by the cardholder as well. It is used for such e-commerce scenarios as a one-time purchase. Card-on-file one-time purchases and recurring transactions and installments were also previously used with this POS entry mode, but got assigned separate entry mode values to better identify them. The e-commerce condition is usually denoted by values of 09 or 81.

Contactless chip—this condition is used when the PAN is entered via the contactless data transfer method, but utilizing the chip on the card and, consequently, passing full ICC data. The condition is also possible if a mobile device which is equipped with a secure element, and therefore capable of performing full-grade EMV transactions, is used for payment at the point of sale. This condition is commonly encoded with the value of 07.

Contactless magnetic stripe—the condition corresponds to situations when the PAN data is auto-entered using contactless data transfer method but under magnetic stripe data rules. A contactless mag-stripe read can occur either when the card or card reader do not support full-grade chip contactless transaction or when a mobile device with no secure element is used to perform a contactless payment transaction. In addition to various implementations of contactless magnetic stripe, the introduction of payment network tokenization has been accompanied by the introduction of conditions indicating PAN auto-mapping (applicable to issuers only). The contactless magstripe condition is usually designated with the value of 91, with several additional codes in use by different implementations.

Other conditions—that are not particularly common but are supported by most dialects include auto-entry with a bar-code reader or an optical reader.

Data Element 23—Card Sequence Number The format of this element is n - 3. It holds a packed BCD value of the card sequence number.

The value is mandatory in EMV full-grade chip transactions. In such cases the chip on card provides the value in a binary byte and the terminal is responsible to encode it in BCD format. Like all BCD values, it is left-padded with zeroes. Thus, for example, if a chip returns sequence number of 0x0A (decimal 10), it should be encoded in this data element as 00 10.

Data Element 25—POS Condition Code The element is not consistently used by various implementations. However, when schemes elect to encode these conditions in different and often proprietary formatted fields, the overall set of possible conditions is largely the same.

Data Element 35—Track 2 Data This element was originally designated to contain full Track 2 data exactly as read from the magnetic stripe (see section 2.4.2 for details). However, additional applications for the field have emerged, which do retain the same original field format. In particular, chip-based transactions generate Track 2 data as well.

Exact encoding of this data element depends on the implementation. In certain cases, the element is encoded as ans-37 and both 'D' and '=' symbols are allowed as field separator characters. In some other implementations, the field is n - 37 with the exception of 0xD (decimal 13) being allowed as the field separator.

When populating the field, the beginning and ending sentinels as well as the LRC character are removed.

Data Element 36—Track 3 Data This element contains Track 3 data as read from the magnetic stripe (see section 2.4.3 for details). It is usually defined as ans-104 and is supposed to contain the Track 3 value without beginning and ending sentinels and without the LRC character. However, as both the field and the entire magnetic stripe technology are phased out, some implementations do not support the field any longer.

Data Element 37—Retrieval Reference Number This element contains a number that is used with other key data elements to track all transactions in a cardholder transaction set. It is usually defined as an-12, however, not all the implementations support alphabetic characters as part of the element. The value is usually assigned by the acquirer, but can also be assigned by the merchant or electronic terminal.

To achieve the best interoperability between card schemes, it is preferable to populate this data element with numeric values only.

A possible and quite popular way to generate RRN values is according to the following format: YDDDnnxxxxxx

Here, Y denotes last digit of the year. Positions marked as DDD are populated with a numeric ordinal date, sometimes also called the Julian day. It is an ordinal integer value, assigned to each day of the year, starting with 1 to denote January 1. The value is zero-padded to the length of three and represents the value of data element 7. For instance, a value of 9 corresponds to January 9th and is represented as 009. The value of nn can be set to the hour of the transaction as taken from data element 7. Finally, the last six positions, denoted as xxxxxx, are set identical to data element 11.

Therefore, a transaction that took place at 10 am on February 13, 2012, having the STAN (data element 11) value of 429132, will is assigned RRN value of 204410429132, where 2 is the last digit of the year, 044 is the ordinal number of February 13th, zero-padded to length of three, the subsequent 10 corresponds to the hour and the value of 429132 is copied from the STAN.

Data element 38—Authorization Code This element is defined as an-6 and contains a code that is returned by the issuer in case the transaction is approved fully, partially or under condition of ID check. In dual-message systems, the code is retained by the acquirer and is later submitted alongside clearing records, as an additional proof of transaction authorization. If returned as part of the original authorization response, it is also sent as part of the reversal message.

The element can contain between 2 to 6 characters, depending on the implementation and a particular issuer, but cannot be all spaces or zeros.

In case of voice authorization, when the transaction authorization is made via a phone call to the issuing bank, the issuer provides an authorization code for the acquirer to use it during the transaction presentment.

Data element 39—Response Code This data element is defined as an-2 in most implementations, but also occurs as an-3 in dialects based on later revisions of ISO-8583, with two-character response codes that by far are more widespread.

The Response Code element defines the result of a request message or message disposition. It is populated by the entity that provides the response, i.e., either by the payment scheme system or by the issuer. It is used both in administrative and technical messages as well as in financial requests and advices.

A transaction or other request can be approved in full, approved conditionally, approved partially, referred to issuer or declined.

Full approval is indicated by response code of 00. In case of pre-authorizations or account validation requests, response code 85 ("No reason to decline") can be also returned by the issuer or payment the scheme. Both values of 00 and 85 can indicate the success of the original request. There are additional approval codes in certain implementations.

Conditional approval is not supported by all the schemes, however, certain solutions can respond with code 08—"Honor with ID". This response code, naturally applicable in the card-present environment only, instructs the merchant to check the cardholder ID and confirm that the full name on the corresponding document is identical to the cardholder's name as seen on card or extracted and displayed on the terminal based on track 1 data (see section 3.3.4).

In case of a partial approval, the response code can assume values of 10 ("Partial approval") or 87 ("Purchase amount only, no cashback allowed"). In these cases, the approved amount will be returned in data element 4 ("Amount, transaction"), with the original amount provided in data element 54 (see section 3.3.4).

Referred authorization receives a response code of 01 or 02, whose meaning is "Refer to card issuer". Upon receiving the code, the shop attendant can place a phone call to the issuer (by calling the acquiring bank that performs a subsequent call or sets up a call conference with an issuer representative, as necessary) for clarifications. Like in the case with voice authorizations, successful transaction receives an authorization code as a proof of the authorization (see also section 3.3.4).

Besides providing some insight into reasons for declines, there are reason codes which may or must prompt additional action on behalf of the card acceptor. For instance, response code 04 ("Capture card") instructs an automated terminal or an ATM not to return the card to the cardholder, and a store attendant may use this indication to retain the card in case it is physically safe. Response codes 41 ("Lost card") and 43 ("Stolen card") are supposed to be handled in a similar way, providing additional details about the reason for the card retainment.

Furthermore, certain solutions have special decline codes for card-on-file/recurring scenarios, notifying the processor that the current and future authorizations have been revoked and the card data should be removed from the processor database.

Data element 41—Terminal ID Data element 41 is defined as ans-8 and contains the identificaton value of the terminal that is operated by a card acceptor. The value is used in conjunction with data element 42 (Merchant ID) and is utilized when just the value of card acceptor ID is not sufficient to uniquely identify the physical or virtual terminal. The value is expected to be space-padded from the right to full length of the field. The terminal ID is also sometimes referred to as TID. Terminals that are equipped with a printer are required to print the value on paper slips.

Data element 42—Merchant ID Data element 42 is defined as ans-15 and contains the identificaton value of the merchant/card acceptor operating the terminal. It is sometimes referred to as MID or as the Card Acceptor ID and can represent a merchant, a specific merchant location, or even an individual terminal, depending on the design of the specific merchant-side solution.

Although the value can contain alphabetic and even special characters, certain card schemes rely on it for merchant registration for various programs and therefore, utilizing numeric-only values in this field is usually the safest option.

This element is used in conjunction with Data Element 41 to uniquely identify the specific terminal that is used to process the transaction.

Different card acceptor applications rely on either the terminal ID or the merchant ID as a unique identifier of the card acceptance terminal entity, as long as the combination of both has a one-to-one correspondence to actual terminals used.

Data element 43—Card Acceptor Name/Location Card Acceptor Name/ Location field is defined as ans-40 in ISO 8583 1978 revision. It is sometimes referred to as "Billing Descriptor" and contains a string that is eventually displayed on the cardholder statement.

In the card-present environment, this field must contain the merchant's "Doing business as" name, city and country, with exact lengths of each subfield slightly varying between implementations. In the card-not-present environment, a phone number is often populated in the city part of the field, to provide the cardholder with the ability to get in touch with the merchant quickly.

In certain cases, processors are allowed to set values in this field dynamically. However, scheme rules prescribe that all messages should still carry a well-defined prefix to simplify the identification by the cardholder.

Data element 45—Track 1 Data This element contains Track 1 data as read from the magnetic stripe (see section 2.4.1 for details). This field is defined as ans-76 in most implementations. In certain cases, special requirements are imposed on the field separator character. When populating this field, the beginning and ending sentinels as well as the LRC character are removed.

Data element 52—PIN Block This element is binary and is a 64-bit or 8-byte binary string. It contains the encrypted PIN block. For details on the format of the unencrypted EPB and the PIN encryption and translation processes, see 13.

Data element 54—Additional Amounts The element has variable length and can range from an-20 to an-120 in 20-symbol increments. Each 20-character value has the same structure: positions 1 and 2 contain the account type (such as default, checking or saving account), positions 3 and 4 contain amount type (such as account balance, previously requested amount or a surcharge), positions 5 through 7 contain currency code of the amount, position 8 contains the amount sign, C for positive and D for negative value, and positions 9 through 20 contain the actual amount, with implied exponent according to the currency.

This field is utilized in multiple use cases. In many solutions in case of a partial approval the original requested amount is returned in this field. In another popular scenario, the issuer may decide to return the account balance alongside the transaction response or list the balances on several accounts. Various issuer surcharges can also be returned as an additional amount in data element 54.

For example, if the account type is "checking" (20), the amount type is "available balance" (02), the currency is Euro (currency code 978) and there is a positive balance of 200 euro on the account, a single 20-symbol string is formatted as 2002978C000000020000.

Data element 55—ICC Data This element contains the ICC data as transmitted by the card's integrated chip via contact or contactless means. The element is of variable length and can contain up to 255 binary bytes or 510 nibbles. While the element itself is generated during the exchange between terminal and card and is transmitted by the payment solutions unaltered, its length is encoded differently in different implementations, being either a binary 1-byte value or a 2-byte BCD element. The element contains BER-TLV data (see section 11.6).

3.4   Other Card Scheme Services

Besides routing of authorization and clearing messages between the payment network participants, card schemes provide a range of additional services to member institutions.

Stand-in Processing (sometimes abbreviated as STIP) activates in four-party schemes when connection to an issuer is unavailable due to planned or unplanned downtime. In this case, schemes rely on predefined tables of parameters set by the issuer and pre-shared card validation keys and pin validation keys to check card integrity, validate PIN codes and approve or decline transactions. Sophisticated STIP solutions keep track of the total count and amount of authorizations according to various criteria. For instance, it may be possible to define a white-listed card, authorizations attempts which are always approved by STIP, provided they are under a certain threshold. Once the issuer comes back online, the details on approvals and declines performed in their absence are communicated by the STIP service, usually in form of advice messages.

International, Regional and National Settlement services collect and distribute the funds between issuers and acquirers. In certain areas (for example, Iceland) same-day national settlement is performed as it is also mandated by the local law. In certain regions such as the Eurozone most schemes support next-day settlement in the Euro currency. Finally, international settlements perform necessary currency conversions to facilitate the exchange of funds between institutions. Schemes do not support all the currencies as settlement currencies—for example, major schemes performed settlement in Russia in such currencies as euros and US dollars for an extensive period of time which resulted in a double currency conversion for every domestic transaction.

Fraud Prevention services enable online transactions scoring for fraud probability and the exchange of information about fraudulent transactions as well as lost and stolen cards between the payment network participants.

Data Integrity services provide an additional validation layer of transaction formats and data consistency between authorization and clearing. For example, a data integrity rule can check if a transaction marked as a e-commerce in the POS entry mode field arrives with Track 2 data, or another contradiction between various transaction parameters. In that case, the transaction can be either declined online or a notification on the violation of the data integrity rule can be sent to the party.

Payment Network Tokenization service is described in section 4.6.3.

Account-Level Product Management service enables banks to update products associated with a particular card in case a cardholder has met certain spending criteria. The service is typically used to issue a new, VIP card to a high-spending individual without changing its PAN number, since different card products are issued in different BIN ranges. By using an account-level product management service, banks can spare the cardholder the hassle of communicating the new card number to all merchants that store it on file.

Account Updater services enable the exchange of account data between institutions. In case when a card is replaced by a card having a new number (for example, if the account-level product management service was not available or supported and the cardholder had received a VIP card) or an expired card is reissued with the same PAN but a new sequence number and expiry date, this type of service enables the issuer to communicate the new PAN and/or the new expiry date to the acquirer. The update of stored accounts is normally initiated by the acquirer that submits the list of PANs to the payment network service. Then the network distributes inquiries to supporting issuers, collects and aggregates the updates and returns them back to the acquirer.

Recurring Payment Revocation service enables issuers to communicate revocations of recurring authorizations to scheme networks, thus placing the burden of declining those transactions on the network itself. Both the service and the account updater service are described in section 4.6.2.

Address Verification service is described in section 4.5.

CARD-NOT-PRESENT ENVIRONMENT

Chapter 4

Card-Not-Present Environment

CONTENTS

4.1 Introduction

In the card-not-present environment, as the name implies, the actual card or device is not physically present at what is considered the point of sale. In this case, the merchant should either enable communicating the PAN and other card details via a channel (it is predominantly phone, mail or Internet, although in certain implementations mobile and "browser-based" channels are sometimes considered separately) or have those details available from a previous transaction (for instance, have a card stored on file for better customer experience with the customer returning to purchase again, or have a subscription-based service with recurrent billing). The specifics of the conditions are described in section 2.11.

Lack of ability to verify the cardholder identity or the card authenticity (at the very least by scrutinizing card design including hologram and checking the buyer's additional identification document), combined with the attractiveness and fast growth of these remote channels, has stimulated the creation of several technical means whose goal is to improve security of sensitive data and combat payment card fraud in card-not-present solutions.

4.2 Secure Sockets Layer

Initially, e-commerce transactions were submitted over the Internet in plain text and there was no standard encryption protocol commonly supported by browsers and web servers. Card data was prone to eavesdropping and man-in-the-middle attacks, being relatively easy to copy or intercept along many routing nodes between the client's browser and the server. The introduction of SSL (Secure Sockets Layer) by Netscape Corporation made the establishment of a direct encrypted tunnel between browsers and servers possible.

The SSL protocol later superseded by TLS (Transport Layer Security) contains three principal security features. First, during the establishment of the tunnel, the server-side signed certificate is cryptographically validated by the client (the browser). Then a random secret symmetric encryption key is generated and shared between the client and the server. Second, the communications between the client and the server are encrypted using that one-time key. Finally, each message exchanged over the tunnel contains a digital signature.

4.3 3D Secure

The development and dissemination of standardized interoperable means to establish secure communication channels between browsers and card acceptor servers resolved the problem of eavesdropping to channels that transfer sensitive payment data. However, that did not allow any authentication of the cardholder or the card beyond CVV2 (see section 2.5.3). To address the problem, schemes have experimented with various technologies such as SET (Secure Electronic Transaction protocol). Those attempts, however, proved to be unsuccessful untill a non-invasive transparent and browser based 3D Secure method emerged and gained traction.

That XML-based protocol was originally developed by Arcot Systems under the name of TransFort and its use was announced by Visa USA in 2001. It was originally deployed under the name of "Verified By Visa". Later, it was adopted by other major industry players, such as MasterCard (under the name of MasterCard SecureCode), JCB (as J/Secure) and American Express (as American Express SafeKey). As was the case with ISO 8583 financial transaction messages standard, the protocol allows for certain flexibility in implementation and hence the actual solutions slightly vary between card schemes.

The protocol is called "3D secure" where "D" stands for "domain" and denotes a three-domain model, with the domains defined as the acquirer domain, the issuer domain and the interoperability domain. In a nutshell, during a 3D Secure transaction the cardholder, while shopping on an e-commerce website is redirected to an additional authentication page hosted by the issuing bank. The page performs an additional authentication using either pre-shared static or a one-time dynamic password. Then the issuer system generates cryptographic evidence of the authentication later forwarded by the acquirer as part of the authorization request for the transaction. Earlier implementations of the protocol supported the Activation During Shopping (ADS) feature as well. The feature allows the cardholder for whom the authentication is attempted for the first time to be redirected to their issuer's web page to enroll for the service. The enrollment is transparent to the merchant: upon its completion, the merchant sees continuation of the shopping process by the cardholder as if just the authentication of the transaction was performed. That feature led to criticism of the protocol by security experts, since the integration of 3D Secure into merchant flow which was IFRAME-based allowed for easy spoofing of the issuer's website, which in this case would be hard to identify even by a security-savvy cardholder.

4.3.1 Overview

Figure 4.1 contains major functional modules of a 3D secure solution. It has been purposely simplified to display components only relevant for acquiring of payments.

MPI (Merchant Plug-In) is integrated into merchant online stores. It handles communications with the payment schemes and the issuers. It is responsible for checking the enrollment status and then processing card authentication.

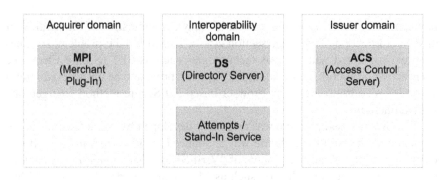

Figure 4.1: Major modules of 3D Secure domains

Directory Server authenticates the merchant and is queried for the enrollment status of the issuer and the specific card by the MPI while also serving as a routing entity for requests to ACS or the Stand-In service.

ACS (Access Control Server) services requests for authentication on the issuer side. It checks the enrollment, performs authentication and generates the cryptographic evidence of transaction authentication. It can also perform service activation during shopping, i.e., allow the cardholder to sign up for 3D Secure during the purchase process.

Attempts/Stand-In Service generates cryptographic evidence of an authentication attempt made by the merchant in cases when the issuer does not support the service, the specific card is not enrolled or when the issuer ACS is unavailable.

The 3D Secure authentication process consists of two steps: participation check and payer authentication.

4.3.2   Participation Check

As part of the step, the issuer and the card participation in 3D Secure service are checked. During the participation check, the merchant also gets authenticated when a certificate that is deployed as part of MPI is validated by the directory server.

The process begins with MPI issuing a request to the Directory Server. If the authentication of the merchant is successful, the Directory Server determines the address of an appropriate ACS, based on PAN data provided by the MPI and forwards the request to it. If no ACS is available or the cardholder does not participate in 3D Secure service, the Directory Server routes the request to the Attempts service instead.

The response follows the route from ACS or the Attempts service to the Directory Server and back to the MPI. If as part of the routing the corresponding system has indicated that no authentication or no attempted authentication response is available, the flow terminates with MPI indicating the status to the invoking application. Otherwise, Payer Authentication commences.

4.3.3   Payer Authentication

During Payer Authentication the MPI redirects the cardholder's browser (usually in an embedded IFRAME) to the issuer ACS.

The ACS performs authentication steps according to the implementation decided upon by the issuer. If the cardholder already participates in the 3D Secure service, the issuer confirms the cardholder's identity using a one-time password texted to the cardholder's mobile phone, a push notification to the issuer's mobile app or a pre-shared static password. If the cardholder has not signed up for the service, the issuer has the option to perform Activation During Shopping.

Due to a high drop-out rate of full 3D Secure transactions, many issuers elect to increasingly rely on risk-based authentication, skipping the authentication altogether in case the transaction is safe according to their own risk evaluation rules.

The issuer can provide an attempted authentication response when for some reason the authentication is not available for the particular cardholder.

As mentioned above, in cases when either the issuer or the cardholder is not enrolled to the service, the Attempts/Stand-In service provides an attempted authentication response. The redirection to the service is handled by Directory Service and is transparent to the MPI.

The ACS or the Attempts/Stand-In service response contains a unique transaction id, the indication of the authentication result (failed, attempted, succeeded) and cryptographic evidence of the authentication or attempted authentication. That response is forwarded back to the Merchant Plug-In by the Directory Server for further use in the authorization request.

4.3.4   Payer Authentication

The ACS or the Attempts/Stand-In service outputs should be included in the authorization message the card acquirer sends to the payment network after the 3D Secure flow completion. Both the data element and the encoding of the values vary between scheme implementations.

The binary evidence can be sent as a binary value, as a hex string (i.e., as a string of ASCII characters 0-9 and A-F representing the numeric values) or in Base-64 encoding (see section 11.5), in either ASCII or EBCDIC character encoding.

The evidence is sometimes referred to as Universal Cardholder Authentication Field (UCAF) or Cardholder Authentication Verification Value (CAVV).

The transaction ID is not mandatory in all cases and also varies in representation.

The 3D Secure authentication attempt status is referred to as "ECI" or "E-Commerce Indicator" and is typically represented as a two- or three-digit code indicating "full authentication", "attempted authentication" and "no authentication" and having values of 05, 06, and 07, correspondingly.

4.3.5   3D Secure Adoption and Challenges

Visa, as well as other card schemes, were interested in promoting the use of 3D Secure protocol in the e-commerce environment. For that purpose, schemes introduced lower interchange rates, benefitting merchant costs, and also announced a chargeback liability shift for certain chargeback reason codes.

However, cardholders did not respond well to the introduction of the 3D Secure authentication. Abandonment rates of shopping carts during online shopping were in double digits or, by some estimates, as high as 40%. It appeared that many cardholders either did not remember or did not renew their pre-shared password.

The situation was slightly alleviated by issuers switching to risk-based authentication, during which the issuer ACS estimates fraudulent transaction risks and in case of low risk provides the necessary cryptogram in a manner transparent to the end user.

That cardholder authentication method became widespread in the United Kingdom dramatically lowering the drop-out rates.

However, the emergence of such multiple Internet-connected devices as tablets and smartphones alongside with an increased sensitivity of merchants to customer experience made the 3D Secure protocol somewhat outdated. It did require the display of an issuer-generated web page (framed or full), a requirement which complicated the development of mobile applications and forced web e-commerce stores to display a payment step that stood in stark contrast with the rest of their user interfaces.

4.4   3D Secure 2.0 (EMV 3D Secure)

To address the 3D Secure challenges, in 2014, Visa and MasterCard developed and contributed to EMVCo, a draft of 3DS 2.0 specification. The specification was published as a standard in 2016, and, unlike the proprietary 3D Secure, the new version of the protocol is provided to the industry royalty-free.

By design the new 3D Secure 2.0 protocol promotes the issuer-side risk-based authentication aiming to identify legitimate transactions correctly and make them as frictionless as possible.

4.4.1   Major Changes in 3D Secure 2.0

The new protocol differs from its predecessor in almost every aspect.

To begin with, it is no longer XML-based but relies on JSON as the format for all its messages. It also utilizes JWE (JSON Web Encryption according to RFC 7516).

The new protocol supports frictionless flow by design, allowing involved parties to avoid the additional redirection to the issuer ACS as well as enabling the transmission of additional user data to the issuer, thus simplifying the task of making a risk assessment.

As for the UI, the protocol continues to support browser-based redirection to ACS, but also introduces native and HTML UI templates for mobile applications, allowing seamless customer experiences on these parties.

In addition to interactive exchanges of (possibly several) challenges and responses between the cardholder and the issuer's systems the protocol allows performing decoupled/out-of-band authentications, whereas the cardholder switches to the issuer's app to confirm the transaction.

Another flaw present in 3D Secure 1.0 was with "disappearing" users when after redirection to an ACS, the merchant storefront could only learn about the outcome of the authentication if its every step worked properly and the user was redirected back to the merchant's web site. In 3D Secure 2.0 the loop is closed with a special new message sent back from the issuer to the acquirer.

Finally, the protocol introduced the support for non-payment authentication and merchant-initiated requests.

In addition to the protocol, the standard includes a definition of SDK for use on mobile devices.

4.4.2   3D Secure 2.0 Actors and Messages

The new standard introduced slight modifications to the terminology. MPI is now replaced with *3DS Server*, merchant storefront is referred to as *3DS Requestor*, while a mobile app on the consumer device is *3DS Client*. Directory server and ACS retained their names from the previous version of the protocol.

As mentioned previously, all messages are JSON objects. A message type is defined by the messageType field.

Any 3DS-related flow is preceded by one or several PReq messages sent by the 3DS Server to Directory Servers it knows. Each DS responds with a PRes message, providing the card number ranges and supported protocols, thus enabling the 3DS Server to route future authentication requests properly (see figure 4.2).

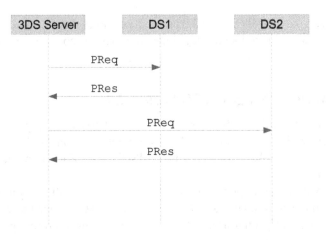

Figure 4.2: PReq and PRes messages

The authentication begins with an AReq message. It contains transaction details, if used for payment authentication, both basic (on par with data sent in
3D Secure 1.0 messages) and extended. In case of mobile SDK, it also contains
cryptographical data used for key exchange. The high-level flow is shown in figure 4.3.

The message is sent either by the merchant's app or storefront to the 3D
Server routing it to the appropriate Directory Server. The latter may either respond to it (scenario 1 in figure 4.3) or forward it to an ACS.

In ARes, the response to AReq, the ACS or the Directory Server provides authentication status as well as corresponding additional details. An authentication
request can be approved by ACS (scenario 2) or an evidence of authentication attempt can be generated by DS (scenario 1). In these cases, the ARes will contain
necessary authentication data. The ACS may decide that a challenge is required.
In that case, the ARes message contains an ACS URL (scenario 2 in figure 4.3).
Finally, the authentication request can be rejected right away and the status value
arrives as part of an ARes message, too.

When as a result of AReq/ARes message exchange the ACS informed the
merchant-side system that a challenge is required, it occurs via a direct interaction between the 3D Requestor and the ACS. In the case of a browser-based flow
the interaction occurs via browser redirection and using HTTP POST requests.
In the case of an SDK or mobile app in general the application sends one or
several CReq messages to the ACS receiving in CRes information regarding the
interaction status as well as necessary details for a subsequent step in it (e.g., first
CRes can contain UI template details, while a second one carries a confirmation
of successful cardholder authentication).

Prior to issuing a final CRes to the 3D Requestor environment (in the form
of a response to CReq or by redirecting the cardholder's browser back to the

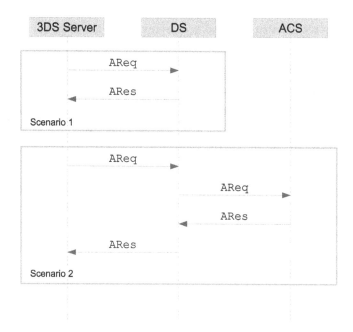

Figure 4.3: AReq and ARes messages

merchant store) the ACS sends a RReq message back to 3D Server via the DS, notifying it of the authentication attempt outcome. The ACS waits for an acknowledging RRes message before sending the final CRes to the 3DS Requestor.

Each transaction performed in the 3DS 2.0 environment gets up to three identifiers: 3DS Server ID, Directory Server ID and Access Control Server ID, if the transaction reaches DS and ACS, accordingly.

It is worth noting that the authenticationValue field containing the cryptographic evidence of the completed authentication can be present either in ARes or in RReq messages but never in CRes.

4.4.3   Browser-based Flow

During initialization the 3DS Server obtains BIN ranges from several Directory Servers. Some of the ranges may include the so-called 3DS Method information.

The 3DS Method is an address to which the merchant's store must perform an HTTP POST request with 3DS Server transaction ID prior to attempting authentication. The purpose of this step is to allow the ACS or another linked system to gather whatever device and browser information it can discern from the HTTP request.

After completing that optional preparation step, the 3DS Server crafts an AReq message that is sent to DS and, through it, to the ACS.

If the ACS doesn't support 3DS 2.0 and an "attempts" service is supported by the DS, it crafts an ARes with corresponding authentication value and sends it to the 3DS Server.

In case the ACS decides to authenticate the cardholder in a frictionless manner, it reports so in the ARes. Otherwise, the ACS can request either a Challenge or a Decoupled authentication. The Challenge flow is shown in figure 4.4.

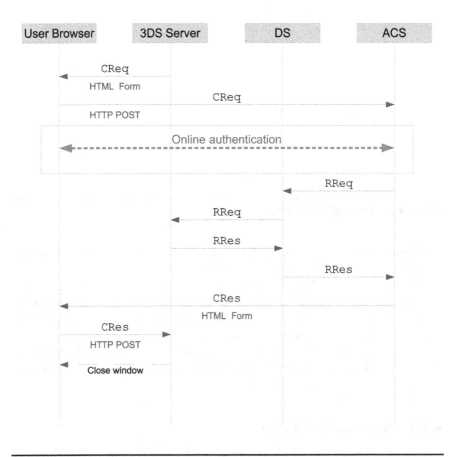

Figure 4.4: Browser-based authentication—Challenge flow

If the ACS has requested a challenge, the 3DS Server crafts a CReq message, encodes it using Base 64 encoding (see section 11.5) and places it in a form which the browser will then automatically post to an ACS URL. The 3DS Requestor environment awaits a RReq message followed by another HTTP POST request by the cardholder's browser, in which the CRes message is included in a similar manner.

The cardholder is redirected to the ACS environment where any necessary authentication steps are performed. Upon completion of the either successful or failed challenge-based authentication the ACS sends an RReq message to the 3DS Server via DS.

In case of a decouple authentication, there are no further UI interactions with the cardholder as part of the 3DS 2.0 flow. The 3DS Server has to wait for an RReq from the ACS, containing necessary details regarding the decoupled authentication outcome.

4.4.4 App-based Flow

The app-based flow begins when the application issues an AReq to the 3DS Server. The latter forwards it to an ACS via a DS. In case of a frictionless authentication, the ARes contain the required authentication value and the flow ends.

Otherwise, if a challenge is required, the app crafts a CReq and sends it directly to the ACS. The CReq contains an indication of supported UI options, including native UI, HTML or both.

The first CRes from the ACS contain the appropriate UI definitions: either an HTML that is rendered as-is or a definition of native UI controls that the application has to render on the mobile device screen.

At this junction, the flow can continue in either Challenge or Out-of-band modes.

In Challenge mode the application captures user input and submits it to the ACS via a CReq message. In native mode, the values of UI controls rendered by the application are used. In HTML mode, the application intercepts the GET or POST request that originates from the HTML form embedded into the UI and sends the value in a CReq request.

The interaction continues until an RReq arrives at the 3DS Server followed by a final CRes sent to the application by the ACS. The interaction is shown in figure 4.5.

In case of out-of-band flow the cardholder follows a push notification or written instructions to switch to another (issuer-provided) app. According to the standard, the SDK sends another CReq request automatically any time the originating merchant application returns to the foreground of the device. The ACS performs cardholder authentication in a separate flow and updates the 3DS Server with a RReq upon its successful completion. The mobile app, in turn, learns of the authentication success once one of CReqs it re-sends returns with authentication results.

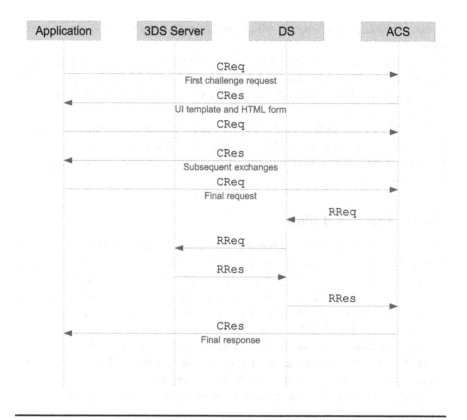

Figure 4.5: App-based authentication—Challenge flow

4.4.5 *Merchant-initiated Transaction (3RI)*

In case of a 3RI (3DS Requestor-Initiated) flow, there is no cardholder UI to be displayed. There are therefore three possible outcomes of such a request: either the transaction is authenticated, thus providing an additional confirmation of, for example, validity of a recurring subscription, or the transaction is rejected, notifying the merchant that their standing order authorization is no longer valid, or, finally, a decoupled authentication launches, verifying cardholder's identity and confirming the transaction via a separate channel.

In case of 3RI, the 3DS Server issues an AReq request. If the request results are in a definitive answer, it is provided back from the ACS in an ARes. Otherwise, if a decoupled authentication is launched, the 3DS Server later receives an RReq message containing the result of the decoupled flow.

4.4.6 EMV 3-D Secure Security

The connectivity of 3DS Servers to DS and between DS and ACS is secured using TLS certificates, as was the case with 3D Secure 1.0. Communication between merchant systems and the 3DS Server is also performed over a secure socket tunnel.

However, in case of 3DS SDK, additional measures to protect the data are undertaken.

The device information 3DS SDK sends alongside 3DS messages is encrypted with a public key of the corresponding directory server. The encrypted data is later sent to the 3DS Server in "SDK Encrypted Data" data element as part of an AReq message. The distribution of said keys is not covered in the standard, but it is assumed that the 3DS Server is capable of providing a public key for the app to use.

To set up of communication between ACS and the application a key exchange mechanism called "Elliptic Curve Diffie-Hellman" is utilized. Using the mechanism the SDK sends a SDK Ephemeral Public Key to the ACS in the AReq message. The ACS responds to it in the ARes with an ACS Ephemeral Public Key additionally signed with a certificate of the DS also known to the SDK. Each side, the SDK and the ACS, can use the pair of ephemeral public keys to construct a mutually shared secret key to encrypt all subsequent CReq/CRes message exchanges.

4.5 Address Verification Service (AVS)

The Address Verification Service is another service provided by schemes that aims to decrease fraud by increasing the number of independent details that can be validated during a card-not-present transaction.

The service allows the validation of some or all of the cardholder personal details, such as the cardholder's name, billing street address and billing zip code, versus data on file at the issuer bank.

During the checkout process the card acceptor, in addition to PAN, captures the expiry date and CVV2, the cardholder's name and billing address (i.e., the address to which card statements are sent by the issuer bank). These additional fields can be sent to schemes either separately from the authorization request or as part of it, receiving a response on address verification results.

A failed cardholder's name or billing address verification does not automatically result in an authorization decline but combined with other suspicious indicators can drive the merchant's decision to decline or cancel the transaction at the front-end.

The card acceptor or the acquirer bank can later use the AVS result to make a decision on either moving the transaction forward or canceling it (by not authorizing or reversing the authorization). For instance, an advanced fraud-prevention system can take into account discrepancies between shipping address, billing address, card country as identified by its BIN and geo-location data based on customer IP address and decide that the overall risk score of the particular transaction is too high.

Adding more fields to be manually populated by a customer increases a possibility of getting a false negative response for a valid transaction. To avoid issues related to human mistakes or differences in spelling AVS validation is performed using the so-called condensed format. In most implementations the service extracts numeric symbols from the provided street address, in order of appearance and compares them to the data stored on file for the cardholder rather than comparing the full street address to the one stored in the issuer systems

As an example consider a cardholder whose address is "1600 Pennsylvania Ave NW". While registering the address in the issuer system, it is to be stored both in full and condensed format as "1600 Pennsylvania Ave NW" and "1600". During the verification the customer can spell the address as "1600 Pennsylvania Av." or "1600 Pennsylvania Ave" but as the numerical parts match the field passes verification.

A request to validate the address is usually bundled with the authorization request and the result of the address verification arrives in a proprietary field varying per solution but in general, reflects the street address status and zip code. Each of those can roughly have the following conditions: "provided and matched", "provided, not matched", "provided, not validated" and "not provided". Depending on the specific implementation, certain combinations of the conditions can be coalesced into one. Furthermore, in some cases there are separate indicators for domestic and international address validation results.

Most AVS implementations limit the validation to the street address in condensed format and zip code. The service is widespread in the United States, the UK and Canada with less traction elsewhere in the world.

4.6 Tokenization

A token in the payment industry is a surrogate value used instead of an actual PAN to perform payment transactions. Originally used in the card-not-present environment, tokenization uses have been extended to the card-present environment with contactless technology. As tokens are very application-specific and in many cases are bound to a single card acceptor, relying on tokenized PAN values reduces fraud risk that follows from data theft, and a token obtained from one merchant is not usable with other merchants.

The card data can be tokenized on either acquirer/processor side or in the payment network. The former is widespread; the latter is emerging but gained significant traction with technologies like Apple Pay™ or Samsung Pay™ based on the EMV Tokenization standard.

The core difference between two approaches to tokenization is shown in figure 4.6.

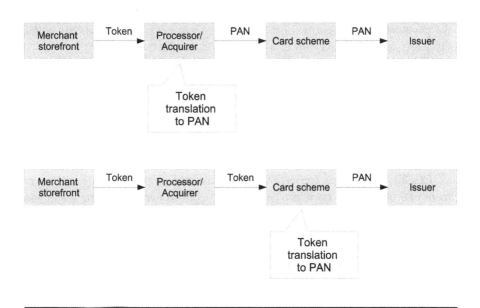

Figure 4.6: Processor and payment network tokenization

4.6.1 Processor Tokenization

Consider the business scenario of such a subscription-based service as utilities or a magazine subscription with monthly billing. Every month at a certain date (after closure of a billing cycle in case of utility bills), the cardholder needs to be charged a particular amount to the card stored with the processor on behalf of the service provider. To do that the processor's system should forward a properly formed authorization or clearing request to the scheme which, inevitably, has to contain a full PAN.

That means that the PAN must be stored for the duration of subscription, potentially until its expiry alongside its expiry date. Besides, such additional authentication and fraud prevention means as CVV2 validation, the address verification and 3D Secure are available with the first transaction in the series or upon subscription setup, but the values are not stored for subsequent transactions. As CVV2 value is used to confirm the card validity, once stored, it does not make subsequent transactions any more valid but increases a risk of theft;

address data may change during the lifetime of a subscription causing false negative responses, and the 3D Secure process generates cryptographic evidence of cardholder identity at the time of the transaction which is not valid for reuse.

In a solution which stores such sensitive data as payment card details, data in the storage itself (i.e., database files on a disk array) is vulnerable for data theft. Hence, a solution that became widespread in the industry was not to store the payment data in clear-text but to encrypt it while it is stored and only handle clear-text data in memory for as a short period of time as possible.

This can be achieved, for instance, by utilizing an HSM. For the purpose of describing the data flow let us assume that the LMK is the active HSM master key and that DEK denotes "data encryption key", a generic-purpose key that is generated by the HSM and whose clear-text form is never exposed.

The tokenization solution stores a single DEK_{LMK} (a DEK encrypted by LMK) but certainly a full solution deploys multiple DEKs at least for key rotation purposes.

Consider a business scenario when a consumer signs up for automatic payment of a utility bill. There are two possible options here: either the cardholder signs up for a future payment or the cardholder pays one of the bills immediately. In either case the card acceptor captures the PAN and card expiry date and gathers data for additional cardholder and card validity checks: the cardholder also provides CVV2, enters a billing address for an AVS check and, for the sake of the example, performs a 3D Secure authentication.

To better illustrate the principles, assume that consumer data and the billing processes are performed in a merchant-owned billing system, external to the card payment processor, an entity responsible for handling the payments itself.

Prior to the token creation the processor performs either a Purchase transaction or an Account validation transaction, depending on whether there is a payment happening simultaneously with storing the card on file or not, correspondingly. The processor sends the PAN, expiry date, CVV, billing address and 3D Secure authentication data to the payment scheme and upon the successful completion of the operation performs the following steps:

1. Sensitive data such as CVV, address, and 3D Secure cryptographic value is discarded.

2. The PAN and expiry date are combined into a vector V and sent to the HSM alongside with DEK_{LMK}

3. The HSM decrypts DEK_{LMK} with the LMK stored internally and then encrypts vector V with the DEK.

4. The HSM returns V_{DEK}.

5. The solution stores V_{DEK} in the database and assigns a token value T to it.

6. The token value is returned to the invoking application.

At a later stage upon the closure of a utility billing cycle, the merchant-owned billing system decides to bill a certain card. The billing system extracts the value of T and sends it to the processor alongside necessary additional transaction details (amount etc). Upon receiving this request, the processor performs the following steps:

1. The value of T is used to retrieve V_{DEK} from the database.

2. V_{DEK} and DEK_{LMK} with the LMK are sent to HSM for decryption.

3. The HSM decrypts DEK_{LMK} with the LMK that is stored internally, then uses clear-text DEK value to decrypt V_{DEK}.

4. The clear-text value of V is returned to the caller system.

5. The processor system does not store the V value but extracts the PAN and expiry date data from it and transmits it to the payment scheme directly.

An automatic billing system acting at the backend and having no interaction with the customer at the point of payment cannot obtain and therefore provide a CVV value. With 3D Secure 1.0, no authentication was also possible. With 3DS 2.0, it is possible to initiate a 3RI flow (see section 4.4.5), during which, either the ACS will approve the transaction or it will reach out to the cardholder for a decoupled authentication. However, in the scenario of recurring utility bills this scenario is unlikely.

Therefore, such a transaction (a subsequent recurring transaction) is transmitted with the PAN and expiry date only. However, the original account validation or purchase did contain confirmation of the card validity and cardholder identity, hence the issuer can still ensure the validity of the request, provided that this transaction is properly matched to the first transaction in series. In most card scheme solutions, in order to simplify the task transactions are marked as recurring with a proprietary flag or value.

That differs from the card-on-file scenario. To illustrate it consider the following example: a merchant, an online e-commerce store, offers its customers to save their payment card for future ease of payment. This, too, can be done independently or jointly with a purchase. In the scenario the tokenization happens in exactly the same manner: the cardholder and the card are authenticated with available and supported means, and the card number and card expiry date are securely encrypted and stored in the processor system. However, subsequent re-use of stored values is interactive and happens with a subsequent purchase: the merchant can prompt the cardholder for such additional authentication as reentry of the CVV value or a challenge-based 3D Secure authentication. Then the data can be sent to card schemes alongside the PAN that was stored on file. This option improves security but slightly impairs usability, hence many merchant solutions do not support it. To distinguish an automated recurring transaction from a card-on-file transaction certain card scheme protocols support a proprietary flag (see also Standing Authorisation in section 2.11).

4.6.2 Revocation of Authorization and Account Updater Services

A cardholder who provides card details to a merchant or a services company is charged recurringly until the contract has terminated. However, when a card is no longer valid (for instance, it has expired or was stolen and had to be blocked and replaced by the issuer), all future recurring transactions are going to be declined.

To reduce the number of unsuccessful authorization attempts some schemes provide special decline codes allowing issuers to distinguish generic declines from those following from one of the specific use-cases mentioned above. They are often called "revocation of authorization" and upon receiving such a code, the entity storing the tokenized account details on file should cease their recurring PAN authorization attempts. In some cases schemes further unburden issuers by allowing them to define PANs lists for which the recurring authorizations are declined by scheme networks without reaching the issuer.

The mechanism only provides the indication of a revoked PAN authorization during an authorization attempt. However, a card can be renewed (issued with a new card sequence number and new expiry date) or a new card can be issued for that cardholder (and in this case the cardholder uses a new PAN). A simple response code cannot carry the details and for such cases schemes have deployed "account updater" services.

A typical "account updater" service is a file-based card scheme service receiving a PANs list and expiry dates from merchants either directly or via their acquirers. Then the service distributes inquiries to issuers, gathers back the results and responds with a file that, in a nutshell, contains a brief status of each submitted account. An account can be valid and have a new expiry date, or a new PAN value and expiry date, and corresponding values are available in the scheme response.

Upon receiving a response file, the processor or other entity keeping the PANs on file should update expiry dates and PAN numbers as instructed. The implementation of the service proactively informs the processor of legitimate changes on the cardholder account, helping avoid "Do not honor" and "Revoke authorization" declines upon future authorization attempts.

4.6.3 Payment Network Tokenization (EMV Tokenization)

Card data tokenization on the processor side has several disadvantages.

Special provisions must be made to secure the data on the processor side properly. However, even with all the necessary compliance measures in place, abundance of recurring billing setups by companies and online stores capable of card-on-file shopping means that the cardholder's PAN is distributed across multiple different systems beyond the cardholder's and cardholder's bank control.

In order to provide the stored card data always be up to date, issuers, schemes and processors must all implement account update services (see section 4.6.2) which are not ubiquitous.

Even though many payment platforms are built with processor tokenization support in mind, the variety of token formats means that systems have to be adopted to either pass through token values or at least carry an indicator distinguishing a one-time transaction from a tokenized one. Also, there are no provisions for standardized processor token formats in the payment industry.

To address the challenges, return control of card data to issuers and cardholders and enable such new payment methods as Apple Pay, schemes and the EMV consortium have introduced payment network tokenization—a method when the token complies with the standard PAN format but is translated to the actual PAN number by the network.

The EMV consortium standard governing payment network tokenization is plainly called "EMV Payment Tokenization Specification", which is somewhat counterintuitive since the bulk of EMVco-standards govern purely card-present transactions.

At the first glance, the method does not make a lot of sense as a PAN is a cardholder-provided number (all-digits, 13 to 19 positions in length) that is securely stored on file by a processor and sent as-is to the payment network, but so is a network token. However, unlike the "general-purpose" PAN number embossed on the card, written on the magnetic stripe, stored in the ICC and used as the primary key for the customer account, the token might be short-lived and limited to a particular channel and payment method.

To support payment network tokenization, schemes have introduced dedicated BIN ranges reserved for tokenized PANs (at the moment of writing tokenized PAN values are assigned the "2" IIN). As BIN tables are updated frequently all players in the card payments industry face little challenges with introducing the new feature passive support, simply enabling the PANs pass-through from the new range through their systems and into payment networks.

4.6.4 Payment Network Tokenization in Mobile Payments

As mentioned above, a network token can be tied to a particular device and a particular data entry mode. Consider the following scenario:

■ The manufacturer of the mobile device or the payment application or framework provider register the owner of the device to a cloud-based payment service. The device owner is authenticated using such means as the device PIN code, a static or a one-time password or using a biometric method.

■ The owner of the device registers their payment card or cards to the payment service. The process can and usually is accompanied with such methods of additional authentication as CVV2 and 3D Secure. The validation of the cardholder billing address can also be performed in the process.

■ Upon registration, a payment network token for the card is generated and stored on the mobile device securely. In addition to the token, a cryptographic key can also be transferred and stored on the mobile device, to be used as part of dCVV.

■ During an m-commerce payment the token value instead of the original PAN is sent to the online store.

■ On paying in store, and this is where the innovative nature of the method truly shows, the token value alongside a dynamic CVV (see also Dynamic CVV) is transmitted to a terminal using contactless magstripe data entry mode. The token number, which is unique to the specific device, is transmitted in the NFC band as part of contactless magstripe data alongside additional cryptographic evidence in the DD part of Track 2 data vector (see section 2.4.2). Since the data is packed into existing, ISO 8583-compliant data fields, contactless POS devices, processor and acquirer systems as well as card scheme networks face no issue with transmitting the transaction to the participating issuer all the way through.

Such modern mobile payment technologies as Apple Pay, Samsung Pay and others rely on this data flow to facilitate card-present payments.

CARD-PRESENT ENVIRONMENT

Chapter 5

Contact Chip Transactions

CONTENTS

5.1 Overview

5.1.1 Introduction

Introducing an entirely new complicated technology profoundly affects card issuers as well as acquirers and requires a nearly complete renewal of terminal, network and card production inventory and is an expensive and disruptive move. However, in the eyes of major industry stakeholders the move was justified for two reasons: combatting fraud and allowing smarter offline authorizations.

A card having a magnetic stripe is not hard to skim and replicate, and as the prices for electronics plummeted and skimming devices grew smaller, it became possible for fraudster waiters to swipe it on their way to the cashier inconspicuously. After such a swipe the card could be replicated and reused for fraudulent purchases.

Magnetic stripe technology made offline transactions authorization possible but imposed high risks on scheme participants as no limits for the numbers or amounts of offline authorizations could be efficiently imposed.

To address both issues scheme participants undertook a major technological transition to integrated circuit cards (ICCs), embedding in effect a small and very secure computer into each card.

Thus, the card becomes smart enough to maintain internal counters in a manner independent from the capabilities and integrity of a particular terminal and rely on cryptographic methods to authenticate cards and transactions. In addition, as faking a chip card is extremely hard, issuers are able to delegate some authority to the card itself allowing it to approve transactions offline.

The terminal, in turn, has to be sufficiently sophisticated to be able to participate in a meaningful dialog with the card, including not only the obvious ability to physically communicate with the chip on it via contact or contactless link but also support the appropriate communication protocol and application-level logic, including cryptographic means of data encryption and signature validation.

5.1.2 "ICC" vs. "EMV card"

In the context of payment the, terms "ICC" and "EMV card" are frequently used interchangeably. That, however, is imprecise.

The term "ICC", if used more accurately, refers to an ISO/IEC 7816-compatible chip card also called *smart card*. The term "EMV card" refers to a card that is compatible with a version of the EMV specification. It follows that every EMV card is an ICC but not necessarily vice versa.

To begin with, all GSM SIM cards are built using the ICC technology and essentially are ICCs with smaller form factors. But even without considering this example the area in which ICCs are used go way beyond boundaries of the EMV standard.

Smart cards can be used as means to achieve higher security during authentication, for example, to facilitate single sign-on in sensitive environments. Also, most HSMs rely on proprietary smart card solutions to store key components.

Governments are increasingly using smart cards for identification. For example, Turkey has relied on ICCs for its drivers' licenses since 1987, and EU countries such as Belgium and Estonia have transitioned to smart card government IDs.

ICCs were (and still are, although decreasingly) used as electronic wallets not requiring a connection to a bank or processing host in order to perform a payment.

Smart cards are also widely used as transit tickets especially since contactless technology was introduced and gradually became affordable. Tapping a card on a terminal is much faster than having the bus driver punch a hole in a multi-ride ticket.

Furthermore, as it is described in more detail below, due to the fact that an ICC can host multiple applications, a single card can perform multiple functions.

Thus, many educational institutions around the globe have introduced student cards providing secure student identification and serving as a digital wallet for purchase of goods and services around the campus. Banks sometimes issue payment cards with applications from several card brands bundled together. In some regions banks issue a combined transit/payment card that can be used both as a transit pass and a payment card (such as OysterPass card in London or Troika card in Moscow).

In subsequent chapters we cover a minimum necessary subset of ICC ISO standards and refer to EMV standards when the latter supplants or extends the former.

5.1.3   ICC Architecture Overview

As mentioned above, the notion of an Integrated Circuit Card means that a "small and secure" computer is embedded into a plastic card. Its physical structure is covered in section 5.2.1.

As one expects from a computer, it is able to run one or many applications, and a standard describes means to select an application and then exchange messages with it.

Applications utilize an API provided by either a native operating system or a framework on top of it. Naturally, there are multiple operating systems and frameworks, listing and describing which is beyond the scope of the book. However, one particular framework stands out: there is a JavaCard specification describing a Java edition for smartcard integral chips.

In a contact-based scenario when the card is inserted into a reader, the terminal provides power to the chip, and the terminal application communicates with the ICC via physical contacts on the card. In a contactless scenario the communication and the power are provided wirelessly.

The ICC hosts a file system containing "dedicated files" (similar to folders with extra data) and "elementary files" (simple files). Dedicated files can be referenced to via an application ID (see below on application selection). Elementary files can be accessed by terminal application directly to retrieve necessary data from the ICC application.

The terminal application sends commands (instructions) to the card application to which the latter responds with status codes and relevant data. EMV specification defines a subset of ICC commands used for the interaction with an EMV application.

Furthermore, the EMV specification defines a tag-level-value format for its data, defines all supported tags and tag combinations (EMV templates) as well as adds the notion of DOLs (data object lists)—a way for terminal-card interaction, whereas the card informs the terminal of expected tags and their allocated lengths, and the terminal responds with the unformatted packed data.

The architecture is described in more details in section 5.2.

5.1.4 Card-Terminal Interaction

A terminal can possess a variety of input interfaces, including a contactless sensor, chip reader and magstripe reader. A card can be tapped on the terminal, inserted into the reader and swiped on it.

Assuming a card supporting all the three entry modes, a tapped or inserted card initiates the relevant application selection and interaction process.

However, as described in section 2.4.4, a chip-enabled magnetic stripe card contains the value of 2 or 6 as the first digit of the service code. Upon reading a magnetic stripe card with this value, a chip-enabled terminal must prompt the cardholder or shop attendant to use chip interface instead.

It is only after an attempt to use the chip fails that the terminal should allow using of the magnetic stripe, a condition called *magstripe fallback*. To simulate this behavior during testing, one could swipe the card, then, when prompted, insert it into the chip reader wrong side first, after which the terminal, unable to distinguish an honest chip transaction attempt from said fake, finally allows the magnetic stripe to work.

The process of terminal, merchant and cardholder working out the data entry method used during the transaction is sometimes called *technology selection*.

Each EMV transaction is performed by means of interaction between an application hosted in the terminal (the *terminal application*) and an application hosted in the card (the *card application*).

Cards carry no battery and exclusively rely on the terminal to provide power. Thus, any chip or contactless interaction of the terminal and the card begins with the terminal providing the power to the card. In the contact environment, the terminal proceeds by sending a signal on the card's RST line to which the card responds with a very short ATR (answer-to-reset) communication.

From that point and until the transaction is completed, interrupted or cancelled, the communication between the terminal and the card is controlled by the terminal (see figure 5.1).

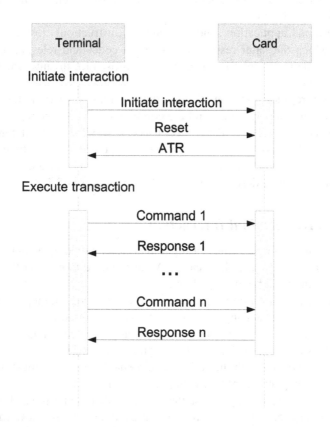

Figure 5.1: Flow of terminal-card interaction

The contactless terminal-card interaction flow does not contain an explicit reset of the contactless card at the start of the communication. Instead, the reader polls its field to identify devices and their physical link types (see section 6.3.2).

5.2   ICC Architecture Details

5.2.1   Chip and Antenna Hardware

The transition from a magnetic stripe card to a chip-enabled one meant adding an ICC to the usual card making it a flavor of an ISO 7816 compatible smartcard.

The chip is essentially a small computer embedded into the plastic. It is powered externally and communicates with reader devices via a set of conductive zones located about 1 cm from the top and 1 cm from the left side of the card. The standard defines 8 external contacts numbered from C1 to C8 out of which C4 and C8 are reserved for future use and another one—C6—formerly used for Vpp (EEPROM programming voltage) is deprecated.

The contacts are listed in table 5.1.

The integrated circuit on a contact chip contains ROM (read-only memory), RAM (random access memory) and EEPROM (electrically erasable programmable read-only memory). The RAM is wiped between activations of the integrated circuit, the ROM is pre-programmed during the card manufacturing and the EEPROM is rewritten repeatedly during the lifetime of the chip.

Table 5.1: ISO 7816 chip contacts

Contact	Designation	Use
C1	Vcc	Power connection through which voltage is supplied to the chip.
C2	RST	Reset line through which the chip can be reset to its initial state.
C3	CLK	Clock signal line through which the chip microprocessor and its communication line is synchronized with the reader device.
C4	RFU	Reserved for future use.
C5	GND	Ground line to provide common electrical ground between the chip and the reader device.
C6	Vpp	Programming power connection—formerly used for older cards and is deprecated now.
C7	I/O	Input/output line that provides the half-duplex communication between the chip and the reader.
C8	RFU	Reserved for future use.

The contactless card contains a somewhat different integrated circuit and is sometimes called PICC or Proximity Integrated Circuit Card and an embedded antenna. ISO/IEC standard 14443 governs contactless cards and readers.

Contactless cards operate at radio frequency of 13.56 MHz (RFID frequency) and NFC (Near-Field Communications standard) is partially compatible with ISO/IEC 14443, allowing NFC-capable devices to operate as contactless cards. The feature enables mobile in-store payment applications.

Contactless cards receive the required power for operation from the current induced in the antenna by the electromagnetic field of the proximity reader. There are two contactless card types, and they are denoted in the standards as Type A and Type B. Among the differences in signal modulation between the two types, the radio field of the reader is turned off for short periods of time during the signal transmission for Type A cards, and so a Type A PICC must contain capacitors to sustain the functioning of the circuit.

5.2.2   ICC File System

Regardless of the underlying operating system implementation, each ICC contains a file system whose organization is defined by ISO/IEC 7814-4.

The ICC can contain two types of files: elementary files (EF) and dedicated files (DF). The file system is hierarchical having DFs roughly corresponding to folders and EFs—to files of a file system—on a personal computer. That is, a DF can contain sub-dedicated files or subfolders and both a top-level DF and its subfolders can contain multiple elementary files.

The root dedicated file of the hierarchy is called the master file (MF).

As an ICC can contain multiple "folders" and applications, the EMV standard defines ADF (application definition file) serving as a data container or a home folder of a single card application and DDF (directory definition file) is a folder containing other folders or applications. Specific sub-DFs and EFs under an ADF contain data specific for and internal to that application, while EFs under the master file (MF) can contain data common to all applications on the card.

5.2.2.1   Dedicated Files and AID

A dedicated file can be referenced using either a *fixed file identifier (FID)*, an *application identifier (AID)* or a full path of fixed file identifiers. The standard actually speaks of "DF Name" rather than application ID, but from practical point of view the terms are interchangeable.

The FID is a 2-byte value which can be thought of as a reference to physical location of the dedicated file. For instance, the master file always has FID of 0x3F00, the first dedicated file immediately beneath it has a FID of 0x7F01 and so the forth so a terminal needs to know the exact structure and order of the DF tree on the card to be able to reference it correctly. That requires a certain level of knowledge of card internals complicating interoperability. In contrast to it, the AID or DF name is a byte string of up to 16 bytes which does not depend on the application location in the chip file system.

To better understand the difference between the two reference methods, consider the task of invoking a browser from within a program on a personal computer to navigate to a website. Knowing the full path to the browser executable is one way of launching it, but it requires some knowledge regarding browsers deployed on the particular machine as well as their executable locations and filenames. That is similar to referencing a dedicated file using FID or an FID path.

Alternatively, many operating systems provide URL handlers and a program could invoke a generic URL handler and pass the web page address to it leaving it to the OS to locate and launch the correct browser.

The AID can be either registered or proprietary. Its format and registration process are defined in ISO/IEC 7814-5.

Obviously, the proprietary AID can be of arbitrary format occupying anywhere between 1 to 16 bytes.

A registered AID consists of two parts: the registered application provider identifier (RID) and the proprietary application identifier extension (PIX). The rationale behind that is as follows: first, to avoid AIDs colliding each application provider is assigned an RID by a registering entity. Then the application provider can optionally use the PIX to identify individual applications.

The structure of a standard compliant AID is shown in figure 5.2.

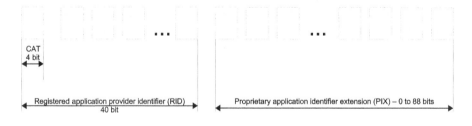

CAT
4 bit

Registered application provider identifier (RID)
40 bit

Proprietary application identifier extension (PIX) – 0 to 88 bits

Figure 5.2: ISO/IEC 7814-5 compliant AID

CAT denotes registration category. It is a 4-bit field with all possible values listed in the ISO/IEC 7816-5 standard. Two of those are worth mentioning here: A for international registration and D for national registration.

In the case of international registration, the RID consists of a 4-bit registration category indicator, with A coded as 1010 and the identifier itself consisting of 9 BCD digits spanning 36 bits. The PIX that can optionally follow the RID can be anywhere between 0 to 11 bytes (in whole bytes).

In the case of national registration, the RID consists of a 4-bit registration category with indicator, D coded as 1101, the country code of the national registration authority in the form of ISO 3166-1 numeric country code in BCD format, spanning 12 bits, and the national identifier in form of a single or multiple fields as defined by the specific registrar.

For example, an international AID can look like A0000000031010 (this is a Visa standard application ID). Here A means international registration, digit sequence 000000003 is the RID and digits 1010 are the PIX for this specific application.

Similarly, here is an example of a domestic AID: D268000001. D means national registrar and 268 is the ISO country code of Georgia. That particular AID is reserved by the Ministry of Finance of Georgia for fiscal cash registers.

5.2.2.2 Elementary Files

Card elementary files can be of several types and be used for one of two purposes. They are listed below for the sake of completeness, however, the technical details are rarely required by a processor or an acquirer as the specifics are abstracted away by the terminal and card applications.

An elementary file can be either *internal* (used by application only and containing implementation-specific and/or sensitive data) or *working* (containing data used by the terminal application during a data exchange with the card).

An elementary file can furthermore be of one of the following types as described in ISO/IEC 7816-4:

Transparent, consisting of a sequence of bytes. It is transparent to the operating system, as its format is raw data the card OS does not need to handle referring its contents as-is to the invoking application.

Linear fixed, consisting of fixed-length records.

Linear variable, consisting of variable-length records.

Cyclic, a type of linear fixed file having a cyclic structure: after the file is full and each record has been written to it any subsequent attempt to write a record overwrites the oldest record in the file.

Elementary files can be referenced via either a FID (a 2-byte value) or a short file identifier (SFI), which is a number between 1 and 30.

To reference an elementary file with its FID, a terminal must know it in advance. That requires awareness of the card application internals and is a barrier for interoperability. Due to that, in such interoperable environments as those conforming to EMV specifications the other method is preferred.

As for the SFI method, some (maybe not all) elementary files on a card are assigned a short number that can be communicated to the terminal in the form of a single file listing. Then, the terminal can use the shortcuts to reference to individual files.

5.3 Flow of a Chip Transaction

5.3.1 Overview

Throughout interaction, the terminal keeps track of the transaction status and the results of various verification steps in special registers, TVR (Terminal Verification Result) and TSI (Transaction Status Information).

Prior to the terminal application starting to interact with the card application, the latter needs to be chosen from the list of applications available on a particular card. The step is called *application selection*. A card can contain a quick index of all EMV applications on it (called PSE which stands for Payment System Environment), or a terminal determines available applications by using its own internal supported list and querying for card applications one by one. The step is described in more detail in section 5.3.5.

As part of the application selection, the terminal can get a list of data fields that the card application requires to process the transaction. The terminal sends the data prescribed by the list to the card application to initiate them. The step is called *initiating application processing* and is described in more details in section 5.3.6. During the initiation, the terminal also receives a set of flags describing various supported functions (mostly related to authentication and risk management), the *application interchange profile*, and a small "catalog" of application elementary files, the *application file locator* with data required for transaction processing.

Once the list of necessary application elementary files is known to the terminal application, it *reads application data*, combines all the data from all files into a single data objects heap and validates the presence of mandatory data objects in it. See section 5.3.7 for details.

Upon reading application data successfully, the terminal can perform the cryptographic *offline card authentication*. Several methods of varying complexity are available according to the EMV standard and the terminal picks the more advanced one out of the list of mutually supported ones. The process is described in section 5.3.8.

After the the terminal and the card negotiated the authentication method, the terminal *checks processing restrictions*, verifying the application version, the application effective and expiry date and the validity of the transaction type for the card application. This step is detailed in section 5.3.9.

Once the terminal makes sure that the transaction can proceed according to the processing restriction, it consults the list of *cardholder verification methods* (the CVM list) and the rules for their selection, picking the first one that matches the terminal capabilities, the terminal and required transaction type and the requested transaction amount. Refer to section 5.3.10.2 for a description of this step.

When EMV technology was first introduced, a large proportion of terminals were not able to authorize each transaction online by sending it to the issuer.

Consequently, the standard allows offline authorization of card transactions while providing guiding rules on when the terminal should go online for authorization nonetheless. The process of applying the rules to determine whether a transaction must be authorized online is called *terminal risk management* and is described in more details in section 5.3.11. The step can be taken anywhere between the moment the terminal reads the application data and the moment it first requests an application cryptogram.

Upon completing cardholder verification and terminal risk management steps, the terminal and the card negotiate the method to approve or decline the transaction. The terminal makes the preliminary decision by taking into account the acquirer preferences, the issuer preferences and the results of the previous steps assembled in TVR. The process is called *terminal action analysis* and is described in section 5.3.12.

Once the terminal has made a preliminary decision, it communicates it to the card in the form of a GENERATE AC command (GAC). The command can also include some data for offline card authentication (see section 5.3.8.7). The card and the terminal decide how to process the transaction further. There are several types of cryptograms which the terminal can request and the card can decide to downgrade in response (for example, refusing to perform an offline authorization and forcing an online one). If the authorization is performed online, the terminal can further ensure the issuer authenticity by either using optionally the EXTERNAL AUTHENTICATE command, followed by second GENERATE AC command to the card or by combining the two. The process is described in 5.3.13.

In case of a transaction involving online processing the issuer can send an update to the card, securely modifying the card's data (resetting counters, thresholds, modifying PIN value or performing other solution-specific activities). Such an update is called an *issuer script* and there are two types of them: scripts sent to the card before an authorization response, and those sent to the card after an authorization response. The process is described in section 5.3.14.

The second call of the GENERATE AC command concludes a contact EMV transaction.

5.3.2 Card Interface

5.3.2.1 Answer-to-Reset

The card communicates with the terminal after it has been inserted into it or tapped on it by receiving its commands and returning command responses (see also section 5.1.4).

All ISO/IEC 7816 standard-compliant cards share the same communication format between the terminal and the card. The specific electronic signals and transmission protocols are described in part 3 of the ISO/IEC 7816 standard.

However, for the purpose of a better understanding of the card interface, it is important to highlight a few key facts about the lower-level data transmission that may not be entirely transparent at a higher applicative level.

For the sake of simplicity consider a contact scenario.

After the contacts are connected to a card-accepting device and power and clock signals are provided to the card, the I/O contact is put into the receiving state by the device and it sends a signal on card's RST contact. The signal causes a reset of any transient state of the card and its initialization in preparation for the command exchange that follows it.

Upon completing the reset the card transmits back via the I/O line, the ATR (Answer-to-Reset) message which among some additional data lists supported data transmission protocols. The protocols are encoded as a 4-bit value denoted as T.

The two most relevant possible values of T are $T = 0$ and $T = 1$, which denote asynchronous half duplex character transmission protocol and asynchronous half duplex block transmission protocol, correspondingly.

The $T = 0$ character (byte) protocol is typically supported by weaker card hardware and it does not allow data transmission in both command and its response (see section 5.3.2.2). The $T = 1$ block protocol has no such restriction.

5.3.2.2 Command and Response

Any application protocol is implemented as a series of commands and command responses. Each such message is called an application protocol data unit (APDU). A command is called C-APDU (command application protocol data unit) and is always sent from the terminal application to the card application. The card application responds to a command with R-APDU (the response APDU).

Card commands are grouped into instruction classes. To specify a command, it is necessary to send its command class denoted as CLA and the specific instruction code within that class denoted as INS. The protocol allows sending two single-byte parameters (P1 and P2) with each command as well as providing an additional variable-length field with additional parameters.

The R-APDU for each command consists of an optional variable-length data field and a mandatory trailer with two status bytes, SW1 and SW2 containing the command result.

The layout of the two APDUs is shown in figure 5.3. Optional fields are enclosed in square brackets.

The C-APDU fields are:

CLA command (instruction) class, mandatory 1-byte field.

INS command (instruction) code, mandatory 1-byte field.

P1, P2 mandatory single-byte parameters of the instruction. If a specific instruction does not require the parameters they must still be sent.

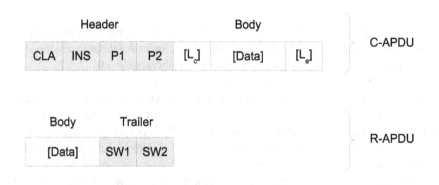

Figure 5.3: Layout of C-APDU and R-APDU

L_c optional length field, indicating number of bytes in the following data field of the command. According to the ISO/IEC 7816-4 standard the field can be 1 or 3 bytes, but in EMV applications only 1-byte length values are used. If the field is present, it must be followed by the data.

Data optional data string provided as additional input data to the card application.

L_e optional length field of up to 3 bytes specifying the maximum length of the response data field in bytes expected for the command. The EMV standard specifies 1 byte as the field maximum length. If the field is present and equal to zero, then the terminal is ready to receive the maximum (256) bytes of data in the response APDU.

If a C-APDU contains a single byte in the optional body, it is assumed to be L_e. The R-APDU fields are:

Data optional variable-length body whose length must be less or equal to L_e if the latter has been specified in the command.

SW1, SW2 mandatory status words occupying 1 byte each.

The ISO 7816 standard only defines the basic commands any compliant card must support. Further standards such as the EMV card standard define additional commands that should be also supported. Finally, each operating system and application can and often does have private use commands only supported by the particular brand of card OS and by the specific application.

5.3.2.3 CLA Format

The CLA byte format assigns its most significant nibble to command type. The EMV specification only uses two out of the possible values for that nibble, namely, 0 for inter-industry commands (those shared with ISO/IEC 7816 standard) and 8 for EMV proprietary commands.

The least significant nibble has bits 3 and 4 allocated to defining the secure messaging format and bits 1 and 2 used to specify the logical channel.

The EMV specification only uses two types of secure messaging format denoted as Format 1 and Format 2.

Standard-compliant secure messaging denoted as Format 1 where each element of the command data strictly corresponds to BER-TLV format (see section 11.6), enciphered or plain-text data fields are passed in appropriate tags, and the message authentication code is provided as yet another standard tagged value. The values for bits 4 and 3 of the least significant nibble of CLA for this format are 11.

Proprietary secure messaging denoted as Format 2 assumes that the data does not comply with BER-TLV encoding rules. It is passed to the card application as is, and the card and terminal application should be able to handle the format details. The MAC for such a message must always be the last 4 to 8 bytes of the data. Values for bits 4 and 3 of the CLA nibble for the format are 01.

The ISO/IEC 7816-4 standard allows multiple logical channels to exist during a single terminal-card session simultaneously allowing up to four parallel links between the terminal applications and the card applications. The EMV standard only utilizes single logical channel, so the values for bits 2 and 1 of the lesser CLA nibble are always 00.

It follows that in an EMV application, the CLA can only assume hexadecimal values of 04, 0C, 84 and 8C.

5.3.2.4   INS Values

The full table of supported INS values as well as the values reserved for future use can be found in Book 3 of the EMV specifications, and some specific commands are mentioned further when appropriate. However, to illustrate the principles of INS code allocation and command list utilization, consider the following examples given in table 5.2.

The table shows two commands: the SELECT command that helps pick an application close to the beginning of a terminal-card interaction, and the GET PROCESSING OPTIONS command that is the main Entry Point to an EMV transaction flow. As defined by the most significant nibble of the SLA, the former is ISO-defined, and the latter is EMV-specific.

Table 5.2: Sample INS values

CLA	INS	Meaning
0X	A4	SELECT
8X	A8	GET PROCESSING OPTIONS

5.3.2.5 *SW1 and SW2*

All the valid values of SW1 and SW2 status word bytes are defined in ISO/IEC 7816-4 standard and mentioned in EMV Book 1 and Book 3 or both.

The outcome of a command execution can be identified by examining SW1. Table 5.3 contains the major groups of status words values.

5.3.2.6 *SFI*

As mentioned previously (see section 5.2.2.2), for the sake of the access simplicity, elementary files on the ICC can be accessed using a Short File Identifier or SFI. During the application selection process (see section 5.3.5), the terminal learns the SFI of the application elementary file (AEF) for the application it is supposed to access.

The AEF is a linear fixed or variable-length file with each record containing tag 70 template (see section 5.3.3 for details). Upon learning the SFI of the file the terminal should access it uses the READ RECORD command to retrieve the data from it.

The EMV standard reserves AEFs with SFI between 1 to 10 for EMV standard data, SFI ranges 11 to 20 are reserved for proprietary data as specified by individual payment systems and ranges 21 to 30 are designated for the issuer-specific elementary files.

5.3.3 *EMV DOLs and Tags*

The EMV specification for data values is based on BER-TLV format (see section 11.6). That simplifies interoperability greatly as the data format (its order) is

Table 5.3: Selected SW1 and SW2 values

Status word	Meaning
9000	Normal process completion. The process has completed successfully. SW2 must always be 00 in this case.
62xx and 63xx	Warning status. The process has completed with a warning.
64xx and 65xx	Execution error. The process has been aborted because of an error during process execution.
67xx to 6Fxx	Checking error. The process has been aborted due to a failed check. Unknown or erroneous command parameters, data that wasn't found and other conditions that precluded execution of the process all fall into this category.

flexible and, furthermore, a terminal or card application can parse a stream of data by looping through the steps of the parsing tag/parsing length/reading tag value.

However, a fixed format has less overhead and can be parsed faster provided that it is well known to both the terminal and the card applications. The EMV standard contains the means for a card to request a set of data fields to be provided to the card application from the terminal in a fixed format. For that purpose, the EMV standard has defined DOL (stands for *data object list*).

A DOL is basically a list of tags and lengths the terminal is expected to provide in return. Upon receiving the DOL, the terminal should gather and concatenate all the requested data trimming or pad with zeros the fields which are too long, too short or absent from the terminal.

In other words, the TLV (tag-length-value) of data elements are split between the card and the terminal. The card holds a list of TL's concatenated as $TL_1 || TL_2 || \ldots || TL_n$, and the terminal is expected to provide a string of V's concatenated as $V_1 || V_2 || \ldots || V_n$.

The following DOLs are defined in the EMV specification:

Processing Options Data Object List (PDOL) used with the GET PROCESSING OPTIONS command. See sections 5.3.5.4 and 5.3.6.

Card Risk Management Data Object Lists (CDOL1 and CDOL2) used with the GENERATE AC command to generate application cryptograms.

Transaction Certificate Data Object List (TDOL) used to generate transaction certificate hash values, sometimes also used for the application cryptograms generation.

Dynamic Data Authentication Data Object List (DDOL) used with the INTERNAL AUTHENTICATE command.

Individual EMV tags can be seen as fields of a particular scalar data type. The tags are grouped into templates roughly corresponding to compound data types. The Data Elements Dictionary section of the EMV Book 3, Application Specification, lists all the possible templates and tags in a single comprehensive table. The table, as seen in version 4.3 of the EMV specification, contains the following columns:

Name specifies data element name.

Description specifies data element description.

Source specifies whether the tag can originate from the ICC, the terminal, the issuer or their combination.

Format specifies the field format, and its conventions are also brought in EMV Book 3, Application Specification.

Template contains the tag or tags of EMV field templates which can contain the current item as a sub-element, if applicable.

Tag specifies the actual tag value for the data element.

To understand the convention better, let us follow the example of tag 9F42. According to the specification, it is the Application Currency Code data element with data length of 2. It is a packed numeric 3-digit number, and it denotes a currency code according to ISO 4217. From the table we also learn that the value originates from the card (the Source column says ICC). Finally, looking at the Template column we see that the tag can appear as part of template 70 or 77.

To locate the fields, it is possible to use the EMV specification data element table by tag number. For instance, according to the table the EMV data element having tag number 70 is the READ RECORD response message template. Thus, we know that the Application Currency Code can be returned by the READ RECORD command.

5.3.4 Terminal Verification Results (TVR) and Transaction Status Information (TSI)

During processing of a single transaction the terminal stores the results of various steps and decisions in two status registers: TSI and TVR.

The Transaction Status Information (TSI) contains 2 bytes of which only first 6 bits are used. The bits are set according to the steps performed by the terminal during the transaction starting at the offline data authentication (bit 8), followed by the cardholder verification (bit 7), card risk management (bit 6), issuer authentication (bit 5), terminal risk management (bit 4) and, finally, issuer script processing (bit 3). The rest of the register bits are reserved for future use.

The TSI contains high-level indications of completed transaction stages while more details about the decisions and checks are stored in the Terminal Verification Results (TVR) register consisting of 5 bytes each roughly corresponding to a stage in TSI.

Byte 1 of the TVR contains flags for offline data authentication results (e.g., bit 7 of the byte is set if the SDA has failed, see section 5.3.8.5, for example), byte 2 contains flags for various processing restrictions (for example, bit 6 is set if the application is not yet active, date-wise), byte 3 contains the cardholder verification flags (such as bit 3, "Online PIN entered"), byte 4 contains bits for terminal risk management decisions (see section 5.3.11), and byte 5 captures the issuer authentication and script processing flags.

The TVR register is eventually used to determine whether the transaction is to be declined offline, authorized offline or sent to the issuer for authorization by applying bit masks to its value and thus determining the course of action (see section 5.3.12). The EMV standard also recommends including the TVR in CDOL1/CDOL2 values sent as an input to the GENERATE APPLICATION CRYPTOGRAM command (see section 5.3.13.2).

5.3.5 *Application Selection*

The Application Selection process is described in the EMV Book 1, ICC to Terminal Interface (as opposed to the rest of the transaction flow handled in the EMV Book 3, Application Specification).

As an ICC can host multiple applications the terminal has to select one of them to communicate with during the particular transaction. To achieve that the terminal builds a candidate list and then selects the one that it is going to interact with during the session. The terminal also learns some details regarding the application and the data it requires during the selection process.

The EMV standard provides two supported ways to enumerate applications present on an ICC. A terminal can either try to read a special file, the Payment System Environment (PSE), using a sequence of READ RECORD commands or query the card for applications on it with a sequence of SELECT commands.

According to the EMV standard the presence of PSE is not mandatory. If present, it is a file having a DF name of 1PAY.SYS.DDF01. A terminal that supports application selection via the PSE (also called indirect application selection) first issues a SELECT command trying to locate it and if successful can read and parse it building the list of its candidate applications in the process. A PSE can contain multiple ADFs (containing AID in tag 61) and DDFs (containing its DDF name in tag 9D and in addition sometimes including multiple subordinate ADFs and DDFs).

If the PSE is not present on the card or the terminal is not programmed to utilize it, the terminal has to query the ICC for the list of applications known to the terminal one by one using the SELECT command. The process is called *direct application selection* and can be quite lengthy as there might be a big number of applications that appear on the terminal list but are not supported by the particular card. The terminal has to send one AID after another, and the card returns a successful response to each SELECT command if the AID parameter of the SELECT command matches an AID of the card application precisely. The process is called *complete* or *full name matching*.

To optimize the procedure in case of such a scenario the EMV standard allows optional *partial name matching* of applications.

In the case of partial matching the terminal could send a prefix (partial name) instead of sending a full application name to the ICC and the ICC returns applications which full AIDs match the prefix.

Consider some scenarios for various cases with direct/indirect application selection and complete/partial name matching given in sections 5.3.5.1 and 5.3.5.2. It is assumed that the terminal supports PSE and partial name matching. Note that the flows only cover basic scenarios and are not provided for the cases when an application or card is blocked and they do not describe any terminal-side logic associated with the rules for adding an AID to the candidate list.

5.3.5.1 Indirect Application Selection

1. The terminal sends a SELECT command with filename value to 1PAY.SYS.DDF01 and P2 parameter set to "first and only occurence".

2. The card responds with SW1/SW2 words set to 9000 (Success), and data containing FCI of the PSE (tag 6F). This result means PSE is present on the card.

3. The terminal sends a READ RECORD command with P1 set to 1 (first record in file) and P2 set to the SFI of the DIR file of the PSE (as returned in FCI).

4. The card responds with SW1/SW2 set to 9000 (Success) and with FCI of the entry (tag 6F).

   If the entry is an ADF (contains tag 4F), the application should join the candidate list. If the entry is a DDF (tag 9D), it is descended into, like a filesystem folder: terminal addresses it with SFI received in previous step, then scans it with READ RECORD command.

5. The terminal repeatedly sends READ RECORD command with P1 set to n (for n-th record in the file) and P2 set to the SFI of the DIR file.

6. The card responds with SW1/SW2 set to 6A83 ("Wrong parameters P1 P2; record not found").

   This result means there is no n-th record in the file.

5.3.5.2 Direct Application Selection

1. The terminal sends a SELECT command with filename value to 1PAY.SYS.DDF01 and P2 parameter set to "first and only occurence".

2. The card responds with SW1/SW2 set to 6A82 ("Wrong parameters P1 P2; file not found").

   This means there is no PSE on the card.

3. The terminal sends a SELECT command with the filename parameter set to the first AID on the list of AIDs the terminal supports.

4. The card responds with SW1/SW2 set to 9000 (Success), but the returned AID is longer than the one provided by the terminal.

   This means that the card has performed partial matching on the application ID prefix.

5. The terminal sends a SELECT command with filename parameter set to the same AID as before, and P2 set to 02 (Next occurence).

6. The card responds with SW1/SW2 set to 9000 (Success) and returns another matching AID.

   The terminal repeatedly sends a SELECT command with filename parameter set to the same AID as before, and P2 set to 02 (Next occurence).

7. The card responds with SW1/SW2 not equal 9000 (Success).

   This means there are no more matching AIDs on the card.

8. The terminal continues with the next AID it supports.

5.3.5.3   Final Selection

Upon completing the list of supported candidates and assuming that there are some applications supported by both the terminal and the card, the terminal can either prompt the cardholder to select an application, confirm the application use or make the choice automatically.

The FCI of each application includes tag 87, "Application Priority Indicator", determining for each application whether its use requires the cardholder confirmation, as well as defining the order in which the list of applications should be presented to the cardholder.

This process is covered in more detail in the EMV Book 1, subsection 12.4, Final Selection, of section 12, Application Selection.

Once the application to be used is identified, the terminal sends a SELECT command to finalize the selection receiving the application FCI in the command response.

It is worth noting that successfully selecting an application does not guarantee that the terminal is actually fully compatible with it. It is possible that during the Processing Restrictions step (see section 5.3.9) the terminal might discover that it cannot support the application version.

5.3.5.4   File Control Information (FCI)

The FCI can contain several optional elements which can be found in the EMV Book 3, Annex A Data Elements Dictionary under template A5.

Optional elements under FCI include "Language Preference" (tag 5F2D) containing an ordered list of preferred interface languages the terminal should use while presenting prompts to the cardholder.

There are also "Application Preferred Name" (tag 9F12) and "Issuer Code Table Index" (tag 9F11) elements defining the application name and the code table in which the application name should be shown to the cardholder on the terminal display.

As for those three elements, issuers can influence customer experience in multi-language environments or when the cardholder is abroad: thus, for example, an owner of an Israeli-issued card travelling in France can see the terminal prompts in English.

The FCI can also contain the data element "Processing Options Data List (PDOL)" in tag 9F38. The element is used to initiate the application processing (Initiate Processing) and contains a list of tag-length identifiers of data elements the terminal has to provide.

The list usually contains data elements describing the terminal environment, its type and capabilities, the country or the merchant category code and is personalized on the card by its issuer.

5.3.6 Initiate Processing

This step is described in the EMV Book 3, Application Specification.

To initiate processing the terminal resets its internal status registers (TVR and TSI, see section 5.3.4) and sends the GET PROCESSING OPTIONS command (colloquially referred to as GPO).

The GPO command has a single data object having tag 83. If no PDOL is available in the application File Control Information (see section 5.3.5.4), the element is sent empty. Otherwise, the values of data elements requested in PDOL are padded as needed and concatenated to form a single string of data (see 5.3.3 for illustration).

In response to the GPO command the card application replies to it with its supported application functions in the business context and the data regarding available application elementary files (AEFs) in detail. The former is referred to as *Application Interchange Profile* (AIP) and the latter is *Application File Locator* (AFL).

The details can be provided either in concatenated form under tag 80 or under tag 77 in separate tags, tag 82 for AIP and tag 94 for AFL.

5.3.6.1 Application Interchange Profile

The AIP consists of 2 bytes of which the first one is only currently in use. The byte contains the indication of supported static and dynamic offline card authentication, cardholder verification, support of issuer authentication and flag for terminal risk management.

Table 5.4 describes the AIP bits from leftmost to rightmost. If a bit is set to 1, the appropriate function is supported.

5.3.6.2 Application File Locator

The AFL contains an array of entries of 4-byte length, each describing the location of data entries the terminal should read from the card.

The entries are structured as follows:

■ Byte 1 encodes the SFI (see section 5.3.2.6) of the relevant application elementary file (AEF).

■ Bytes 2 and 3 encode the first and last AEF record the terminal should use for processing.

■ As not every record should be considered for the purpose of offline static data authentication as opposed to overall processing, byte 4 specifies the last AEF record that should be used for offline static data authentication.

The terminal uses the data in the file locator to read and parse records from application elementary files at the next step of an EMV transaction or Read Application data (see section 5.3.7).

The terminal also relies on each entry's byte 4 to compose a data authentication input vector byte sequence used during offline static card authentication (see section 5.3.8.5).

For example, if an entry has the form of 0D 01 06 04, the terminal should access file identified by SFI of 0D using the records from first to sixth for its general application data needs but only use records 01 to 04 for offline data authentication.

Table 5.4: Structure of Application Interchange Profile

Bit	Usage
Bit 8	Reserved for future use
Bit 7	SDA supported. The application supports offline static data card data authentication (see section 5.3.8.5).
Bit 6	DDA supported. The application supports offline dynamic data card data authentication (see section 5.3.8.6).
Bit 5	Cardholder verification is supported. See section 5.3.10.
Bit 4	Terminal risk management is to be performed. See section 5.3.11.
Bit 3	Issuer authentication is supported. A card can authenticate issuer cryptogram using either a second call to GENERATE AC command or using a dedicated EXTERNAL AUTHENTICATE command (see also section 5.3.13.2).
Bit 2	Reserved for future use.
Bit 1	CDA supported. The application supports offline combined data card data authentication (see section 5.3.8.7).

5.3.7   Read Application Data

Once the application selection has been completed and the AFL has been provided to the terminal application (see section 5.3.6.2), the terminal can read application data. The data accessible to the terminal can be split across several application elementary files (AEFs).

The terminal application iterates over AFL entries. Each entry contains the AEF Short File Indicator to be read, as well as the range of records to be read from the AEF. The terminal application reads each AEF issuing a READ RECORD command for each record in the relevant range for the file. In response to the READ RECORD command the card returns the READ RECORD Response Message Template which has tag value of 70. The terminal application parses the sub-elements of the template and adds them to a common EMV data objects heap for future processing, discarding any element it is not familiar with in process but keeping optional elements in the heap.

Once the reading process is complete, the terminal application is able to confirm whether the card provided all the mandatory data objects The EMV standard mandates the presence of Application Expiry Date (tag 5F24), Application Primary Account Number (PAN) (tag 5A), and two DOLs—Card Risk Management Data Object List 1 (tag 8C) and Card Risk Management Data Object List 2 (tag 8D).

In addition to the mandatory objects that must always be present in application data, the terminal also verifies objects depending on the provided AIP. For instance, if the card application states it supports cardholder verification by setting bit 5 in the AIP byte 1, then application data must also contain the Cardholder Verification Method (CVM) List (tag 8E). Depending on the stated support for offline authentication (SDA, DDA, combined DDA), relevant data objects must also be present in the application data.

5.3.8   Offline Card Authentication

Prior to the introduction of chip technology, card authentication hardly existed. A hologram embedded in the card was supposed to be validated by all shop attendants at all stores. Except for the hologram image, there were no other means to confirm the card genuineness, and even that protective measure was not properly enforced by sales personnel.

As for chip technology, the terminal is able to authenticate the card cryptographically in every EMV transaction whether it is contact or contactless or online or offline one. To do so, scheme public keys are loaded into each EMV terminal. The card delivers a digital signature to the terminal which the latter verifies with a scheme public key. Certainly, scheme private keys are not used to produce cards directly but there is a key chain of trust between the scheme and the issuer keys allowing proper signature validation (see section 5.3.8.2).

The process is called "offline data authentication" and terminals can chose to skip the step relying on issuer card authentication instead (and thus performing online card authentication).

Offline card authentication can be performed using one of the following standard methods (if supported by the card and the terminal):

Static data authentication (SDA). A static data authentication value is precalculated by the issuer and written on the card. It is read and validated by the terminal upon every transaction, thus confirming the authenticity of data written (personalized) on the card by the issuer. That type of authentication is potentially vulnerable to replay attacks but requires less sophisticated software and allows for weaker hardware on both the card and the terminal.

Dynamic data authentication (DDA). A dynamic data authentication (DDA) value is calculated by the card upon each transaction using random data from both the card and the terminal. Successful dynamic data authentication means that in addition to the valid origin of the card it has not been modified after its personalization.

Combined data authentication (CDA). In essence, that authentication method does not differ from the DDA method, except that the card authentication value is generated together with the application cryptogram (see also section 5.3.13.2).

If either the card does not support the offline data authentication (see section 5.3.6.1 for bits that indicate this) or the terminal is "online only" or there is no mutually supported offline card data authentication method, the terminal skips the entire offline authentication stage, setting the relevant bit (offline data authentication was not performed) in the TVR (see section 5.3.4).

The terminal chooses to process static data authentication when it is supported both by the card and the terminal and neither DDA nor combined data authentication are mutually supported. In case of multiple options, the standard prescribes combined data authentication as the preferred method, followed by dynamic data authentication and then followed by static data authentication.

5.3.8.1 Common Steps of Offline Authentication

Roughly all offline authentication methods follow the same flow with the first few identical steps for both static and dynamic data authentication methods.

The terminal starts by recovering the keys it needs to authenticate the card. Using the keys, the terminal calculates a cryptographic signature independently from the card and validates the results. If the signature, present or returned by the card, is validated by the values calculated by the terminal independently, the authentication is successful.

The generic process of key recovery is described in section 5.3.8.3, and the generic process of signed data validation is described in section 5.3.8.4.

As the first step common to all authentication methods when the issuer public key is recovered using data read from card during the Read Application Data stage and based on public CA certificates provided by card schemes (in this context in the EMV standard, they are referred to as *Certification Authorities* or *CAs*).

Public CA certificates are pre-loaded in each EMV terminal by the acquirer while the the issuer public key is personalized on the card by the the issuer.

That is the last step of static data authentication and the flow ends as the terminal uses the issuer key to decipher static authentication signature from the card and validate it using data elements read from the card.

For dynamic data authentication the terminal uses a similar method as with the issuer public key to recover the card public key and then continues with generating dynamic authentication data sending them to the card using an appropriate command, and validating their result using the card public key and data elements read from the card.

Upon completing the authentication the terminal sets the "Offline data authentication was performed" bit in TSI to 1.

If one of the authentication methods fails, the terminal sets bits "SDA failed", "DDA failed" or "CDA failed" of the TVR to 1. Otherwise, all the three bits are reset to zero.

5.3.8.2   Key Chain of Trust

Exchanging messages securely using asymmetric cryptography requires pre-sharing of public keys between participating entities. That is trivial for two parties, but in case of a large number of participants in a message exchange, the number of required key exchanges grows fast: in a theoretical network with two issuers and two acquirers one needs to exchange four pair of keys, which is a nuisance; a hundred participants require 2,500 key exchanges which is simply not feasible.

To make asymmetric cryptography scalable, all practical asymmetric algorithms support a form of delegation of trust in which an entity trusted by many participants of message exchanges can sign keys thus witnessing their validity. Consider the tree of participants in figure 5.4.

To ensure that each member of the hierarchy except its root is able to validate a digital signature of any other member of the hierarchy, it is sufficient to distribute the public key or keys of the tree root also known as the Root Certificate Authority or Trusted Certificate Authority.

For example, all banks (L1 nodes) trust the scheme (root node) and exchange keys with it. In principle, banks do not exchange keys with each other. If such a bank encounters a message signed by another bank's key, it cannot validate the

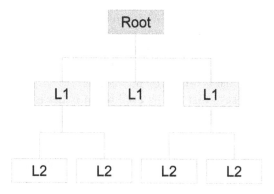

Figure 5.4: Key hierarchy

signature and confirm that it belongs to the counterpart bank, but it can check that the message was signed by a key that, in turn, was signed by the scheme. The transitive relationship is referred to as a *key chain of trust*.

That ability to overcome the problem of scale comes in especially handy with billions of cards and hundreds of thousands if not millions of EMV-capable terminals.

Each card communicates with the terminal it has been tapped on or inserted into while cryptographically signing exchanged messages. It is obviously not feasible to have all cards and all terminals exchange an individual pair of keys. However, in the diagram above, cards and terminals roughly correspond to L2 nodes, banks are L1 nodes and the scheme is the root authority. Therefore, approximately, the following procedure takes place in case of protected EMV cards against counterfeits [1]:

- The scheme generates its root key pair and stores the private key as a very closely guarded secret distributing its public key throughout the entire network: to all banks and especially all terminals that aim to process cards of that particular scheme.

- Each issuer generates a key pair it would like to use for card personalization, sends its public key to be signed by the scheme and gets it back with digital signature of the scheme and the root authority of the hierarchy applied to it.

- Each card personalized by that issuer contains its own key which, in turn, is signed by the issuer's private key.

---

[1] The described scenario lists the full set of keys used for Dynamic Data Authentication (DDA). Static Data Authentication (SDA) does not involve card-specific keys.

When the card communicates with a terminal, the terminal seeks to establish trust with the card, or confirm its authenticity otherwise. The terminal has the scheme public key deployed in it. It cannot directly validate the private key of that particular card, but using the scheme public key, it can confirm that the card was issued by a bank that is trusted by the scheme.

Full hierarchy of keys that can be used by an issuer is shown in figure 5.5. The exact usage and purpose of these keys is described later.

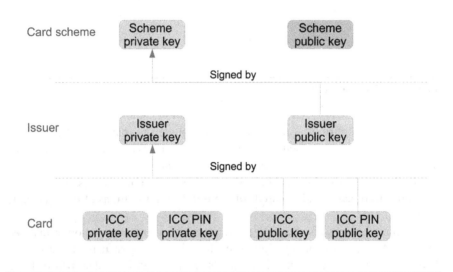

Figure 5.5: Scheme, issuer and ICC keys hierarchy

5.3.8.3   *Public Key Recovery*

Under aforementioned scenarios, terminals have to recover issuer public keys and ICC public keys. The recovery algorithm used for both types of keys is very similar:

1. The terminal retrieves the key certificate from the card. The *key certificate* is a data structure that includes part of the key or more rarely the whole key encrypted with a private key to which the terminal has a matching public key.

2. If the entire key is too long to fit into the certificate, the remaining bytes of the key (*key remainder*) are provided by the card in unencrypted form.

3. The terminal decrypts the certificate using the public key it has. The result of the decryption has to start with constant data header (0x6A) and data

trailer (0xBC) which, if not matched, cause the terminal to consider the entire process of card authentication as a failure.

4. If the data header and the trailer of the decrypted certificate are valid, it is separated into two parts. The first part, commonly denoted as M_R, is the unencrypted certificate containing some additional data about the format, owning entity (BIN or PAN), expiry date and, most importantly, leftmost digits of the public key. The second part or the last 20 bytes of the value is commonly denoted as H and is the hash value for the recovered full certificate.

5. The terminal combines the decrypted certificate with the Key Remainder, applies a specified hash function to it and compares the result with H. If the result matches, the terminal considers the key recovery successful, extracts the key part from the certificate and combines it with the clear-text key remainder and the key exponent values to obtain the full key.

6. The terminal performs such additional validity checks of the certificate as its expiry date, BIN, etc. and if all are passed, accepts the key for further processing.

As mentioned above, card schemes issuing root key pairs function as Certificate Authorities with the EMV standard. The pairs are then handled thus:

■ The public keys of card schemes are distributed publicly and are usually accessible on card scheme websites. They are preloaded into terminals by respective terminal network operators or acquirers. Each compliant terminal must be able to hold an array of CA root keys and each card application indicates to the terminal the index of the key it requires to use, using the "Certification Authority Public Key Index" data object (tag 8F).

■ Private keys of card schemes are shared with no one. Issuers submit their issuer public keys to card schemes and receive signed certificates back. Then the certificates are used to personalize the issuers' cards.

Note that the full key recovery algorithm is described in more details in EMV Book 2, Security and Key Management, in chapters Static Data Authentication and the Digital Signature Scheme Giving Message Recovery section of Security Mechanisms Annex. It is also repeated there for dynamic data authentication.

In addition to the aforementioned keys, the card can contain (and the terminal may have to recover) an ICC PIN encipherment key. It is recovered using issuer public key. Full hierarchy and order of recovery of keys that can be used with a particular ICC application is shown in figure 5.6.

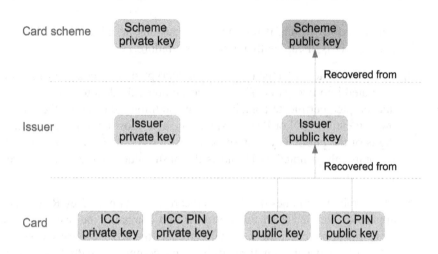

Figure 5.6: Recovery of keys

5.3.8.4 *Signed Data Validation*

In all data validation scenarios the terminal obtains—either by reading from the card a static value or by receiving a response to a command—a data field with signed data it needs to validate the use of a previously recovered public key.

As a prerequisite, the terminal obtains a public key it uses for data validation. The validation process happens as follows:

1. The terminal computes the data byte string that should be signed and validated. That step differs between static, dynamic and combined data authentication methods, see details below, and the byte string is further referred to as a *data authentication input vector*.

2. The terminal obtains the signed data string from the card. The step also differs per method.

3. As a result of the two steps above, the terminal has a string of clear-text data M, a vector of signed data S and a public key K in its memory that should be used for data validation.

4. The terminal uses the public key to decipher the signed data. The result should contain the data header (0x6A) and the data trailer (0xBC). If the actual result differs, the validation is considered as failed.

5. The terminal strips the header and the trailer and then refers to the last 20 bytes of the data as hash code H. The terminal concatenates all deciphered data except the hash and the sentinel bytes with the data authentication

input vector it prepared at step 1 and uses an appropriate hash algorithm to calculate its hash value.

6. Then it compares the hash to the recovered H value. If the values match, the signed data have been validated successfully.

5.3.8.5 Static Data Authentication (SDA)

As mentioned in the section on the Application File Locator, each entry in AFL mentions a short file identifier, the first and the last records in a file which are to be read by the terminal as well as the last record of the file that is relevant for offline authentication.

Usually, the terminal combines all the records thus prescribed into the data authentication input vector while other reading application data, for efficiency.

In addition, if the optional "Static Data Authentication Tag List" (tag 9F4A) is present, the terminal appends the AIP to the data authentication input vector, as the optional tag is only allowed to contain the tag value for AIP[2].

The terminal needs to recover the issuer key from the card following the steps described in section 5.3.8.3 when it uses a card scheme public key (identified by "Certification Authority Public Key Index", tag 8F) to recover the issuer key from "Issuer Public Key Certificate" (tag 90), "Issuer Public Key Remainder" (tag 92) and "Issuer Public Key Exponent" (tag 9F32).

Then the terminal performs signed data validation as described in Signed Data Validation, with static records (and optional AIP) it concatenated and using the issuer public key as the validation key. Data object "Signed Static Application Data" (tag 93) contains the signed data for validation, and if the card supports SDA, it is mandatory for the object to be present on the card.

5.3.8.6 Dynamic Data Authentication (DDA)

Dynamic Data Authentication (DDA) greatly improves data exchange security by introducing, as the name implies, dynamic elements to the authentication process. It puts additional demand on the computational power of both the terminal and the card as well as introduces an additional step in the transaction flow slightly slowing it due to a communication overhead.

The data authentication input vector for DDA is defined by the Dynamic Data Authentication Data Object List (DDOL) (see section 5.3.3) provided by the card in data element 9F49. If the element is not present, the terminal is allowed to revert to an acquirer-defined default DDOL.

DDA differs from SDA in several aspects.

First, the DDOL is composed by the terminal dynamically and can contain multiple transaction-specific details. The EMV standard also requires that

---

[2]The older version of EMV specification did not require AIP inclusion in static data for authentication, and the optional tag has been introduced to allow simultaneous support of both its newer and older flavors.

"Unpredictable Number" (tag 9F37) should be always present in any DDOL, regardless of whether it is provided by the card or used by the terminal by default. The "Unpredictable Number" is defined as "the value to provide variability and uniqueness to the generation of a cryptogram" and is usually a random number generated by the terminal in a manner independent of other transaction details.

Second, to validate the signed dynamic authentication data, the terminal uses the ICC public key and not the issuer public key. To obtain the ICC public key the terminal first uses a card scheme public key to recover the issuer key as described in section 5.3.8.3 and then uses the issuer public key to recover ICC key.

Finally, rather than referring to a static value already read by the terminal during the Read Application Data stage of the transaction, the signed value is obtained from the card using a special command called INTERNAL AUTHEN-TICATE. In addition to the unpredictable number provided by terminal, the card also generates and returns an "ICC Dynamic Data" (tag 9F4C) value defined as "Time-variant number generated by the ICC" and can be either a simple counter incrementing on each DDA or transaction attempt or a random number.

The Dynamic Data Authentication flow steps are performed as follows:

1. The terminal uses a procedure described in section 5.3.8.3 to reconstruct the issuer public key from the "Issuer Public Key Certificate" (tag 90), "Issuer Public Key Remainder" (tag 92) and "Issuer Public Key Exponent" (tag 9F32) using a card scheme public key identified by "Certification Authority Public Key Index" (tag 8F).

2. The terminal repeats the same procedure to reconstruct the ICC key from the "ICC Public Key Certificate" (tag 9F46), "ICC Public Key Remainder" (tag 9F48) and "ICC Public Key Exponent" (tag 9F47), using the obtained issuer public key in step 1.

3. The terminal prepares a data authentication input vector according to either ICC-provided DDOL or acquirer default set in the terminal. Along the way the terminal also generates a random number (the Unpredictable Number) and includes it in the data string.

4. The terminal issues an INTERNAL AUTHENTICATE command to card. The command's P1 and P2 registers are set to 0, and its data are the data sequence prepared, based on the DDOL in use. In response the card sends back either "Response Message Template Format 1" (tag 80) or "Response Message Template Format 2" (tag 77). Format 1 only contains the signed dynamic application data whereas format 2 may contain additional elements.

5. The terminal uses the ICC public key to validate the signed data, as described in section 5.3.8.4.

5.3.8.7 Combined Data Authentication (CDA)

Combined data authentication (CDA) optimizes the transaction flow of dynamic data authentication for cases when the card's computational power is high enough and the overhead of exchanging commands with the terminal becomes a bottleneck. During CDA there is no separate exchange of commands for the sole purpose of offline card data authentication.

In other words, CDA is (almost) as fast as SDA and as secure as DDA.

Instead of managing a separate list of data elements and using a dedicated command, the card uses the data already provided by the terminal during the "Generate Application Cryptogram" step (see section 5.3.13). It calculates the signature for the data authentication input vector composed of PDOL, CDOL1 and/or CDOL2 data object lists as well as the tag, lengths and values of elements to the relevant command. For CDA to work, the issuer must include "Unpredictable Number" in both CDOLs, thus making sure the terminal is able to generate and send it off.

Besides the aforementioned differences, the CDA flow is similar to DDA one:

1. The terminal uses the procedure described in section 5.3.8.3 to reconstruct the issuer public key from the "Issuer Public Key Certificate" (tag 90), "Issuer Public Key Remainder" (tag 92) and "Issuer Public Key Exponent" (tag 9F32) using a card scheme public key identified by the "Certification Authority Public Key Index" (tag 8F).

2. The terminal repeats the same procedure to reconstruct the ICC key from the "ICC Public Key Certificate" (tag 9F46), "ICC Public Key Remainder" (tag 9F48) and "ICC Public Key Exponent" (tag 9F47) using the issuer public key obtained at step 1.

3. Depending on the transaction flow during the first or second GENERATE AC command the terminal sets a bit in the command's P1 parameter asking the ICC to perform CDA.

4. The terminal uses the input it sent for the command (PDOL and the corresponding CDOL) and, unlike other data authentication methods, the tag, lengths and values of ICC response data to the GENERATE AC command to generate the data authentication input vector.

5. The terminal uses the ICC public key to validate the signed data as described in section 5.3.8.4.

It is worth noting that in the EMV Contactless world, there is a notion of *fast DDA* or *fDDA*. That offline card authentication method algorithm is identical to that of CDA. However, due to some differences in the transaction flow, the POS usually reads the data it needs to validate after it receives the signed data value and not prior to it.

5.3.9   Processing Restrictions

During the Read Application Data step, the terminal receives certain data regarding the card application used to determine whether the application is of correct version, can be used for that type of transaction (referred to as *Application Usage Control*), is already effective and has not yet expired.

5.3.9.1   Application Version Number

To determine the application version, the terminal checks whether the card application provided the data element "Application Version Number" (tag 9F08). If the number is not present or matches the one found in the terminal, the applications are compatible and the transaction continues. If the version number as provided by the card differs from the one in the terminal, the version check fails and the terminal sets the appropriate bit ("ICC and terminal have different application versions") in the TVR.

5.3.9.2   Application Usage Control

A card application can contain an "Application Usage Control" (tag 9F07) data element having the length of 2 bytes. Its bits correspond to various scenarios for application usage such as "valid for domestic cash transactions" or "valid for international services". It also contains "valid at ATMs" and "valid at terminals other than ATMs" flags.

The terminal starts the usage control check by inspecting the latter two flags and determining whether the transaction can proceed based on the terminal type. If the "Issuer Country Code" data element (tags 5F28, 5F55 or 5F56 in different formats) is present in the application data, the terminal based on its own location data determines whether the transaction is international or domestic, and, finally, checks the transaction type.

For instance, consider POS located at a store in Germany and a card issued in Iceland and a cardholder attempting to purchase goods without a cashback amount. The terminal first checks that the card application is valid for non-ATM terminals. If the flag is set, the terminal compares the issuer and its own country code determining the transaction as an international one and not domestic one. Then to allow the transaction it checks whether at least one of "Valid for international goods" or "Valid for international services" bits is set in the Application Usage Control.

In case the usage is not allowed for the card application, the terminal sets the appropriate bit ("Requested service not allowed for card product") in the TVR.

5.3.9.3   Application Effective and Expiration Date

If the card data contain the "Application Effective Date" (tag 5F25), the terminal checks whether it is less or equal to the current date. If there is a future application effective date, the terminal does not allow the transaction to proceed, setting "Application not yet effective" bit in the TVR to 1. If there is no application effective date on the card, the application is considered effective.

After checking the effective date, the terminal checks whether the "Application Expiration Date" (tag 5F24) is not exceeded (i.e., is later than the current date or or equal to it). If it is exceeded, the check has failed and the appropriate bit ("Expired application") is set in the TVR.

5.3.10 Cardholder Verification

The card application usually contains a "Cardholder Verification Method List" (CVM List) (tag 8E) data element, defining the rules according to which the terminal should select the card verification method or methods to use. The data element contains two amount fields referred to as X and Y and a list of the cardholder verification rules (CVRs), which is a variable-length array of 2-byte values.

5.3.10.1 Amount Fields

The first 8 bytes of the CVM List data element contain two amount fields. Each amount field is encoded in binary format with implicit decimal point. Each amount is expressed in "Application Currency Code" (tag 9F42) stored on the card and retrieved during the Read Application Data step.

For example, if the application currency is Euro (978) then the value of 0x07BA for the first amount field corresponds to the amount of 19.78 EUR.

Specific cardholder verification rules refer to the first and second amount as X and Y to define the conditions under which a said rule is applicable.

5.3.10.2 Cardholder Verification Rules

Each of the cardholder verification rules consists of 2 bytes, with the first one specifying the CVM to be used, and the second one specifying the condition under which the verification method is to be applied. The first byte is called Cardholder Verification Method code (CVM code) and the second byte is called Cardholder Verification Method Condition code (CVM Condition code).

The leftmost bit (8) of the CVM code is reserved for future use.

Bit 7 of the CVM code, if set to zero, indicates that the terminal should end the cardholder verification stage if the CVM fails. If the bit is set to 1, the terminal can continue to the next CVM on the list if the method failed.

Bits 6 to 1 of the CVM code represent the method supposed to be applied. They are listed with the corresponding bit values below:

Failed CVM processing (000000). The method is used to force CVM failure in the terminal. For example, it can be the terminating member of a CVM list to make sure that the cardholder verification is considered failed if no other matching CV rule was previously found.

Cleartext offline PIN (000001). The PIN is transmitted by the terminal to the card unencrypted for offline validation.

Online PIN (000010). PIN as entered by the cardholder is transmitted to the issuer for validation in the form of an encrypted PIN block (EPB).

Cleartext offline PIN and signature (000011). That is a combination CVM of clear-text offline PIN and signature.

Enciphered offline PIN (000100). The PIN is enciphered by the terminal and then sent to the card for offline validation.

Enciphered offline PIN and signature (00101). That is a combination CVM of the enciphered offline PIN and signature.

Signature (011110). A slip is printed by the POS, the cardholder has to sign it and the shop attendant is expected to compare it to the signature on the card signature strip. As of April 2018, most major schemes no longer require that shops accepting EMV cards store the signature slips.

No CVM (011111). No verification of the cardholder is performed.

These CVMs are also described in section 2.7.

Besides the standard codes mentioned, the EMV specification reserves ranges 000110 to 011101 for future use and allocates ranges 100000 to 101111 and 110000 to 111110 for use by individual schemes and individual issuers, correspondingly. The value of 111111 has a special meaning for the CVM results data element (see section 5.3.10.3).

The CVM condition codes include the following key values:

Always (0x00). Indicates that the CVM should be always attempted.

If terminal supports the CVM (0x03). Indicates that the CVM should only be attempted if supported by the terminal (or, in other words, it is acceptable to skip this method if the terminal does not support it, e.g., is unattended/has no printer for a signature slip).

If unattended cash/If manual cash/If purchase with cashback (0x01/0x04/0x05) Applicable in the corresponding cash-related scenario.

If no cash involved (0x02). In the standard the value is officially referred to as "not unattended cash and not manual cash and not purchase with cashback". In practice, it applies to the most widespread type of card-present transaction—the basic POS purchase.

If under/over value (0x06/0x07/0x08/0x09). The rule is applicable if the transaction is in application transaction currency (transaction currency code equals application currency code) and is under X value (0x06), over X value (0x07), under Y value (0x08) or over Y value (0x09).

The value ranges 0xA to 0x7F are reserved for future use by the EMV standard while range 0x80 to 0xFF is allocated for proprietary use by payment schemes.

Upon the completion of cardholder verification, the terminal should set bit "Cardholder verification was performed" to 1 in the TSI. If the CVR list is not present in the card application data or does not contain any rules the bit is set to zero.

In addition, the terminal performs special handling of a condition when PIN entry is requested but PIN pad is not attached or functional by setting bit "PIN entry required and PIN pad not present or not working" of the TVR to 1.

5.3.10.3   CVM Results

The results of the last executed cardholder verification are stored in data element "Cardholder Verification Method (CVM) Results" (tag 9F34). The data element contains three bytes: the CVM Code of the verification method that was performed, the CVM Condition Code that was fulfilled and the CVM Result byte carrying the CVM status: 0 for unknown (such as signature), 1 for failed and 2 for successful CVM.

If no actual CVM was performed, the CVM code is set to 0x3F (bit value 00111111, with lower 6 bits corresponding to the reserved value of six 1 bits). Byte 2 and byte 3 of the CVM Results data element are set to 0 ("always attempted" and "failed"), correspondingly.

5.3.10.4   Example of a CVM List

For the sake of the example, let us assume that the application currency is the euro.

Consider the CVM list in figure 5.7, and let's review it according to the format mentioned above.

The first 4 bytes are "amount X" and "amount Y", which are 0x4E20 and 0xC350, or 20000 and 50000 decimal, and correspond to amounts of 200 and 500 Euro.

The CVM rule list contains five rules.

Rule 1 in bytes 5 and 6 contains the value of 0x0201. Byte 1 is the CVM code, binary 00000010. The 0 of bit 7 means the terminal cannot proceed to the next CVM rule if that one fails, and value of 000010 corresponds to online PIN. Byte 2 value, 0x01, indicates that the rule applies for unattended cash (in other words, ATM).

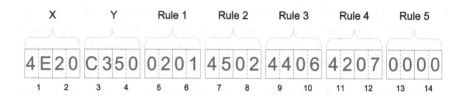

Figure 5.7: Example of a CVM list

Rule 2 in bytes 7 and 8 contain the value of 0x4502. The CVM code is binary 01000101, corresponding to "enciphered offline PIN and signature" and bit 7 means the terminal can proceed to the next CVM rule if that one fails. The CVM condition, 0x02, means that is a POS transaction.

Rule 3 in bytes 9 and 10 contain the value of 0x4406. The CVM code binary value is 01000100, corresponding to "enciphered offline PIN". Bit 7 allows the terminal to attempt the next CVM if that one is not supported. The CVM condition, 0x06, specifies that the rule applies for transactions under value of X or below 200 Euro.

Rule 4 in bytes 11 and 12 contain the value of 0x4207. The CVM code binary value is 01000010, corresponding to "online PIN" and allowing to skip to the next CVM rule if failed, and the CVM condition means "over value of X" or above 200 Euro.

Finally, rule 5 in bytes 13 and 14 contain 0x0000. That means "failed CVM processing", no skipping to the next CVM and is applicable "always".

Let us consider several possible scenarios under which the card can be used.

Scenario 1 Assume that the card is used to withdraw funds in an ATM. Rule 1 CVM condition code applies for unattended cash and in this case is attempted by the terminal.

Scenario 2 Assume that the card is used to withdraw funds in an ATM but this time the online PIN verification fails: either the PIN pad is not functional or connection to a card scheme network is not available. The terminal is not allowed to proceed to the next rule, and it considers CVM failed.

Scenario 3 Assume that the card is used for a purchase of 150 euro at a store. The terminal skips rule 1, since the transaction does not involve a form of cash withdrawal and proceeds to rule 2. The terminal attempts to validate the enciphered offline PIN and collect the cardholder's signature.

Scenario 4 Assume that the card is used for a purchase of 150 euro at a store but the POS has no printer attached. The terminal skips rule 1 since it is not applicable for retail stores. It attempts rule 2, but seeing there is no printer considers it failed. Bit 7 of the rule's byte 1 allows the terminal to proceed to the next rule or rule 3. The rule is applicable for any transaction of less than amount X, i.e., 200 euro, and is therefore applicable here. Under the rule, the terminal performs the online PIN validation without capturing the signature.

Scenario 5 Assume that the card is used for a purchase of 250 euro at a store but the POS has no printer attached. The terminal skips rule 1 since it is not applicable for retail stores. It attempts rule 2, but seeing there is no printer considers it failed. Bit 7 of the rule's byte 1 allows the terminal to proceed to rule 3, but since its CVM condition is for transactions under 200 euro, it is skipped as not applicable and the terminal considers rule 4. Rule 4 is applicable for transactions over amount X and, therefore, in this case, it prescribes online PIN validation, which the POS is to attempt.

Scenario 6 Assuming that PIN validation fails in scenario 4 or there is no connectivity in scenario 5, the terminal reaches rule 5 which is always applicable and always fails.

To rephrase the above logic, the set of rules:

■ Prescribes online PIN and online PIN only for any ATM cash withdrawal.

■ Always attempts to collect the signature and validate offline PIN for any in-store purchase.

■ If an in-store terminal does not support the signature collection, the rules allow enciphered offline PIN validation for transactions under 200 euro and force online PIN validation for transactions over 200 euro. Note that the rule is also applied if the transaction is a manual cash withdrawal or a cashback purchase.

■ If the above validation methods do not work, the CVM fails.

5.3.10.5 Offline PIN Verification

During the offline PIN verification process the terminal application and the card application interact to validate the PIN without involving the issuer. As already mentioned above, the offline PIN can be validated in plaintext or enciphered mode. The mode refers to communication between the terminal and the card only as no PIN details are sent elsewhere.

The card keeps track of the number of PIN attempts made.

There are three ways for offline PIN verification CVM to fail:

■ The terminal does not support it either permanently (not implemented or no PIN pad) or temporarily (PIN pad not working or missing). In this case the terminal sets "PIN entry required and PIN pad not present or not working" bit of the TVR to 1.

■ All attempts to verify the PIN have failed, the card could not decrypt the enciphered PIN or decided to block the PIN upon the first entry. In this case, the terminal sets "PIN try limit exceeded" bit of the TVR to 1.

■ Merchant/customer decided to bypass PIN entry. The condition was designated by the standard to be used for new cardholders and during transitions to PIN CVM in cases when the cardholder realizes they have forgotten or do not know the PIN. In this case, the terminal sets "PIN entry required, PIN pad present, but PIN was not entered" bit of the TVR to 1, thus informing the issuer that the PIN entry was voluntarily bypassed.

Overview

To verify the type of PIN verification as the first step the terminal can retrieve the number of PIN attempts remaining. That can be done by issuing a GET DATA command to the card with P1 P2 set to 9F17 (data element "Personal Identification Number (PIN) Try Counter"). If the value returned by the card application is zero, PIN attempts are exhausted and the CVM has failed. The step is not mandatory since, as it can be seen below, the VERIFY command is able to return the number of remaining PIN tries in its status words.

Otherwise, the terminal needs to verify the PIN. PIN verification is done using the VERIFY command. The VERIFY command is issued with P1 set to 00 and with P2 set to either 0x80 for plaintext or 0x88 for enciphered PIN[3]. The command can provide three optional responses:

■ The card application returns a success response code (SW1/SW2 equal to 9000). That means the PIN was verified and the EMV transaction can proceed.

■ The card application returns a checking error (SW1/SW2 of 6983 or 6984). That means the card application blocked the PIN at the first try or failed to decipher the PIN block. In either case, there is no point to retry the PIN validation and the PIN validation should be considered a failure.

■ The card application returns a warning error (SW1 equal to 63). That means a particular PIN verification attempt has failed. In this case, SW2 is in the form of Cn, where n indicates the number of PIN attempts remaining (C2 for 2 attempts, C1 for 1 attempt, C0 for no attempts remaining).

If the PIN is to be enciphered, the terminal issues a GET CHALLENGE command to obtain necessary data for the encipherment.

---

[3] Although the EMV standard mentions value of P2 = 00 according to ISO/IEC 7816-4 standard, it is not used in EMV applications.

Cleartext Offline PIN Verification

To perform the cleartext offline PIN verification the terminal prompts the card-holder for the PIN value and then issues a VERIFY command to the card with P2 value set to 0x80. The PIN value entered is packaged into a ISO-9564 Format 2 PIN block (see section 13.1 for description of PIN block formats).

Enciphered Offline PIN Verification

The PIN is enciphered with a public key which should be personalized on the card. Furthermore, to avoid replay attacks the terminal uses an unpredictable number provided by the card as part of the enciphered PIN envelope.

To recover the key the terminal first checks the presence of "Integrated Circuit Card (ICC) PIN Encipherment Public Key Certificate" (tag 9F2D), "Integrated Circuit Card (ICC) PIN Encipherment Public Key Exponent" (tag 9F2E) and "Integrated Circuit Card (ICC) PIN Encipherment Public Key Remainder" (tag 9F2F) elements.

If present, the terminal applies the algorithm described in sections 5.3.8.3 and 5.3.8.6 to recover the issuer public key and then utilizes the issuer public key to recover the ICC PIN encipherment public key used to encipher the PIN block.

If the elements are not present in the card application data, the terminal checks whether elements "ICC Public Key Certificate" (tag 9F46), "ICC Public Key Remainder" (tag 9F48) and "ICC Public Key Exponent" (tag 9F47) are present in the card application data. If they are available, the terminal recovers the ICC public key and uses it to encipher the PIN block instead of a dedicated ICC PIN encipherment key.

In addition to the recovery of the PIN encipherment key, the terminal issues a GET CHALLENGE command to the card. The command has no command data. The card responds with a random sequence of 8 bytes, data element "Unpredictable Number" (tag 9F37), which the terminal, in turn, uses as described below. To prepare input data for the enciphered PIN, the terminal appends:

■ Data header (0x7F)

■ PIN block according to ISO 9564 format 2.

■ ICC unpredictable number as returned by the GET CHALLENGE command.

■ Random padding to the full length of the public key used for encipherment.

The result is encrypted using either the ICC PIN Encipherment Public key or ICC Public key depending on whether the former is or is not present in the application data. The encrypted outcome is sent to the card in VERIFY command with its P2 value set to 0x88.

5.3.10.6 Online PIN Verification

For online PIN verification the terminal must capture the PIN entered by the cardholder and ensure it is transmitted securely to the card issuer. Online PIN verification, if supported, can fail in two cases:

- The PIN pad is not present or malfunctioning. In this case the terminal sets "PIN entry required and PIN pad not present or not working" bit of the TVR to 1.

- PIN entry is bypassed. In this case the bit "PIN entry required and the PIN pad present but the PIN was not entered" of the TVR is set to 1.

The EMV standard does not mandate a particular format in which the terminal can transmit the PIN to the terminal management system. However, once the transaction reaches a scheme network, the PIN block must be generated according to the formats 0, 1 or 4 (see section 13.1) and encrypted with a Zone PIN Key (see section 8.3.2).

5.3.11 Terminal Risk Management

5.3.11.1 Offline Authorization and Terminal Risk Management

At the time when the EMV technology was incepted and rolled out an electronic terminal was not necessarily able to maintain a permanent connection to the network and authorize each transaction online. Nowadays, when terminal manufacturers offer various wireless connectivity options as a standard package, offline authorization is becoming a niche feature for specific applications.

Offline authorization is a feature allowing a card to make decisions on transactions without consulting the issuer based on some rules (implemented as a set of thresholds and counters). A card can decide to either authorize the transaction offline at the spot, force the terminal to go online in front of the issuer, or instruct the terminal to attempt an online authorization and if the connection is not available, approve the transaction offline anyway.

In the world of EMV, "Terminal risk management" refers a set of checks a terminal should perform to selectively force online authorization of a particular EMV transaction. Technically, the terminal gathers the results of risk checks in TVR bits and then applies bit masks to determine the way to handle the transaction further based on the acquirer and issuer's preferences. See section 5.3.12 for a detailed process description.

There are three major types of risk checks. They are: the *floor limit checking* when the terminal goes online for transactions over a particular accumulated limit, *random transaction selection* when the terminal relies on a random number to authorize a particular transaction online, and *velocity checking* when the terminal checks a soft and a hard limit for number of offline transactions that are allowed since an online card authorization.

The floor limit and random transaction selection parameters are set by the acquirer according to the card scheme rules. The velocity checking parameters are defined by the issuer.

5.3.11.2   Floor Limit

The floor limit value refers to a minimum transaction amount above which any transaction must be authorized online or declined by the terminal. The floor limit is typically set by a specific acquirer for merchants within overall limits pre-scribed by relevant card schemes. The acquirer can elect to lower the floor limit to zero for a particular terminal solution thus flagging all the transactions to be authorized online or declined.

The EMV standard recommends but not mandates maintaining a log file on the terminal to avoid "split sales", a behavior type when multiple transactions just under a limit are made to circumvent the threshold. If the terminal manages such a log, it should add the latest value from the log to the current transaction amount in order to determine whether the sum of the transaction is above or below the floor limit.

To illustrate that consider the following example. If the floor limit is 25 euros and the requested amount is 15 euros, the transaction is below the floor limit. However, if there has been a recent transaction of 15 euros recorded in the log, the terminal shall consider the amount of 30 euros with regard to the floor limit.

If a particular transaction amount or the sum of amounts exceed the floor limit, the terminal sets the "Transaction exceeds floor limit" bit of the TVR to 1 which, in turn, may force the transaction online authorization.

5.3.11.3   Random Transaction Selection

The random transaction selection process performs a random selection of trans-actions under a certain transaction amount, called "Threshold Value for Biased Random Selection" (herein referred to as BRS threshold). A certain percentage of transactions with amounts not exceeding the threshold value are chosen for online authorization. For amounts exceeding the BRS threshold value the per-centage goes up linearly up until the floor limit (over which it is, naturally, 100% as all transactions are authorized online).

To determine whether a transaction should be flagged to be sent online the terminal generates a random number between 1 and 99. Then the terminal com-pares it to the target percentage for the transaction amount and if the number does not exceed the target percentage, decides to authorize the transaction on-line. In particular, that means that the higher the target percentage is, the higher the proportion of transactions to be authorized online is.

For transactions of amounts not exceeding the BRS threshold, the random selection according to a parameter called "Target Percentage to be Used for Ran-dom Selection" is performed. For transactions exceeding the BRS threshold, a bias up to the value of "Maximum Target Percentage to be Used for Biased Random Selection" is added.

Let B be the BRS threshold, X the transaction amount, F the floor limit, T the target percentage for random selection and M the maximum target percentage for biased selection. To perform the random selection the terminal has to calculate E or the effective target percentage.

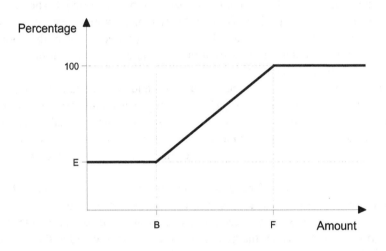

Figure 5.8: Effective target percentage

In these terms, the following formulas define the values for effective target percentage:

- If $X < B$, then $E = T$ (the value is too low and the percentage is fixed)

- If $F > X >= B$, then $E = T + \frac{(X-B)}{(F-B)} \times (M - T)$ (linear bias is added to the fixed percentage)

- If $X >= F$, then $E = 100$ (the value is over the floor limit and all transactions must go online)

This dependency is illustrated in figure 5.8.

5.3.11.4   Velocity Checking

Velocity checking is performed in terms of the number of transactions since the last online authorization. Its parameters are personalized on the card by the issuer in such data objects as "Lower Consecutive Offline Limit" (tag 9F14) and "Upper Consecutive Offline Limit" (tag 9F23).

If these elements are present, the terminal issues GET DATA commands to the card requesting the values of "Application Transaction Counter (ATC)" (tag 9F36) and "Last Online Application Transaction Counter (ATC) Register" (tag 9F13). ATC counts transactions performed by the card application, and the register contains the ATC value of the last transaction authorized online.

The terminal subtracts the register value from the ATC and compares it to the lower and upper consecutive offline limits. If the difference exceeds the lower consecutive limit, the terminal sets the TVR bit "Lower consecutive offline limit exceeded" to 1. If the difference exceeds the upper consecutive limit, the terminal sets the TVR bit "Upper consecutive offline limit exceeded" to 1. Finally, if the ATC is equal to zero, the terminal sets the TVR bit "New card" to 1.

5.3.12 Terminal Action Analysis

Upon completing the previous steps, the terminal makes a preliminary decision about the fate of the particular transaction. The terminal can decide to decline it offline, authorize it offline or attempt an online authorization. The decision is made based on the combination of rules set by the issuer, the rules set by the acquirer and the values in TVR aggregated as part of the transaction's previous steps.

The rules are called *action codes* and are stored in two groups of three registers each. There are issuer action codes which can be personalized on the card and acquirer action codes stored in the terminal. Each group of the registers encodes actions defined by the issuer and the acquirer if the corresponding TVR bit is 1, hence the name. Each register has the same length of 5 bytes as the TVR.

There are three types of registers: action code denial, action code online and action code default. The "denial" registers specify conditions under which a transaction must be declined offline. The "online" registers specify the conditions under which a transaction must be authorized online. The "default" registers specify the action when the terminal intended to send the transaction online but failed to do that for a technical reason.

The issuer's registers are personalized in such data elements as "Issuer Action Code—Denial" (tag 9F0E), "Issuer Action Code—Online" (tag 9F0F) and "Issuer Action Code—Default" (tag 9F0D) on the card. Their acquirer-defined counterparts are called Terminal Action Code—Denial, Terminal Action Code—Online and Terminal Action Code—Default, correspondingly.

To determine the required course of action the terminal can apply a logical OR for each pair of the issuer and terminal registers and then apply a logical AND to the result and the TVR. If the outcome is not zero, the relevant action must be triggered. The EMV standard encourages terminal application developers to optimize the process by terminating a denied transaction earlier during the lifecycle if the appropriate register bits are set (for instance, a terminal can decline an EMV transaction immediately once DDA has failed if the corresponding bit in Issuer Action Code or Denial register is set to 1, thus not extending the interaction any longer).

To illustrate that consider the following examples.

Scenario 1. Bit 7 of the TVR byte 2 corresponds to the "Expired application" condition. Assume the issuer has set its "Denial" counterpart (i.e., bit 7 of byte 2 of Issuer Action Code—Denial register) to 0, "Online" to 1 and "Default" to 0. Under these conditions, if the application has expired, the issuer does not want the transaction to be declined offline and asks the terminal to go online with it but if it fails to do that allows attempting the transaction offline authorization.

Now let us assume that the acquirer has set their Denial bit to 0, Online to 1 and Default to 1. In other words, the acquirer does not want the transaction to be declined on the spot and asks for its online authorization but if it is impossible, prescribes its offline decline.

With such a combination of action codes, the terminal does not decline an expired application immediately (both the issuer and the acquirer set their Denial bits to 0) and attempts to go online (the issuer has set the Online bit to 1) and if the attempt fails, declines the transaction offline (the acquirer has set the Default bit to 1).

Scenario 2. Bit 4 of the TVR byte 2 corresponds to the "New card" condition. Assume we have an issuer which set the "Denial" bit to 0, "Online" bit to 0 and "Default" bit to 0. let us also assume the acquirer is more cautious and their "Online" bit is set to 1 with "Default" and "Denial" bits also set to 0.

With this combination of action codes upon encountering a new card the terminal does not decline it offline (both the issuer and the acquirer Decline bits are 0) and tries to go online (the acquirer Online bit is 1) but if the attempt fails, does not decline the transaction (both the issuer and the acquirer Default bits are 0).

5.3.13   *Generation of Cryptograms and Issuer Authentication*

The terminal can request up to two cryptograms from the card by issuing Generate AC (GAC) commands. Both the first and the second GAC can result in a transaction decline or full authorization in case the EMV transaction can complete.

However, the first GAC can also return an authorization request cryptogram (ARQC). The terminal sends the cryptogram for the issuer's approval and upon receiving a response, the terminal has to complete the transaction by issuing the second GAC obtaining a full authorization or a full decline cryptogram and later transmitting it to the payment scheme for clearing.

That serves the important purpose of making the issuer and the card authentication mutual: if the card does not confirm the issuer's response validity (possible indication of a man-in-the-middle attack), the transaction is rejected.

As mentioned previously (see section 5.3.8.7), the first GAC can also be used for offline data authentication. In a somewhat similar manner it is possible to perform the issuer authentication (i.e., issuer response validation of authenticity) by either a separate EXTERNAL AUTHENTICATE command or as part of the second GAC.

5.3.13.1   Card Action Analysis

Upon making a preliminary decision on the transaction handling method, the terminal communicates it to the card by requesting an application cryptogram of a particular type. They are: TC (Transaction Certificate) indicating an offline authorization, ARQC (Authorization ReQuest Cryptogram) corresponding to an online authorization attempt, and AAC (Application Authentication Cryptogram) or an offline decline.

There is a hierarchical order of cryptograms where TC is the highest one and AAC is the lowest one in the hierarchy. The terminal suggests a particular hierarchy level in the request and the card either responds with the requested cryptogram or downgrades it by responding with a cryptogram of a lower level in the hierarchy.

The process of the card's decision on the manner in which the authorization is supposed to be performed is referred to as *card action analysis*.

There are three possible scenarios for card action analysis.

Scenario 1. The terminal asks the card to generate a TC, thus authorizing the transaction offline. The card can either return a TC forcing an attempted online authorization by returning an ARQC or decline the transaction altogether by returning an AAC.

Scenario 2. The terminal asks the card to generate an ARQC for a further online authorization. The card can either return an ARQC or tell the terminal not to bother, returning an AAC.

Scenario 3. The terminal asks the card to generate an AAC and that is what the card does.

If the terminal returns a TC or an AAC to the card, the transaction is complete. The TC or AAC is later sent to the schemes as part of the transaction details in the clearing file.

A card can decline the transaction for two major reasons: due to some limitation of the transaction environment, such as restriction of a particular type of merchant, or due to an issue with the particular transaction. The standard contains provisions for both scenarios allowing the terminal to display a different message in either case. The card may also ask the terminal to send an advice message about the decline (so far, only "PIN try limit exceed" has been identified as a case when that may be necessary) to the issuer.

5.3.13.2   Generate AC (GAC) Command

As mentioned previously, the terminal can issue the command to the card up to two times. If an attempt is made to issue the command for the third time, the card application responds to it with SW1/SW2 set to 0x6985.

During the first issuance of the GAC command the terminal can request TC, ARQC or AAC from the card by setting an appropriate value in bits 8 and 7 of the command's P1 control parameter. Value of 0x00 corresponds to AAC, value of 0x01 corresponds to TC and value of 0x10 corresponds to a request of ARQC. Furthermore, the terminal, can set bit 5 of the P1 parameter to 1 to request a CDA alongside the application cryptogram in case the requested cryptogram is not an AAC.

The second issuance of the GAC command occurs if ARQC was generated during the first issuance, the terminal was able to transmit the transaction and the issuer provided a response to it. Depending on the issuer's decision, the card can perform the issuer authentication as part of the second Generate AC command.

It follows that during the second issuance of the Generate Application Cryptogram command an ICC can perform up to three distinct operations: combined data authentication, the cryptogram generation, and the issuer authentication.

GAC Data Object Lists

To calculate the input data for the Generate AC command the terminal concatenates a string of values according to set of value definitions it retrieved previously as CDOL1 and CDOL2 (tags 8C and 8D) with CDOL1 used for the first GAC command and CDOL2 used for the second GAC command.

With few exceptions, the standard does not mandate a particular list of fields that are always to be included in a CDOL, however, there is a recommended minimum set of values including the amount(s), date, type and currency of the transaction ("Amount, Authorized", tag 9F02, "Amount, Other", tag 9F03, "Transaction Currency Code", tag 5F2A, "Transaction Date", tag 9A, and "Transaction Type", tag 9C), a few details on the terminal ("Terminal Country Code", tag 9F1A, and "Terminal Verification Results", tag 95, see also section 5.3.4).

To prevent replay attacks the lists of data objects must include the "Unpredictable Number" (tag 9F37) generated by the terminal.

Transaction Certificate Hash Value

In addition to values sent to the card for the purpose of generating the cryptogram directly, the card can also request some additional value fields to be taken into account indirectly via a computation on the terminal side.

That is done by requesting a "Transaction Certificate (TC) Hash Value", tag 98 as part of CDOL1 and/or CDOL2.

Upon encountering the tag in a DOL, the terminal checks the data object list provided in the "Transaction Certificate Data Object List (TDOL)" (tag 97). The terminal concatenates the values of data elements specified in the list and then calculates the hash code for the resulting string. Then the card uses the resulting value to calculate the cryptogram.

Application Cryptogram Calculation Algorithm

To put it simply, an application cryptogram is a MAC (message authentication code) of a certain sequence of data fields computed with a unique key. The key is time-dependent: it is derived based on the ATC.

The standard does not mandate a set of fields for cryptogram generation but it does recommend to include, at minimum, the same values mentioned above as well as the "Application Interchange Profile" (tag 82) and the "Application Transaction Counter" (tag 9F36). That, in particular, means that the recommended data contain some temporary details on a specific transaction, including its date, a random number generated by the terminal and a counter that is maintained by the card. The set of values ensures that no replay attack can be performed with the cryptogram as both the terminal-generated number and the ATC are unique per transaction.

However, the cryptogram generation procedure is even more time-dependent. During the card issuing personalization stage the issuer personalizes an ICC Application Cryptogram Master Key on the ICC. To calculate the cryptogram the card derives a one-time Application Cryptogram Session Key from the master key using the ATC.

While an individual issuer is allowed to decide on a proprietary method and algorithm for key derivation, the EMV standard defines a recommendation.

According to it, in order to derive the key the card pads a two-byte value ATC with zeroes to the full length of the algorithm input block, which in the most common case being triple-DES, is 8 bytes. Then the card generates two blocks of values, F1 and F2, where the third byte (the one right after the bytes allocated for ATC) is set to 0xF0 and 0x0F, accordingly.

The blocks are encrypted using the ICC Application Cryptogram Master Key, each one individually, and the encrypted values are concatenated. The resulting 16-byte vector is used as a double-length 3DES key.

Then, the ICC computes the 8-byte MAC of the data using the just-derived session key (see section 12.4).

Generate AC Command and Combined Data Authentication

As mentioned previously, when requesting a TC or an ARQC the terminal can set bit 5 of the P1 parameter of the GAC command to request a CDA alongside the application cryptogram. Upon receiving the GAC command with the bit set, the card application begins the performance by computing the cryptogram as described.

Then the card generates a 20-byte Transaction Data Hash Code. After that it proceeds to sign it with the ICC Private Key making the resulting value verifiable by the terminal (see description of Signed Data Validation below). The outcome is stored in the "Signed Dynamic Application Data" field (tag 9F4B).

In other words, in addition to the data listed in PDOL, the card additionally signs all the fields returned alongside the cryptogram as well as the cryptogram itself. That makes the CDA the most secure data authentication method and prevents attacks that tamper with such indicators as the cryptogram type flags in the Cryptogram Information Data (see next section).

GAC Return Value

The Generate Application Cryptogram command can return its results in two formats, conveniently called Format 1 and Format 2.

In the case of a Format 1 response the value is a primitive data object or "Response Message Template Format 1" (tag 80). The object is a concatenation of Cryptogram Information Data (CID), Application Transaction Counter, Application Cryptogram itself and optional Issuer Application Data values.

In the case of a Format 2 response, the value is a constructed data object or "Response Message Template Format 2" (tag 77). The object contains full BER-TLV objects which must include "Cryptogram Information Data (CID)", tag 9F27, "Application Transaction Counter (ATC)", tag 9F36 and "Application Cryptogram", tag 9F26. Naturally, CDA can only be used for Format 2 responses while the "pure" cryptogram generation result can be returned in both formats.

The Cryptogram Information Data is a one-byte value carrying bits for a cryptogram type or an indication of whether an advice message on an offline decline should be sent to the issuer. It also has three bits allocated for an optional advice code or decline reason.

ARQC validation and calculation of ARPC

In response to an ARQC cryptogram sent alongside other ISO 8583 data to the issuer, the latter validates the cryptogram and calculates the Authorization Response Cryptogram (ARPC).

To validate the ARQC the issuer first derives the master key corresponding to the particular card (based on PAN and PAN sequence number) and then uses the ATC to derive the session key from it. After obtaining the session key which in the case of using a valid card is identical to the one calculated by the ICC, the issuer host uses the unpredictable number and other data elements that transmitted alongside the ARQC to calculate the application cryptogram value independently. If the value calculated by the issuer matches the one transmitted to it by the terminal, the cryptogram validation is considered successful.

To calculate the ARPC, the issuer host takes the 2-byte Authorization Response Code (ARC) value, pads it with zeroes to the full 8-byte length, XORs it with the ARQC cryptogram and encrypts it with the same session key that was used to validate the ARQC.

The ARPC and ARC values are sent back to the terminal and via it to the ICC in data element 55 of the ISO message as "Issuer Authentication Data" (tag 91) and, optionally, as "Authorization Response Code" (tag 9A). The length of the Issuer Authentication Data element can be between 8 to 16 bytes and while the first 8 bytes always contain the ARPC, the remaining 8 bytes have the structure proprietary to the issuer. However, the first two bytes usually contain the ARC.

Issuer Authentication Commands

Upon receiving a response from the payment network, the terminal seeks to authenticate the issuer making sure that the response comes from a genuine authoritative source and thus also ensuring that the particular store is going to get paid by the issuer for the transaction.

The EMV standard provides two ways to do that. The Application Interchange Profile value on the ICC may have bit 3 or "Issuer Authentication is supported" set to 1 and in this case a separate command or EXTERNAL AUTHENTICATE is used to authenticate the issuer. If the bit is set to zero, the authentication is combined with the second issuance of the GAC command.

Regardless of the way the authentication is performed its process is the same:

1. The ICC decrypts the ARPC received from the issuer using the same session key formerly used to generate the ARQC.

2. The ICC XORs the decrypted result with the ARQC and so obtains a padded Authorization Response Code. It extracts the ARC from the first 2 bytes of the 8-byte result value. Note that for a successful transaction the decrypted ARPC is to be identical to the original (encrypted) ARQC since the transaction approval is indicated by zeroes.

3. The ICC compares the calculated ARC with the one provided alongside the ARPC. If the values match, the issuer is successfully authenticated.

The data required for issuer authentication with the EXTERNAL AUTHENTICATE command is provided as part of the Issuer Authentication Data element. At the very minimum, it includes the ARPC and the ARC.

If the issuer authentication is combined with the second Generate AC command issuance, the issuer adds tag 91 ("Issuer Authentication Data") to CDOL2, thus ensuring that the value is included in the input parameter of the command.

If the authentication using the EXTERNAL AUTHENTICATE command fails, the terminal sets the "Issuer authentication failed" bit of the TVR to 1, and, correspondingly, takes the value into consideration when deciding which second cryptogram to request from the card (TC or AAC). If the combined authentication fails, the card makes the decision on the returned cryptogram type.

5.3.14 Script Processing

As mentioned, the issuer can send issuer scripts to the card alongside a response to an online authorization request.

A possible scenario for such a script could lock a lost or stolen card. For instance, an issuer can receive a call about a lost card. If an attempt to perform a transaction on that card is made, once the transaction is attempted online, a script is transmitted to its card application disabling the card permanently.

To do so, the issuer can transmit two data elements alongside its response to an ARQC cryptogram or "Issuer Script Template 1" (tag 71) and "Issuer Script Template 2" (tag 72). The first template is to be sent to the card before the second issuance of the GENERATE AC command, and the second template is to be sent to the card after the second issuance of the command.

An issuer script template contains optional script identifier ("Issuer Script Identifier", tag 9F18) used by the terminal to collect script results and not sent to the card. After the identifier the script template contains a sequence of "Issuer Script Command" elements (tag 86).

Each issuer script command from the appropriate template is transmitted to the card as-is. The terminal checks the status words of the card response. If a particular script command was successful or ended with a warning, the terminal continues to send another command to the card. If the response contains an error, the terminal does not send further commands to the card setting "Script processing failed before final GENERATE AC" or "Script processing failed after final GENERATE AC" bits in the TVR.

The terminal captures the execution results both for each issuer script and each command in a 5-byte value. Each individual command result is stored as a 5-byte sequence.

The first byte of an individual command result reflects the command execution status and its ordinal number in the template. The command execution status is stored as the most significant nibble (0 means "Script not performed", 1 - "Script processing failed" and 2 for "Script processing successful"). Storing of the command sequence number in its parent script template is optional and the terminal can decide to always return a zero ("Not specified") or provide the command ordinal number in the template within the least significant nibble. In the latter case, the first 14 commands are labeled with hexadecimal values of 0x1 to 0xE, and 15 and all the following commands are denoted with an 0xF.

The trailing 4 bytes contain either the Issuer Script Identifier, if provided, or 4 bytes of 0x00 if no script identifier arrived as part of the specific script template.

Although the EMV standard does not allocate any tag for the issuer script results, card schemes usually require it to be sent to the issuer under a proprietary tag element.

5.3.15 *Transaction Completion*

The second call to the GAC command and the following generation of TC or AAC cryptograms conclude the EMV transaction. The TC is sent to the issuer as further evidence for a valid conclusion of the entire transaction flow.

Chapter 6

EMV Contactless Transactions

CONTENTS

6.1 Overview

RFID and later NFC technology have enabled contactless data transmission over an unlicensed global radio frequency between devices in close proximity, including power supplies using radio waves.

About five years after ISO/IEC 7816 was first released in 1995, the work concluded in ISO/IEC 14443, the standard defining physical characteristics, radio frequencies, transmission protocol, anti-collision measures and initialization of *proximity cards*[1].

At a very high-level view of a contactless interaction several challenges can be identified that to a considerable extent have shaped the differences between the elaborate complex and well-defined "contact" chip EMV transaction standard and the EMV Contactless family of standards.

Unlike the traditional EMV case where a transaction is always initiated by the card reader, a contactless transaction can be initiated by the card entering the polling field of the reader device to which the device only reacts. That is typical for mass transit, parking lots, toll roads payment scenarios, etc.

The card itself stays in the field of the proximity reader for a limited period of time and is moved away by the cardholder regardless of whether the card and the reader have completed the exchange of commands. That takes much less time than an online authorization does to be completed. In other words, by the time a response from the issuer arrives, the card is already away from the reader.

Finally, the card is no longer exactly a card as it might be a mobile phone, a key fob, a wristband or any other item supporting the same physical protocol.

The transaction origination by the card instead of the terminal can be resolved as a minor incremental change to an existing terminal. As for the form factor of the "card" or payer's device apart from the magnetic stripe or integral circuits as long as a particular device conforms to the physical link requirements of ISO/IEC-14443, its form is immaterial.

The short period of time the card is present in the polling field of the reader device, however, is a major difference that has considerably impacted the contactless protocol.

To begin with, the card does not stay in front of the device long enough to receive a response from its issuer. That automatically means that in some cases unless the idea of issuer scripts is to be forfeited by a particular implementation, the cardholder may have to tap the card on the reader twice: the first time to initiate the transaction and the second time to receive the issuer scripts. Furthermore, the EMV transaction protocol may have to be condensed into fewer commands to ensure the limited tap time is sufficient.

The convergence of the payment industry to a single standard happened in several phases. First, as a result of some early experiments the ISO/IEC 14443

---

[1]These differ from *vicinity cards*, which operate at a somewhat greater distance and are covered by ISO/IEC 15693 standard

was developed and accepted by all major industry players. Later schemes proceeded with their individual solutions to the challenges listed previously until finally those were brought under a common umbrella standard of EMV Contactless as alternative Kernels (see section 6.2).

Partly due to the limitations of existing networks and the necessity of costly upgrades across the board, the contactless standard allows two modes of operation: full-grade EMV and contactless magstripe, the latter being similar to part-grade EMV.

6.2   Main Concepts

In its first book *Book A, Architecture and General Requirements* consistent with a top-down approach, the EMV Contactless standard describes the concepts of the card, transaction and POS system.

As mentioned, a card is basically any device, item, object, gadget or under-skin implant[2] compatible with the ISO/IEC 14443 reader physical link requirements.

A transaction defined by the EMV Contactless standard does not differ in principle from a contact chip EMV transaction and hopefully should not require additional elaboration at this point in the book.

Conceptually, a *POS system* consists of a terminal and a reader. In some scenarios the terminal activates the reader and then exchanges some data with it until receiving a Final Outcome from it. The reader communicates with the contactless card and application or applications on it, shows messages to the cardholder, beeps and blinks its LED lights.

As the standard is uniting multiple concurrent (and differing) implementations of a payment protocol over ISO/IEC-14443 physical link, each such implementation is called a *Kernel*. Therefore, the reader inside the POS system communicates not only with one of many possible applications conforming to a single protocol but with many possible Kernels, each of which has a slightly or significantly different set of commands.

Consequently, rather than choosing an application the reader picks a *combination* of an application and Kernel and activates the Kernel (thus allowing the support for multiple sub-protocols in the form of functionally separate but compliant modules). It also performs *pre-processing* (preparatory steps of a transaction) and, finally, informs the terminal of Kernel's instructions on the way to proceed. The set of functions is called Entry Point functionality and the standard

---

[2]In 2015, a man called Vlad Zaitsev implanted silicon-coated internals of a Troika card (combined payment and public transit contactless card) into his palm to "avoid losing an expensive season ticket". Since his skin was too thick for most readers in Moscow, the plan did not work. Still, Vlad's hand definitely meets the criteria of an EMV Contactless "card" as outlined by Book A section 4.1 at the time of writing.

Table 6.1: Kernels and card schemes correspondence

Kernel	Card scheme
Kernel 1	JCB, Visa (special case, fallback from Kernel 3)
Kernel 2	MasterCard
Kernel 3	Visa (preferred choice)
Kernel 4	American Express
Kernel 5	JCB
Kernel 6	Discover
Kernel 7	UnionPay

contains a dedicated book or "Book B. Entry Point Specification" describes its processes in details.

The version 2.6 Entry Point Specification data on Kernels and their corresponding card schemes are listed in table 6.1.

The *Outcomes* are Kernel's instructions to the Entry Point on the way to proceed with the processing. The Entry Point can handle the outcomes itself or forward it to the terminal as the *Final Outcome*. Under certain conditions the Entry Point itself can generate a final outcome (usually when it does not find a matching card application).

It is worth noting that since each "tap" is short and the Kernel activates an online request the card is no longer present in the reader's field when a response to it arrives. In this case, for example, if there are issuer scripts to be processed, there protocol contains means to request a Kernel restart for the second tap, as required to finalize transaction processing.

6.3   Entry Point

An Entry Point can perform up to five steps in a transaction flow. Four of them happen before the control is handed over to a particular Kernel, and the fifth is the processing of Kernel outcomes.

The contactless transaction steps for an Entry Point are *Pre-Processing, Protocol Activation, Combination Selection, Kernel Activation and Outcome Processing*.

Depending on conditions an Entry Point can start processing from each of the first four steps. In the EMV Contactless Standard they are called Starts. An Entry Point can have A, B, C and D Starts beginning pre-processing, protocol activation, combination selection or moving directly to the Kernel activation, correspondingly.

6.3.1   Pre-Processing

The pre-processing step corresponds to Start A of the Entry Point. It is present in cases when the terminal initiates the transaction. The opposite case when the transaction is initiated by a card entering the polling field is sometimes referred to as "AutoRun" and as defined in the standard means that the Entry Point is initiated using Start B (see section 6.3.2).

The pre-processing step is naturally present in variable-value transactions as the POS system needs to define the transaction amount before the actual transaction can commence.

Once pre-processing is completed, the Entry Point activates the contactless reader and proceeds to protocol activation.

6.3.2   Protocol Activation

The protocol activation step corresponds to Start B of the Entry Point.

During the step, the reader begins *polling* of the electromagnetic field in front of it. The reader prompts the cardholder to present the card and then proceeds with the polling. The protocol itself supports two types of physical-level protocols: Types A and B. In accordance with the ISO/IEC 14443 standard, the reader is capable of the collision detection and avoidance in case multiple devices are present in its electromagnetic field.

Upon the protocol activation step completion the reader has detected a single device in its field, identified it and established the physical link dialog with it determining its type (Type A or Type B).

In some cases, the Entry Point can revert to Start B state when a second tap of a mobile device is required.

The step is roughly similar to chip card's reset and answer-to-reset (ATR) interaction but certainly is more complicated due to the nature of the physical link.

Once the physical link is established, the Entry Point proceeds to combination selection.

6.3.3   Combination Selection

The combination selection step corresponds to Start C of the Entry Point. During the step the Entry Point has to select a combination of AID and the Kernel version. The step roughly corresponds to the application selection step of an EMV contact chip transaction, however, there are several key differences driven by the constraints of the contactless environment and its history.

To begin with, one application can be supported by multiple Kernels available at the Entry Point. As also seen above a Kernel can use the Select Next Outcome to instruct the Entry Point to skip to the next suitable combination (same AID and another Kernel).

Furthermore, due to the card's time limit on presence in front of the reader direct selection of the suitable application (direct application selection) by series of SELECT commands on terminal-supported AIDs may prove unwise.

To perform combination selection the Entry Point utilizes a variant of indirect application selection. It reads a Proximity Payment System Environment (PPSE) file from the card that must be present on the card under the name of 2PAY.SYS.DDF01.

A PPSE is expected to contain a list of supported applications, associated Kernel identifiers and priority values (so that a PPSE can contain a single AID with multiple Kernel IDs which can be ordered by priority).

If no Kernel ID is present in the PPSE, the Entry Point relies on the ADF name to pick a suitable Kernel.

Once the Entry Point has chosen a combination, it proceeds to the Kernel activation step.

6.3.4   *Kernel Activation*

The Kernel activation step corresponds to Start D of the Entry Point. Upon Kernel activation, the Entry Point hands over control of communication with the contactless card to the activated Kernel.

The Entry Point may get back to the start after it picked a Kernel and the latter by returning the Select Next Outcome indicated that the next combination must be chosen.

Once the Kernel has completed or terminated its interaction with the card application, it returns the outcome for the Entry Point to handle.

6.3.5   *Outcome Processing*

At this step the Entry Point processes the Kernel Outcome returned by the Kernel. If the outcome is marked as final it is further returned to the terminal by the Entry Point. The outcomes are listed in section6.4.

6.4   Kernel Outcomes

The standard lists seven outcomes some of which can also be returned by the Entry Point itself. Most of the outcomes are returned to the terminal as the final outcome. Outcomes have parameters associated with them which can affect further steps of the transaction processing.

Some analogies between EMV contact chip transactions and a Kernel-card contactless interaction outcome are drawn in the following sections. It is worth emphasizing that the actual command exchange over the contactless interface between a Kernel and a card will possibly, if not highly likely, differ from that of the EMV contact chip.

Select Next The outcome informs the Entry Point that the combination of Kernel and application is not suitable for the Kernel. The Entry Point is instructed to try another combination, if available. If no other combinations are available, the Entry Point returns the End Application outcome as its Final Outcome to the POS system. Otherwise, another combination is tried in a manner transparent to the POS.

Try Again The outcome informs the Entry Point that the Kernel wishes the card to be presented again. That can be a result of such an error as "tearing" (card being taken away too fast).

It can also be used for mobile devices requiring the confirmation code or other form of identification. In such scenarios the Kernel performs the initial exchange with the card (mobile device), then the relevant application on the device requires additional authentication from the user, and, finally, the transaction is retried by the Entry Point.

This outcome is transparent to the POS.

Approved The outcome informs the Entry Point that the transaction has been approved. Upon receiving it, the Entry Point returns it to the POS as the Final Outcome.

The outcome can occur under two possible scenarios:

■ The Kernel has successfully authorized an offline contactless transaction. That is analogous to a TC returned by the first GENERATE AC command of an EMV contact chip transaction (see section 5.3.13.2). However, the actual command exchange between the Kernel and the card possibly differs.

■ The Kernel is invoked following an online request to the payment network for the second time and has decided to authorize the transaction. That is analogous to a TC returned by the second GENERATE AC command of an EMV contact chip transaction. However, the actual command exchange between the Kernel and the card is very probably different.

Declined This outcome informs the Entry Point that the transaction has been declined. Upon receiving it, the Entry Point returns it to the POS as the Final Outcome.

The outcome can occur under two possible scenarios:

- The Kernel has decided to decline the contactless transaction offline. That is analogous to an AAC returned by the first GENERATE AC command of an EMV contact chip transaction (see section 5.3.13.2). As in the case of the previous outcome the actual command exchange between the Kernel and the card possibly differs.

- The Kernel is invoked following an online request to the payment network for the second time and has decided to decline the transaction. That is analogous to an AAC returned by the second GENERATE AC command of an EMV contact chip transaction. As in the case of the previous outcome the actual command exchange between the Kernel and the card is very probably different.

Online Request The outcome informs the Entry Point that the Kernel requested an online request to determine the transaction status. The Entry Point returns it to the POS as the Final Outcome.

However, using a parameter the Kernel can indicate that it wishes to be restarted upon receiving the response (which means that the cardholder will be prompted for a second tap to perform issuer authentication, see section 5.3.13, and/or to process issuer scripts, see section 5.3.14).

The outcome is analogous to an ARQC returned by a GENERATE AC command of an EMV contact chip transaction.

Try Another Interface This outcome can originate from both the Kernel and the Entry Point. It is returned as the Final Outcome to the POS. It can occur under two scenarios:

- The Kernel is unable to complete a contactless transaction with this card, but, from configuration data available to it, is aware of additional interfaces (chip reader, magstripe reader) that are available on the POS. The Kernel has the means to indicate preference for the interface to be tried next.

- The Entry Point wasn't able to identify a compatible application it could use to complete the transaction and is aware of additional interface of the POS.

End Application This outcome can also originate from both the Kernel and the Entry Point. It is returned as the Final Outcome to the POS. There are several positive and negative flows that could lead to this outcome.

Firstly, the Kernel can encounter an unrecoverable error that won't resolve if the transaction is tried again with the same application (and hence returning a Try Again is pointless). Alternatively, the Entry Point can fail to identify a suitable application and, therefore, asks the POS to ask the cardholder to present a different card.

Besides the error conditions, the outcome can happen if the Kernel decides it had completed processing and requires no further action.

The Kernel can indicate the next Start that the Entry Point should use as a parameter of the outcome it sends to the Entry Point. In that manner, this outcome can also be used with mobile devices, as one of the ways to allow the device owner to perform an on-device authentication (confirmation code, passcode, biometry etc.), an alternative to one described in "Try Again Outcome".

6.5   Contactless Magstripe

The EMV Contactless standard and its, in effect, sub-protocols available in the form of Kernels, only affect the outermost edge of the card payments acceptance network. Therefore, data captured at POS during a contactless transaction must travel via existing infrastructure that was not necessarily capable of supporting full-grade EMV transactions at the dawn of the EMV technology.

That gave birth to the so-called Contactless Magstripe POS entry mode whereas the terminal communicates with the contactless card or a mobile device in line with EMV Contactless standard, but the interaction outcome is encoded into a magnetic stripe format and packed into (most often) Track 2 or sometimes Track 1 discretionary data.

In the case of Contactless Magstripe, a verification value often referred to as dynamic CVC is generated and embedded into discretionary data part of Track 2 (see section 2.4.2 for format details). This is done instead of producing a full-grade ARQC cryptogram for transmission to the issuer.

The method is supported by MasterCard, American Express and one of JCB Kernels.

6.6   Cardholder Verification Methods

A cardholder cannot be expected to keep the card in the reader field while punching in the PIN on the PIN pad. Therefore, offline PIN verification methods are not available in the contactless environment.

With a physical card, a contactless terminal can either give up cardholder verification entirely (No CVM method) and request the signature or require an online PIN.

In the latter case after the card is out of the reader field, the terminal prompts the cardholder for a PIN, encrypts it and sends to the issuer alongside other transaction details as part of the online authorization request.

A Kernel can indicate the required CVM-related action to the Entry Point by passing a value alongside its Outcome. The values are described in the Outcome Parameters chapter of Book A of the EMV Contactless standard.

The values requiring a further action are Online PIN and Obtain Signature. The Kernel can also decide on not requiring a CVM (No CVM) or not providing any CVM value whatsoever.

In the case of a consumer device, the Kernel can indicate to the Entry Point that the cardholder has successfully verified their identity by entering a confirmation code or performing some form of biometric authentication on the device via value Confirmation Code Verified.

6.7 Understanding Kernels

Except for the so-called contactless magstripe, a contactless transaction which encountered no protocol issue (software was mutually supported, no software fault or "tearing" of the card from the reader's field happened) results in a cryptogram. It is either approved offline or an ARQC cryptogram is generated.

By and large, a contactless transaction is a trimmed-down version of a full-grade EMV contact chip transaction optimized, one way or another, for the much shorter timeframe of a single tap. In fact, each Kernel is an interesting insight into the way engineers developing a particular card scheme have addressed the constraint.

As communication with the issuer takes more time than the card is expected to be present in the reader's field, in certain cases the cardholder may be required to tap their card a second time to process issuer scripts. In case of a plastic card a second tap is rarely required for a transaction completion.

For mobile devices functioning as cards a second tap is much more common. Since mobile devices are used as means for cardholder verification, from the consumer's point of view a contactless transaction performed with a mobile device requires a first tap or a sort of mobile pin or biometric authentication in a payment app followed by a second tap.

In both cases the Kernel notifies the Entry Point that the Kernel should be restarted and the cardholder should be prompted to present the card again to complete the transaction. That is achieved by setting a value of requested Start as an Outcome parameter the Kernel returns to the Entry Point.

Many of the Kernels the standard currently supports include additional data fields and additional commands defined for the purpose of a specific EMV Contactless implementation. Such data fields and commands are below referred to as proprietary even though formally they are part of the EMV Contactless standard.

6.7.1 Kernel 1—Visa, JCB

Kernel 1 makes two decisions based on the amount to be authorized. If it is below the Reader Contactless Floor Limit, the transaction is authorized offline. If the value is below the Reader CVM Required Limit, no cardholder verification is performed.

Furthermore, the Kernel expects a VLP Issuer Authorisation Code value to be personalized on the card. If the value is absent, transactions are not authorized offline even if they are below the Reader Contactless Floor Limit.

The transaction flow begins with the application selection. After the SELECT command the Kernel sends a GET PROCESSING OPTIONS command to the POS and retrieves the AIP and the AFL. Then it reads the application data invoking READ RECORD commands.

Once the application data has been read, the Kernel makes a decision regarding offline or online transaction authorization.

In the case of an offline authorization, the Kernel relies on the so-called fDDA (fast DDA) for card authentication. From the card's point of view that is a standard DDA, but the Kernel completes authentication after the card has left the polling field. To authenticate the card, the Kernel invokes the INTERNAL AUTHENTICATE command normally only sending the Unpredictable Number as its parameter. The terminal subsequently uses the VLP Issuer Authorisation code, Track 2 and, if available, Track 1 discretionary data in the clearing record. There is no further interaction with the card after the INTERNAL AUTHENTICATE command.

If the decision is to go online, the Kernel invokes a GENERATE AC command. It only expects to receive an ARQC back from the card terminating the transaction in any other case.

The Kernel checks the application expiry date after either INTERNAL AUTHENTICATE or GENERATE APPLICATION CRYPTOGRAM commands. In the latter case no second GAC invocation is performed and no issuer scripts are processed.

6.7.2 Kernel 2—MasterCard

The Kernel supports two processing modes: Magstripe and EMV. Furthermore, it supports some methods to recover from card tearing (premature removal of the card from the reader field) and supports *data storage* or the ability to use the card as a data scratch pad.

The data storage ability comes in two flavors: standalone data storage or SDS requiring a separate set of commands to read and update the data and integrated data storage or IDS providing data access piggybacking on EMV commands of other designation. Data storage of a separate Kernel is not interoperable with another.

In addition to standard EMV commands the Kernel uses several proprietary commands.

The transaction flow begins with the application selection. After the SELECT command the Kernel sends a GET PROCESSING OPTIONS command to the POS and retrieves the AIP and the AFL.

According to the EMV standard bit 8 of the second byte of AIP is reserved for EMV Contactless implementation. As for Kernel 2, it is used to indicate whether the card supports EMV Contactless or not.

In the magstripe mode the Kernel reads card data using the READ RECORD command. Then the Kernel generates an unpredictable number and afterwards uses a proprietary COMPUTE CRYPTOGRAPHIC CHECKSUM command to retrieve the so-called CVC3 or dCVV value from the card. After that it places the unpredictable number and the calculated value into discretionary data of Track2 value it generates,and, if personalized on the card, Track1 as well. Then the values are sent to the issuer for authorization online, conforming to magnetic stripe transaction format but bearing cryptographic checksum generated by an ICC over contactless interface.

The support of contactless EMV mode means that the card can support one of the two formats of data storage. The Kernel and the card also have tools to handle a torn transaction.

If the card supports SDS, the Kernel issues a GET DATA command to retrieve storage contents. It then reads application data using the READ RECORD command. If the data storage is integrated, the Kernel retrieves stored data as part of the READ RECORD command.

With SDS, the Kernel invokes the PUT DATA command to store data on the card.

After reading the data from the card the Kernel may identify a transaction as a "torn" one or the one that was already attempted but did not complete. If the Kernel considers the transaction a torn one, it issues the RECOVER AC command to the card asking not to generate a new cryptogram but to retrieve a previously generated one instead. The card may either respond with a previous cryptogram or return an indication that there is no application cryptogram to recover and the Kernel may proceed with the transaction as a new one.

If the transaction was not identified as torn or the RECOVER AC call returned no cryptogram, the Kernel invokes the GENERATE AC command retrieving a cryptogram from the card. Kernel 2 relies on the standard EMV mechanism of requesting a cryptogram type and having the card comply or downgrade it (e.g., the Kernel can ask for a TC and obtain an ARQC in response). If the data storage is integrated, the Kernel sends the values to store as part of GAC parameters.

According to the output of the GAC command the Kernel either authorizes the transaction offline or decline it or go online for the authorization. The Kernel can also attempt a CDA as part of the GAC call.

If the Kernel failed to receive the cryptogram, it stores the PAN and the card sequence number in an internal log and in the case of a second tap attempts torn transaction recovery.

No further interaction with the card follows the cryptogram generation as Kernel 2 does not support the second GAC or the issuer scripts.

6.7.3 Kernel 3—Visa

Unlike Kernel 1, Kernel 3 provides support for a second tap of the card allowing the issuer scripts to be transmitted to the card, if necessary. The Kernel supports integrated data storage functioning on the similar principles typical of Kernel 2 but is not compatible with it.

A key feature of Kernel 3 is using of its single GET PROCESSING OPTIONS command to perform functions that are divided between GPO, INTERNAL AUTHENTICATE and the first GAC in a regular EMV flow.

When during Entry Point's Combination Selection step the application is selected, the returned FCI may contain a tag pointing to the Integrated Data Storage Directory. If the tag is present, the Kernel operates in IDS mode reading and updating the IDS, as required. If the tag is absent, the Kernel only performs a payment transaction.

After the Application Selection, the Kernel invokes the GET PROCESSING OPTIONS command based on the PDOL obtained as part of the FCI. The PDOL always contains a mandatory proprietary element, 'Terminal Transaction Qualifiers' (tag 9F66) or TTQ, containing the indications of terminal capabilities as well as a bit indicating whether online or offline authorization is required.

In response to the GPO command the card application returns the processing options, fDDA value and an application cryptogram possibly downgrading an offline authorization to an online one. The card also returns a proprietary element called "Card Transaction Qualifiers" (tag 9F6C) or CTQ.

Then the Kernel proceeds issuing READ RECORD commands to retrieve application data from the card. Once the data is retrieved, the Kernel is able to perform offline authentication. If the authentication is successful, the transaction is considered authorized offline or is sent to the issuer for an online authorization attempt.

If both the issuer and the card support issuer update processing, and an online authorization is required, the Kernel instructs the Entry Point via a display message to request the card to be presented again and asks for a return to Start B. The Entry Point handles the online request and restarts the Kernel. Upon restart, the Kernel detects that a response from the issuer has arrived and performs the completion of the previously started transaction instead of starting a new one.

The Kernel issues an EXTERNAL AUTHENTICATE command to the card to check the Issuer Authentication Data. If successful and if the issuer scripts are provided, they are sent to the card.

In case the integrated data storage (IDS) support is indicated in the FCI and the terminal supports it, the flow of the first tap (new transaction) slightly changes. In the IDS mode a proprietary EXTENDED GPO (EGPO) command is sent by the reader instead of a standard GET PROCESSING OPTIONS command. It contains additional data elements allowing the IDS update. Conversely, after the EGPO receives the response the data read by the READ RECORD also contain data from the IDS.

6.7.4 Kernel 4—American Express

Kernel 4 supports both the EMV and magstripe contactless modes. The card indicates the desired mode via AIP where bit 8 of byte 2 is set to 1 in the case of EMV transaction and to 0 for the magstripe.

The Kernel defines *Offline, Delayed and Partial Online* modes of transaction authorization. The offline mode is the standard offline authorization, the partial online corresponds to online authorization with other Kernels and is called partial because no second GAC call is made. The delayed authorization is a special handling of cases in which the transaction is sent to the issuer for reservation of funds at a later stage. In the case of delayed authorization the terminal considers the transaction approved but sends the online message to the issuer once connection is available. The delayed authorization is transparent to the card.

The Kernel also supports a Mobile CVM in form of a code which can be entered into the mobile device for cardholder verification. If a Mobile CVM is required, the Kernel returns a Try Again Outcome to the Entry Point allowing the cardholder to perform verification and tap their device at the reader once again. If a Mobile CVM is performed, the card returnes its results to either GET PROCESSING OPTIONS or GENERATE AC commands.

Among other Kernel special features is the CDOL-Switch which is the name for the card's ability to return different CDOLs in EMV and magstripe modes.

Otherwise, the Kernel command flow follows standard EMV transaction until the first GAC. Only SDA or CDA offline authentication methods are allowed, i.e., no INTERNAL AUTHENTICATE command can be sent to the card (see section 5.3.8).

The Kernel uses READ RECORD calls to read application data in the EMV mode and issues a GET DATA command in magstripe mode to retrieve the ATC.

EMV GAC is similar to the contact EMV command. In magstripe mode a limited set of data elements is sent as input to the GAC command and the cryptogram is handled differently. To begin with, a TC cryptogram, if returned by the card, causes the terminal to decline the transaction. Also, since transmission of the full cryptogram value to the issuer is impossible (hence the magstripe mode in the first place), the cryptogram is encoded into discretionary data section of Track 2 (see section 2.4) by discarding its first 5 bytes converting the value to decimal digits and placing the last five of them in the DD section of the Track 2 data field.

6.7.5   Kernel 5—JCB

Kernel 5 supports both EMV and magstripe modes. A simplified version of EMV mode or the Legacy mode is also defined in the documentation (its key differences are no offline card authentication, no support for offline authorization and no issuer script processing/second tap). The card indicates the desired mode via AIP where bit 8 of byte 2 is set to 1 in the case of EMV transaction and to 0 for the magstripe. The Legacy mode is indicated in the PDOL by an additional data element.

The Kernel also allows for two issuer updates modes: either via a second tap or by continuously holding the card in the reader field. The Kernel must support both options as their choice is indicated by the card. Kernel 5 also supports torn transaction recovery.

Kernel 5 transaction flow in EMV mode is similar to the Contact EMV transaction flow. Kernel 5 only supports CDA mode of offline card authentication (see section 5.3.8) and, therefore, the INTERNAL AUTHENTICATE command is not part of Kernel 5 transaction flow.

The first GENERATE AC command may return a value indicating mobile CVM. In this case, the Kernel returns an End Application Outcome to the Entry Point instructing it to return to Start B and display an appropriate message to the cardholder.

In case the Kernel supports issuer updates, in response to GAC the card may return an "Issuer Update Parameter" (tag 9F60) indicating one of the two supported modes for issuer updates or notifying that no issuer update is required. If updates are required, the card may request the card to be held in the reader field until the the issuer's response arrives. In that case, the Kernel returns an Online Request outcome with the "Present and Hold" parameter. Otherwise, the card may ask for the second tap.

Regardless of the chosen mode upon receipt of data from the issuer the Kernel transmits scripts from the "Issuer Script Template 1" (tag 71) to the card. If the Issuer Authentication Data or Issuer Script Template 2 are present in the issuer response, the Kernel invokes the second GAC command and handles its outcome as with a standard EMV transaction.

In magstripe mode, a MDOL ("Magstripe Data Object List", tag 9F5C) proprietary value can be personalized on the card. It is read by the Kernel at the Read Application Data stage, but if absent, a default set of values is defined in the standard. Then the Kernel issues a GET MAGSTRIPE DATA proprietary command to the card retrieving a full Track 2 image in response. After that the Kernel refers to the last data nibble containing a code for the preferred CVM method to be performed. Magstripe mode transactions are always authorized online.

If the card tears away during the GAC command, the Kernel allows its recovery without generating a new cryptogram. If Kernel 5 considers the transaction as torn, it enters the torn transaction recovery mode. In the mode a proprietary ECHO command is sent to the card after the final SELECT command. If the response to the ECHO command is 9000, the Kernel proceeds with the regular EMV flow but in response to the GAC the card returns its previous cryptogram instead of generating a new one.

6.7.6   *Kernel 6—Discover*

Kernel 6 supports both EMV and magstripe modes. There is also a second magstripe mode called Legacy Magstripe mode. The support for it is determined by AID: there is an AID for EMV and Magstripe modes and another one for the Legacy Magstripe Mode.

The Kernel relies on the GET PROCESSING OPTIONS command to retrieve offline card authentication data as well as an application cryptogram. In EMV mode, the issuer scripts are supported via a second tap. In case of mobile CVM, the Kernel returns the Try Again Outcome to the Entry Point.

After the application has been selected, the Kernel issues a single GPO command. In EMV mode, the GPO command contains the application cryptogram and some data for offline card authentication. The Kernel makes its decision on the next steps (online or offline authorization) based on the type of cryptogram returned in the GPO response.

After receiving the GPO response and in case it contained an AFL, the Kernel issues READ RECORD commands to read data from the card.

In EMV mode, the data read is used to perform offline card authentication.

In magstripe or legacy magstripe modes, the Kernel retrieves Track 1 and Track 2 data from the card in responses to READ RECORD commands.

A card can also support the Dynamic CVV (DCVV) functionality. In that case the PDOL contains an Unpredictable Number, and during READ RECORD a Dynamic Card Verification Value (DCVV) (tag 9F7E) is present in the data read.

Upon encountering the DCVV data, the Kernel places 2 least-significant Unpredictable Number digits it formerly generated and the DCVV value it retrieved from the card in Track 1 and Track 2 values at fixed offsets as defined in the standard.

In case Issuer Script updates are required, after restarting the Kernel transmits them to the card one by one without performing the second GAC call.

6.7.7   *Kernel 7—UnionPay*

Kernel 7 supports EMV mode only. No issuer script processing is supported by it.

It relies on a single GET PROCESSING OPTIONS command to retrieve an application cryptogram. Furthermore, it only uses CDA (in fDDA form) in the case of an offline transaction authorization.

Once the GPO command is issued and the response to it arrives and if the application cryptogram type returned is ARQC, the card can leave the reader field after transmission of the GPO command response.

In the case of a TC returned by the GPO command, the card also computes the offline authentication (fDDA) value. The Kernel proceeds to issue READ RECORD commands until the data required to authenticate the card are fully retrieved.

For mobile devices the GPO command returns a status word of 6986. In that case, the Kernel returns a Try Again Outcome to the Entry Point requesting to restart Start B.

OTHER PROCESSES AND STANDARDS

Chapter 7

Disputes, Arbitration and Compliance

CONTENTS

All scheme members are bound by membership terms and conditions and undergo certification testing prior to go-live or to introduce new services or devices. That ensures the conformance of member systems with formal technical requirements of payment scheme systems.

In addition to the (one-time or periodic) go-live testing, schemes also enforce the authorization, clearing and dispute transactions validity by rejecting poorly formatted transactions automatically or providing their members with reports on data validity or integrity.

However, these technical means cannot cover all possible behaviors (or misbehaviors) of the scheme members, cardholders or merchants including both intentional deviations from the rules and honest mistakes.

To allow scheme participants to raise and manage issues related to such deviations from processing rules schemes support two major processes: *dispute management and arbitration* to resolve disputes between participants and *scheme compliance* to handle non-compliance of parties with scheme rules.

7.1 Dispute Management and Arbitration

7.1.1 Overview of Generic Dispute Lifecycle

Dispute management and arbitration processes slightly vary between schemes but by and large can be described as a subset of the process described in table 7.1 and initiated by the issuer.

The arbitrated flow can potentially contain a step of filing a pre-arbitration case with the scheme when the other party can concede the dispute and avoid the risk of scheme decision not in its favor, which is accompanied by a relatively high fee. It is usually possible to skip the step and go directly for arbitration approaching the scheme dispute resolution team for decision.

Table 7.1: Non-arbitrated dispute lifecycle

Issuer sends	*Acquirer responds*
Retrieval request Request for retrieval of supporting documentation for a transaction.	*Fulfillment, explicit non-fulfillment or no response* Supporting documentation is provided in the case of fulfillment.
Chargeback Actual dispute of the original transaction.	*Representment, acknowledgement or no response* Supporting documentation in the case of representment. If no response, the chargeback is considered accepted by the acquirer. Certain schemes encourage proactive acknowledgement of accepted chargebacks by the acquirer.
Second chargeback Further challenge to the transaction with additional documents to support the claim.	*No response, pre-arbitration or arbitration* In the case of no response, the chargeback is considered accepted by the acquirer.

7.1.2 Retrieval Requests and Fulfillments

As an optional tool for issuers to investigate potential disputes, schemes provide a mechanism often called "retrieval request". As its part the issuer sends a request to the acquirer asking to provide supporting documentation for a particular transaction. The acquirer can typically choose not to respond to a request or to respond by either providing the document(s) or refusing to do so.

The acquirer's response to a retrieval request with documentation is called *fulfillment* and a response without documentation is called *non-fulfillment*. It is not mandatory for an acquirer to respond to a retrieval request.

Typically, the documentation includes sales draft. For e-commerce or EMV transactions in which the cardholder signs no slip, all the data necessary for a draft is found in the acquirer systems or has already been transmitted to the payment network. However, in cases when legacy scheme systems mandate provisioning of a sales draft acquirers generate so-called "substitute drafts" or subdrafts containing all necessary transaction details in an image file.

It is usually in the acquirer's best interest to provide supporting evidence to the issuer as that can help avoid a subsequent chargeback.

7.1.3 Chargebacks and Representments

A *chargeback* is a demand to make good the cardholder's loss on a fraudulent or disputed transaction. Such a demand may or may not follow a retrieval request.

A chargeback is initiated by the issuer on behalf of the cardholder and in full dispute cycle is delivered to the acquirer in form of a financial record that can arrive in an incoming settlement file or in form of a case that appears in an online dispute management system provided by the scheme.

Each chargeback contains an indication of the reason (fraud, technical problem with the transaction or dispute of the transaction between the merchant and the cardholder) and the issuing bank can, in case the rules for the particular chargeback reason require that, provide evidence in form of supporting documentation available via online dispute management system.

A chargeback can be of the full amount of the original transaction or only for its part (if, for instance, only some goods or services have not been delivered and are being disputed). Multiple partial chargebacks are possible for a single transaction provided that the total of all partial chargebacks does not exceed the amount of the original purchase.

Previously, schemes used to define a large variety of various reason codes thus simplifying the classification of chargeback cases on the acquirer side. For example, a situation when the goods have not been delivered by the merchant and a situation when services have not been provided by the merchant are encoded with separate reason codes allowing the acquirer representment rights in case the reason code was not chosen properly. That was subsequently amended and the reason codes for chargebacks were reduced from several dozens to a handful simplifying the job of an issuer and placing more burden on the acquirer's dispute management team.

Once a chargeback is delivered to the acquirer, its amount is collected from the acquirer by deducing it from the corresponding settlement amount (for example, international settlement on the processing date when the scheme sent the chargeback to the acquirer).

If the acquirer agrees with the chargeback amount or decides that the cost of their further steps is higher than the benefit from winning the disputed amount back, the acquirer can either send an acknowledgement of the chargeback or simply do nothing. If a scheme supports chargeback acknowledgements, members are usually encouraged to use them.

The acquirer can choose to either absorb the costs or to roll them on the merchant.

Some of the possible reasons for a chargeback include:

■ Technical faults, errors at the point of sale, wrong currency conversion rates and late presentments of the original transaction.

■ Fraud, transaction not authorized by cardholder, recurring billing for a service that was canceled by the cardholder.

■ Goods or services not delivered or provided, fully or in part.

■ Special/industry specific disputes. For instance, some schemes apply certain rules to charges a car rental business can make to a customer card. Another example is an automatic chargeback right for counterfeit goods.

Should the acquirer disagree with the chargeback, they can perform a *representment* (sometimes called *second presentment*). During a representment the acquirer submits necessary details or documents to the issues via the scheme as well as sends them a financial record. Then, the acquirer is credited the representment amount by the scheme.

Sometimes it is sufficient to simply send a financial record when its fields allow passing enough data for the issuer to process the representment. For instance, if the acquirer has received a duplicate chargeback, no additional documents are needed. If the transaction has already been refunded, the acquirer can provide the reference number of the refund as part of the representment financial record.

In other cases the submission of additional documents may be required. They may include sales drafts with cardholder signatures or other evidence that the goods were indeed shipped or the services rendered. For card-not-present transactions, especially e-Commerce and PIN-based authorizations, when no signature has been provided, the schemes anyway often require that a sales draft should be submitted to the issuer during the representment. Such a sales draft is commonly generated based on the data from the acquirer database and is called a substitute draft or sub-draft.

As for chargebacks, a representation can be partial or full. A representation is considered partial if it does not cover the full amount of the original transaction and is considered full if it does.

To illustrate it, consider the set of scenarios of possible disputes on a 100 EUR transaction by the issuer with a response by the acquirer in table 7.2.

7.1.4 Second Chargeback

In case the issuer disagrees with materials provided with the representation, certain payment schemes allow sending them an additional chargeback called *second chargeback* or *arbitration chargeback*. Upon the second chargeback the issuer is credited with the disputed amount and the acquirer is debited with it.

Schemes may rely on second chargeback as an additional step in the non-arbitrated dispute resolution process, however, the number of card schemes supporting this step decreases over the years.

7.1.5 Allocation vs. Collaboration

In recent years schemes began to deploy a kind of short-circuited process for technical and fraud-related chargebacks.

According to the new rules there is no adversary process in certain cases: the scheme allocates a side that bears the liability for the chargeback. There is no option to proceed in a non-arbitrated manner beyond that point and a challenge to a chargeback requires a much costlier pre-arbitration or arbitration.

To distinguish the short flow from the standard one, schemes use such a term as *allocation* (for scheme decision on chargeback liability) as opposed to *collaboration* (for a full non-arbitrated exchange).

7.1.6 Pre-arbitration and Arbitration

If the scheme members failed to reach a conclusion during non-arbitrated communication, they can turn to the scheme for the case analysis and decision. The

Table 7.2: Partial and full dispute and representment scenarios

	Chargeback of 50 EUR	*Chargeback of 100 EUR*
Representment of 50 EUR	*Partial representment*	*Partial representment*
Representment of 100 EUR	N/A	*Full representment*

process is called *arbitration* and is triggered by the last party in the dispute flow turning for resolution to the scheme. In certain solutions the arbitration step is preceded by the *pre-arbitration* step when the appropriate party notifies its counterpart that it is about to approach the scheme for arbitration providing the last opportunity to agree to the dispute.

As arbitration is a manual process that involves dispute resolution specialists employed by schemes, members are discouraged from unnecessarily relying on them and their effort is compensated by scheme members.

7.1.7   Liability Shift

In certain cases schemes implement some rules denying a certain party its usual dispute rights. These are called *liability shifts* and are used as a tool to motivate institutions towards a certain behavior mostly to implement the latest technological features for fraud prevention and authentication and cardholder protection.

For example (specific rules can change or vary between schemes):

■ If a transaction has been authenticated using 3D Secure (under corresponding brand name) or EMV 3D-Secure, the issuer cannot dispute it claiming that the cardholder does not recognize it. In case a dispute of the sort arrives to the acquirer, the acquirer can represent the dispute on the grounds of liability shift.

■ Likewise, the implementation of EMV technology was accompanied by a liability shift in favor of the implementing party. A transaction processed on a magstripe-only terminal with a card having an embedded chip can be disputed by the issuer for the reason of not being authorized by the cardholder and the acquirer is not able to represent it except for a technicality in the chargeback message itself.

7.1.8   Streamlined Lifecycle

Originally, the dispute lifecycles were identical for technical issues (such as mismatch of attributes between authorization and clearing transactions), fraud-related issues and genuine disputes between merchants and cardholders.

However, with evolution of network authorization and clearing systems towards the increase of data integrity enforcements and validations, schemes began introducing a leaner process for technical issues that can be analyzed and resolved based on transaction attributes only.

The streamlined process implies the allocation of liability upon dispute submission by the scheme. In other words, instead of an exchange of dispute messages and documentation between the issuer and the acquirer upon a chargeback submission by the issuer the scheme, decides on the winning party and performs the corresponding financial movements accordingly.

Following such an allocation of liability both the issuer and the acquirer can appeal asking to move the dispute case to arbitration.

7.2   Compliance

At any time of the dispute management cycle or at any time at all regardless of a particular dispute, a member can raise a complaint regarding scheme rules compliance against another member or the scheme itself.

Typical compliance procedure permits but does not require the complaining member to first notify the complainee with a *pre-compliance* notification describing the non-compliant behavior and allowing the complainee to resolve the matter before the scheme compliance team steps in. The complainee may respond to the complainer, however, should the answer be unsatisfactory, the complainer can proceed with a compliance case that is to be handled by the scheme personnel.

To illustrate it consider the following scenarios.

Scenario 1. An acquirer was repeatedly sending card-not-present and card-on-file transactions even though the result code from the issuer instructed the acquirer that the authorization for the card had been revoked. Each decline triggers a fee the issuer pays to the scheme and the acquirer did not obey the response code and continued attempted authorizations. The scheme authorization service did not block those transactions so the issuer filed a compliance case against the acquirer.

Scenario 2. An acquirer received several chargebacks from an issuer on transactions which having been fully authenticated with 3D Secure should have enjoyed the liability shift (see section 7.1.7) for that particular chargeback reason. A check with transaction investigation tools and the support of the scheme indicated that the transactions had been sent correctly but reached the issuer with the full authentication indicator stripped from them. To prompt action on behalf of the scheme the acquirer filed a compliance case on the scheme.

Chapter 8

Data Security Standards in the Payment Card Industry

CONTENTS

Considering how few details are required to perform a card payment, it is obvious that card and cardholder data security is paramount to combat fraud. Following a significant number of data system breaches, both large and small, the card industry responded by self-organizing into the Payment Card Industry Security Standards Council or PCI SSC. The council was formed in 2006 by American Express, Discover, JCB, MasterCard and Visa, and its goal was to create and maintain data security standards relevant to payment cards.

The principal standard the council develops and maintains is the PCI DSS or Payment Card Industry Data Security Standard providing technical and operational requirements for a proper protection of sensitive and account-related data. The standard provides end-to-end requirements beginning from software, its configuration, operating systems and databases it runs on, policies and procedures around it and all the way through to requirements for physical access to hardware and facilities. The council defines methods for self-assessment as well as for independent audit and maintains a registry of approved assessors.

The PCI SSC also issues and maintains additional standards with notable inclusions of PCI PA DSS (Payment Application Data Security Standard) and PCI PTS (PIN Transaction Security) as well as some more focused standards for point-to-point encryption and HSMs secure handling and management (see section 8.3.1).

8.1 PCI Data Security Standard (PCI DSS)

The PCI Data Security Standard covers technical and operational requirements designed to protect account data. It defines the cardholder data environment or CDE as people, processes and technologies that store, process or transmit cardholder or sensitive authentication data. Consequently, its requirements cover all the components either included in or connected to the cardholder data environment. For instance, if a machine does not store, handle or transmit account data but resides on the same network segment as another machine does, PCI DSS requirements extend to the machine anyway.

8.1.1 Account Data

The PCI Data Security Standard explicitly defines which data values are considered account data. Account data consists of cardholder data and sensitive authentication data.

Cardholder data or CHD is the Primary Account Number (PAN), cardholder name, service code (see section 2.4.4) and card expiration date. The latter three values are only considered CHD if stored together with the PAN. It is permitted to store cardholder data, and there are additional PCI DSS requirements which apply it that case. The standard also requires rendering the PAN unreadable which is ubiquitously achieved by masking all but the BIN (first six) and the last four digits of the account number. Requirement 3.3 of the PCI DSS standard prohibits to display more than these digits to anyone but personnel with a legitimate business need.

Sensitive authentication data is defined as full track data (including track 1, 2 and 3), CVV2 data, the PIN and the PIN block. Unlike cardholder data that can be stored, it is forbidden to store the sensitive authentication data including strongly encrypted form.

8.1.2 Levels of Compliance and Assessment Process

The PCI DSS standard does not define any "level of compliance" and an entity either complies or does not with PCI DSS requirements but there is a distinction made for methods to assess and certify the compliance. A merchant, processor, institution or another entity can follow one of the two paths to certify its compliance: an audit by a Qualified Security Auditor (QSA) or a completion of a Self-Assessment Questionnaire (SAQ).

Upon completion of a SAQ, the merchant or processor authorized personnel sign an Attestation of Compliance (AOC) document who thereby commit to both levels of compliance as stated in the attestation and the action plan to become fully compliant in case certain requirements are not fully met, as needed.

Upon completing an audit by a QSA, the auditor prepares a Report of Compliance. It may contain committed action plans with specific dates for full compliance as well as well-defined compensatory controls.

A QSA can also be involved in completing an SAQ in case the entity that undergoes self-assessment so desires.

Payment schemes typically group entities involved in processing into several groups or "levels". These levels are not part of the PCI DSS standard, and despite widely accepted definitions are set by schemes at their own discretion. The highest level of PCI DSS compliance is usually dubbed level 1 and requires an annual audit by a QSA while some lower levels may require initial QSA audit followed by self-assessment or even require annual SAQs only.

Schemes typically assign levels based on the annual volumes of card-present and card-not-present transactions processing which can be counted regardless of the payment scheme (e.g., Visa can request the full volume of processing including MasterCard, American Express, etc., to assign the level of required compliance). It is also typical to tolerate a bigger number of card-present transactions versus a much smaller number of card-not-present transactions for the same level of compliance so that the processing volumes of tens of thousands of e-commerce transactions require adherence to the same rules as the processing of hundreds of thousands of card-present transactions.

Entities are required to perform internal and external vulnerability scans at least quarterly and after every major change in the solution. Internal scans can be done by an internal team while external scans are to be performed by an Approved Scanning Vendor (ASV). Although the requirement is part of the PCI DSS QSA evaluation it can also be required in some cases involving an SAQ (see section 8.1.3.

The SAQs, AOCs or ROCs with ASV scan reports as required and according to the specific situation are submitted to processors, acquirers or card schemes for the required compliance review and confirmation.

8.1.3 Self-Assessment Questionnaires

SAQs depend on an entity's specifics and its card processing environment. Most SAQ types were defined for specific types of merchants and are focused on the requirements relevant for those merchant types.

Most SAQ types do not allow any cardholder data storage in merchants' systems: merchants that store cardholder data automatically require the SAQ D questionnaire covering the largest scope.

Card-not-present merchants should use either the lighter SAQ A/SAQ A-EP questionnaires or the fuller SAQ D for Merchants questionnaire. Card-present merchants can be required to perform self-assessment based on SAQ B/SAQ B-IP/SAQ C/SAQ C-VT, SAQ P2PE questionnaires or default to the full SAQ D for Merchants questionnaire.

SAQ A questionnaire applies to non-face-to-face merchants who have fully outsourced their processing to a PCI-DSS compliant entity and perform no cardholder data processing, transmission or storage.

SAQ A-EP questionnaire applies to merchants who did likewise but possess a website that can impact a payment transaction security

SAQ B questionnaire applies to card-present merchants only, utilizing imprinters or having a dial-up connection to their processor.

SAQ B-IP questionnaire is designed for card-present merchants whose terminals are PCI PTS approved and connected to the processor via an IP connection but store no cardholder data.

SAQ C questionnaire applies to card present merchants using payment systems connected to the Internet.

SAQ C-VT applies to merchants who key in cards (in a card-present environment) into a virtual terminal provided by a third-party processor.

SAQ P2PE questionnaire is designated for card-present merchants having a PCI-SSC listed fully-managed hardware P2PE–compliant terminal system.

SAQ D the most comprehensive questionnaire of the family, exists in two flavors: SAQ D for Merchants and SAQ D for Service Providers. Entities storing cardholder data are to self-assess using the corresponding SAQ D questionnaire regardless of the card presence in their transactions.

8.1.4   PCI DSS Principles

PCI DSS standard lists six core principles subdivided into requirements that, in turn, contain multiple nested sub-requirements including well-defined testing and assessment procedures and compliance criteria. Both best practices and the detailed sub-requirements are listed in the most recent PCI DSS standard. However, as the standard is structured around these core principles there is value in a top-down review of the principles and requirements.

Regardless of the security aspect defined in the PCI DSS standard, it has to be securely deployed (user access rights restricted, firewalls configured, antivirus installed), any changes to it must have a documented business reason, follow a well-defined procedure and leave a paper trail (access request process, firewall configuration process, antivirus definitions update process) as well as to be periodically assessed for compliance and vulnerabilities (by means of scanning and disabling inactive user accounts, performing internal and external vulnerability and penetration tests, reviewing firewall configurations, etc.).

Build and Maintain a Secure Network and Systems

The principle translates into two requirements: "Install and maintain a firewall configuration to protect cardholder data" and "Do not use vendor-supplied defaults for system passwords and other security parameters".

The requirement to maintain a firewall configuration to protect cardholder data (Requirement 1) contains some sub-requirements covering key network segments which should be separated by firewalls, processes for justifying, documenting, reviewing, approving and revisiting any change in firewall configuration, requirements for proper synchronization of router and firewall configuration across different instances and networks and requirements for portable devices connected to the cardholder data environment.

The requirement to not use vendor-supplied defaults for passwords and other parameters (Requirement 2) contains some sub-requirements which in addition to the obvious detailed description of the general requirement also prescribe that each host on the network should provide a single major service (e.g., NTP or DNS) and that all other services on that host should be disabled.

Protect Cardholder Data

This principle translates into two requirements: "Protect stored cardholder data" and "Encrypt transmission of cardholder data across open, public networks".

The requirement to protect stored cardholder data (Requirement 3) contains several sub-requirements. First and foremost, sensitive authentication data (see section 8.1.1) cannot be stored. Second, cardholder data storing must be kept to a minimum necessary, including both well-defined and well-maintained retention policies as well as hashing, truncating or encrypting the PAN. Finally, for any encryption scheme used the encryption keys must be securely handled and rotated in a timely manner.

The requirement to encrypt data transmission across public networks (Requirement 4) prescribes encrypting the PAN data during transmission using strong cryptographic methods as defined in PCI DSS glossary and never transmitting a full unencrypted PAN using such means as SMS or instant messenger. The latter requirement applies less to systems and more to working processes of people supporting and maintaining these systems.

Maintain a Vulnerability Management Program

The principle translates into two requirements: "Protect all systems against malware and regularly update anti-virus software or programs" and "Develop and maintain secure systems and applications".

The requirement to protect systems against malware (Requirement 5) prescribes deploying and regularly updating proper anti-virus software that cannot be disabled by end users.

The requirement to develop and maintain security systems and applications (Requirement 6) contains some sub-requirements pertaining to two processes. It prescribes tracking, prioritizing and patching vulnerabilities in third-party vendor software, including timelines for security patches. It also goes into great details describing secure methods for custom code and in-house software development, maintenance and deployment.

To comply with PCI-DSS requirements for custom code, its development and testing should be properly separated from the production environment. Special attention should be paid to developer and testing accounts needed to be disabled prior to production deployment. Furthermore, the code must undergo a mandatory security code review by a trained reviewer who, in turn, should keep up to date with the most recent secure coding practices.

Implement Strong Access Control Measures

The principle translates into three requirements: "Restrict access to cardholder data by business need to know", "Identify and authenticate access to system components" and "Restrict physical access to cardholder data".

The requirement to restrict access to cardholder data on a need-to-know basis (Requirement 7) also requires that the default level of access to cardholder data is always "deny all".

The requirement to identify and authenticate access to system components (Requirement 8) prescribes having a unique identifier assigned to each user. It prohibits the use of group accounts and shared passwords, restricts direct (as opposed to via an application) access to database with cardholder data to database administrators and requires all non-console administrative access to be protected with a multi-factor authentication. There are also some sub-requirements for password policies, removal of inactive accounts and lock-outs of inactive user sessions.

The requirement to restrict physical access to cardholder data (Requirement 9) covers three major areas with its sub-requirements. A facility entry control to limit and monitor physical access to systems in the cardholder data environment is required as well as the rules to identify and authorize visitors to the facilities. Another set of sub-requirements covers classification, storage, shipping and destruction of media that contains cardholder data. Finally, there are sub-requirements to protect devices interacting physically with the card from tampering, including inventory, separation of access and proper training of handling employees.

Regularly Monitor and Test Networks

The principle translates into two requirements: "Track and monitor all access to network resources and cardholder data" and "Regularly test security systems and processes"

The requirement to track and monitor access (Requirement 10) prescribes creating and maintaining an audit trail of user activity which should also be periodically reviewed for any suspicious activity.

The requirement to regularly test security systems and processes (Requirement 11) demands regular scan for unauthorized wireless access points and networks, quarterly internal and external network scans for known vulnerabilities, and penetration tests.

Maintain an Information Security Policy

The principle is listed as Requirement 12 in the PCI DSS standard.The requirement is defined as "Maintain a policy that addresses information security for all personnel" and mandates the creation and maintenance of an information security policy published to all personnel, including full-time and part-time employees, contractors and resident consultants. The requirement also mandates a periodic risk assessment process and an incident response action plan.

8.2 PCI Payment Applications Data Security Standard (PCI PA DSS)

PCI PA DSS applies to software vendors developing payment applications. According to standard's definition a payment application is one that "stores, processes or transmits cardholder and/or sensitive authentication data".

The key difference between PCI PA DSS and PCI DSS is that the former applies to an individual application while the latter covers the entire solution or even full scope of the company systems.

It is possible to have an application that is fully PCI PA DSS–compliant but deployed and used in such a manner that it fails PCI DSS requirements. Conversely, it is possible, though certainly not advisable to use a non-compliant payment application but to comply with PCI DSS standard by deploying compensating controls.

One such method is actually described in the PCI PA DSS standard: a terminal application not PA DSS–compliant on its own may reside on a device that complies with the PIN Transaction Security standard and therefore may comply with PCI DSS through the combination of application and hardware security controls.

The PCI PA DSS standard uses the same cardholder and sensitive data definitions as PCI DSS standard and has a similar assessment process.

During a PCI DSS audit having PCI PA DSS certificates for all relevant applications (ones that in the solution store, process or transmit CHD or SAD) significantly shortens the certification process as the assessor does not have to look into each individual application having received the results of an assessment already performed.

It follows that having a PCI PA DSS certification is highly recommended to any vendor of payment applications.

8.2.1 PCI PA DSS Requirements

The PCI PA DSS standard contains 14 requirements further subdivided into lower-level requirements and accompanied with testing procedures and guidance. PCI PA DSS requirements are also explicitly mapped to corresponding PCI DSS requirements.

Requirement 1—"Do not retain full track data, card verification code or value (CAV2, CID, CVC2, CVV2), or PIN block data"

Requirement 1 is not to retain any sensitive authentication data, namely full track data, CVCs, or PIN block data. The requirement makes exception for software made for issuers. If the software has other intended uses, it should either never store or verifiably delete the SAD after authorization.

The requirement also demands sensitive authentication data removal during the software upgrade process in case such data was stored by the previous version of the software. Finally, the requirement lists the measures that should be taken in case some authentication data must be stored for debugging or troubleshooting purposes.

The requirements aim to ensure that the most sensitive data is protected from possible compromise by its absence from the application.

Requirement 2—"Protect stored cardholder data"

Requirement 2 demands the cardholder data protection. The vendor must provide guidance to their customers regarding data cleanup after the retention period expiration, making sure the PANs are normally masked and the full values are only visible to personnel with actual business need to access them, and render PAN unreadable anywhere it is stored.

The application must protect cryptographic keys it uses to secure cardholder data and ensure necessary framework of key generation and management processes as well as provide mechanisms to reliably render obsolete keys irretrievable. Although many of the means can be implemented in software, using such secure devices as HSMs wherever possible is usually a better way to support the requirements.

The requirement provides framework to protect cardholder data from compromise if it has to be stored in the application.

Requirement 3—"Provide secure authentication features"

Requirement 3 describes secure authentication and authorization features of the software such as individual user accounts, password policies (including complexity and length requirements and history), secure password storage, inactive session expiry and user lockout mechanisms. The requirement prescribes fine-grained access management within the application, including limiting access of user accounts to the minimum necessary application features. In addition, default accounts, group accounts or generic accounts are prohibited.

The requirement aims to define requirements for user access and authorization following the industry best practices. It should also be considered in conjunction with requirement 4, speaking about logging: if each user is identified individually and authenticated in a reliable manner, then logging full activity of each user creates an audit trail that is very useful for forensics in case of a compromise.

Requirement 4—"Log payment application activity"

Requirement 4 describes necessary logs the application must be capable of writing. The requirement is to log all user activity, including failed and successful attempts to access cardholder data, all actions of application administrators, and any attempt to access audit logs themselves or alter logging mechanisms.

In conjunction with requirement 2 (protection of cardholder data) and requirement 3 (user authentication features) the requirement ensures the availability of an audit trail in case a user tries either to access cardholder data when they really should not be accessed or to tamper with evidence of such access.

Requirement 5—"Develop secure payment applications"

Requirement 5 speaks about the best practices concerning the application development process. According to it, the application development must take into consideration the full scope of PCI DSS requirements and the processes must be in place to ensure the code avoids common code vulnerabilities. Security training, security reviews of each application version and code reviews are also required.

In addition to making sure the code is initially written in a secure way, the requirement elaborates the way it should be kept secure including the requirements for source control and version management ensuring the integrity and a change management process that makes sure no unauthorized change can be made into the application.

The sub-requirements under requirement 5 give special consideration to the way SAD is stored in memory demanding that is explicitly documented.

Finally, there are requirements for test data: no live PANs must ever be used in test environments and, conversely, all the test data and test accounts must be removed from the application prior to its deployment into production.

Requirement 6—"Protect wireless transmissions"

Requirement 6 covers minimum steps that must be taken in case the application uses wireless transmissions including the cases when the application is not explicitly designed for use with a wireless communications network. Applications that are explicitly designed for wireless technology or are bundled with it must have vendor defaults changed and must use best practices for authentication and encryption (e.g., WEP is explicitly forbidden in the standard).

In case the application was not explicitly designed for wireless technology but since can be possibly used with the wireless infrastructure, the implementation guide prescribed by the standard must contain details on security of wireless networks.

Requirement 7—"Test payment applications to address vulnerabilities and maintain payment application updates"

Requirement 7 prescribes security testing of the payment application but, more importantly, outlines the vulnerability and risk management processes, including a requirement of timely security patching of the software and documentation of security vulnerabilities in release notes.

While requirement 5 makes sure the payment application is written with security in mind and no malicious code is purposely injected into software versions, requirement 7 makes sure the application stays secure: the application is explicitly tested for security and in case an issue is found it is fixed with due haste.

Requirement 8—"Facilitate secure network implementation"

Requirement 8 describes the way the application must make sure it does not interfere with secure network implementation according to PCI DSS standard. For instance, the application must not require antivirus to be turned off to function, rely on a non-secure system process or use a port utilized by a standard security protocol in the PCI DSS environment.

Requirement 9—"Cardholder data must never be stored on a server connected to the Internet"

Requirement 9 is perhaps one of the standard shortest ones in terms of sub-items. Beyond the self-describing title, the requirement goes on to elaborate that if the application requires Internet connectivity, it must allow any server-storing cardholder data (e.g., database server) to be deployed in a different network segment.

Requirement 10—"Facilitate secure remote access to payment application"

Requirement 10 deals with remote access to the payment application from outside of the customer environment. It prescribes multi-factor access to any personnel accessing the application either the vendor's or the customer's ones. It goes on to detail requirements in the case of remote access to customer systems by vendors for support and update purposes. For example, if downloads to the customer environment without using of a VPN are required, the necessary remote access must be turned on immediately before and turned off immediately after the download.

Requirement 11—"Encrypt sensitive traffic over public networks"

Requirement 11 does not explicitly prescribe the use of TLS over various types of networks but mentions it in its sub-items and the enclosed guidance several times. The requirement demands that any sensitive data is encrypted in transmission and, furthermore, that if such data as PANs is distributed over end-user channels (such as emails), strong cryptography is used to protect it.

Requirement 12—"Secure all non-console administrative access"

Requirement 12 mandates strong encryption of any administrative access not via console. For instance, to quote an example from the standard, telnet is not to be used while SSH is to be used instead. Furthermore, multi-factor authentication is required for all the personnel with non-console administrative access to the application.

Requirement 13—"Maintain a PA-DSS Implementation Guide for customers, resellers, and integrators"

Requirement 13 mandates that a vendor should maintain a detailed guide on the secure implementation of the application in the PCI DSS compliant environment.

Requirement 14—"Assign PA-DSS responsibilities for personnel, and maintain training programs for personnel, customers, resellers, and integrators"

Requirement 14 mandates recurring training programs for all the actors mentioned in the title with training and training materials review to be conducted annually.

8.3 Key Management with Hardware Security Modules (HSMs)

8.3.1 Hardware Security Modules (HSMs)

Hardware security modules provide payment industry actors with a high level of security by performing all encryption-related operations in a protected environment. HSMs are equipped with a variety of sensors and are able to destroy their contents if an attempt of unauthorized access is made or if the device is being tampered with. For example, HSMs have built-in vibration sensors that would react if an attempt to remove the HSM from the server rack is made, and there are special product lines of hardware security modules for seismically active areas.

All sensitive data inside an HSM is protected by one or more master keys, referred to as Local Master Key or *LMK* or Master File Key or *MFK*. Multiple LMKs can co-exist in an HSM simultaneously. To enable administrative access to an HSM for generation of other, derived keys, an LMK is written into at least two smart cards which, if lost, render the specific LMK slot unusable.

At least two physical keys are typically used to switch an HSM into the administration mode and temporarily turn off some of its protection mechanisms.

Even the owner of the HSM, once it is properly deployed, is limited in his control of the module in comparison to a standard server or an appliance. If a financial institution somehow lost all of it's smart cards with an LMK component, even the relatively straightforward process of relocating a hosting facility would require involvement of military forces trained in disarmament of undetonated munitions (i.e., people who are able to move an object VERY carefully).

As a rule, HSMs utilize two types of keys—data encryption keys, used to calculate card validation values, pin verification values, decipher and translate PIN blocks etc, and key encryption keys (KEK), used solely to encrypt and secure data encryption keys.

The KEKs themselves are stored outside of the HSM under LMK and the data encryption keys are, in turn, encrypted using KEK and then used to encrypt or decrypt the data. As LMKs are kept highly secure, both KEKs under LMK and data encryption keys under KEKs are allowed to be stored in a database or on a file system external to the HSM.

To illustrate the principle, consider the CVV validation scenario. The CVK is encrypted using the LMK. The resulting value, CVK_{LMK}, is stored externally in a database and is associated with a certain PAN range. Once a transaction arrives at the issuer host, the CVV data from Track 2 discretionary data subfield is transmitted to the HSM alongside the CVK_{LMK}. The HSM first deciphers the actual CVK and then uses its value to validate the CVV.

As for a more complicated scenario, consider a case of PIN translation when there is an incoming encrypted PIN block (EPB) encrypted with an acquirer worker key (AWK1) and the processing platform has to send the PIN block under another worker key (AWK2) to the payment scheme. In this case, both worker keys are stored under LMK in a database external to the HSM and the invocation of the PIN translation function has the following parameters: EPB_{AWK1}, $AWK1_{LMK}$, $AWK2_{LMK}$. The output of the translation operation is EPB_{AWK2} while the unencrypted values of both worker keys and the EPB do not exist outside of the HSM.

8.3.2   HSM Keys and Algorithms

Table 8.1 summarizes some of the key types that are mentioned above and below, including alternative terminology.

Various scenarios that occur in payment industry utilize different encryption algorithms. For acquiring of card payments, however, only algorithms relevant to PIN translation require the HSMs use and understanding and, consequently, only they are covered herein.

To protect PIN blocks and PIN keys, the 3-DES algorithm (see section 12.2) with single, dual and triple-length keys is used[1]. As the PCI DSS standard in its definition of "strong cryptography" mandates the minimum effective key strength of 112 bits, the single-length DES keys are not PCI DSS–compliant and should not be used in production. They are easier to manage and use during their development and testing and, if at all, should only be utilized during such activities.

Therefore, valid keys are binary strings of length 8, 16 or 24. It is easy to see that a single-length key can be "disguised" as a double- or triple-length key by repeating the first 8 bytes. However, HSMs detect and prohibit the use of such keys in secure production mode

---

[1]The latter two options are sometimes also denoted as 2TDES and 3TDES, correspondingly.

Since DES is a block cipher with 8-byte block size, keys can be encrypted by other keys without padding. An HSM may export the keys in enciphered form using different formats such as key blocks under various standards or using proprietary representations sometimes referred to as "key schemes". The widely accepted ANSI X9.17 standard often assumed by default requires just the 3-DES encryption with the appropriate KEK.

8.3.3 *Variants and Key Blocks*

To make sure keys are properly secure and less vulnerable to attacks their use must be appropriately limited. Naturally, a key that is never used is a key that is very hard to compromise. A wider use of a key beyond the necessary would increase possible points of attack on it as well as allow an attacker to gather more data for known-plaintext attacks. In a sense, keys form a hierarchy: the

Table 8.1: Key types and roles

Key type	*Name(s)*	*Key role*
Master key	LMK (Local Master Key) MFK (Master File Key) KKM (Key encrypting Key Master)	The key is used to derive and encrypt other sensitive keys. Besides being stored inside the HSM, it is usually stored on external media (smart cards) as two or more separate components. It is only used for the encryption of keys and never is for the encryption of actual data.
Zone master key	ZMK (Zone Master Key) KEK/KK (Key Encryption Key)	A zone master key is used to establish mutual trust in a trust zone. It is used for the encryption of keys and not used for the encryption of data.
PIN key	ZPK (Zone PIN Key) PEK (PIN Encryption Key) AWK (Acquirer Worker Key) IWK (Issuer Worker Key)	The key is used to encrypt and decrypt a PIN in a PIN block.
Data key	DEK/DK (Data Encryption Key)	It is a generic name of an encryption key used to encrypt generic data.

master key resides at the top of it, key encryption keys are found under it and worked keys used to encrypt data are at the lowest level. Obviously, an attacker has more opportunities to gather values for an attack on a key used to encrypt data. If the key is only used for that purpose, its compromise is remedied by a swift rotation of data encryption keys, which is easy to perform if the KEKs are still intact. However, if the key is also used as KEK, the damage will be much more profound.

To limit the key use beyond their original purpose some proprietary representations involved the application of a *variant* when a pre-defined value is XOR-ed with the key during its 3-DES encryption. Since one bit of each byte of a 3-DES key is used for parity, an attempt to use a variant-encrypted key when an ANSI X9.17 key is expected is likely to result in a parity check error. As it is still theoretically possible that a variant key would pass parity check and would be used for an additional purpose, the method is deprecated and phased out to be replaced with *key block*.

In the case of a key block, a key is wrapped into a structure of data containing information about its purpose, its length, the encrypted key itself plus a signature, usually a strong hash, sometimes referred to as *key block authenticator*. In this manner, a key purpose may be learned from the header, and secure devices will not permit the use of the key beyond what is defined in the key block. The structure of the key block is shown in figure 8.1

Key block header	Encrypted key value	Key block authenticator

Figure 8.1: Structure of a key block

8.3.4   Trust Zones

In business scenarios when two HSMs need to share a key for data encryption (for example, in PIN translation, when an encrypted PIN block is re-encrypted by an HSM during the relay between payment network segments or during the exchange of CVKs between issuers and schemes for stand-in processing), zone notion is used. As with local keys, there is separation between key encryption keys and data encryption keys.

The process of establishing a trust zone between HSMs includes two steps. First, a Zone Master Key or ZMK is securely shared between two HSMs. The typical process is usually as follows (any party can initiate it):

1. Party A key custodians (see section 8.3.7) generate a ZMK in the form of clear-text components.

2. Key custodians of Party A securely combine the components to generate a ZMK under LMK of Party A's HSM.

3. Key custodians of Party A securely hand over their respective key components to key custodians of Party B.

4. Key custodians of Party B securely combine the components to generate a ZMK under LMK of Party B's HSM.

At this point, both parties possess a shared KEK which can be utilized to exchange worker keys (in the case of PIN translation, they are denoted as AWKs or ZPKs or acquirer worker keys or zone PIN keys).

Upon establishing the shared secret, the parties can use the HSM to generate such a key under LMK and ZMK. The key as it is encrypted using a strong cryptographic method can be sent over a public network (for instance, emailed).

The process of generation and exchange of ZPKs usually happens as follows (it can be initiated by any party regardless of the initiator in the previous step and regardless of the sender and the receiver of the actual pin block):

1. Party A key custodians generate a ZPK in encrypted form under LMK and ZMK. The former is used by party A host systems and is either used to encrypt EPBs outgoing to Party B or decrypt EPBs incoming from party B depending on the direction of the data flow.

2. Party A key custodians retain the ZPK under LMK and send the ZPK under ZMK to party B.

3. Party B key custodians import the ZPK under ZMK into party B's HSM which yields ZPK under LMK of party B. The key is used by party B host systems to either encrypt outgoing EPBs in the direction of party A or decrypt incoming EPBs from party A depending on the direction of the data flow.

8.3.5 Key Components

As mentioned previously, zone secrets (the key encryption keys known to parties within a trust zone) have to be generated, delivered and deployed using clear-text data due to the fact that a mutually shared secret is only established between the parties. This sensitive clear-text data exchange is performed according to the principles of multi-party split knowledge. Several officers of the financial institution, usually at least three, use the HSM as part of a key ceremony to generate clear-text components of a future key (see section 8.3.7) each.

The clear-text components are binary strings typically represented in hexadecimal format and written down physically on specially designed forms. The length of these components is identical to the length of the future key and is 32 in case of dual-length and 48 in case of triple-length keys.

Upon generating clear-text components, they are reimported into the originating HSM to form a ZMK under the LMK of the sender and to generate a key check value of the full key.

The key custodians of the originating institution send the components alongside the key check value to the key custodians of the recipient institution using special precautions usually in tamper-evident envelopes via three different delivery methods and on different dates.

Then the receiving party uses its HSM to recombine the keys into a fully functional ZMK. While the procedures around the process are somewhat elaborate and involve significant paperwork, the mathematical principle behind the key import from clear-text components is simple: they are XOR-ed together to form a single key. The import process typically produces a ZMK under LMK of the recipient and also generates a KCV which is compared to the one enclosed with the delivery to confirm that the process was completed properly.

8.3.6 PIN Security Requirements

To ensure that PIN values are duly protected, card schemes have imposed security requirements and defined testing processes for these requirements. With time as the PCI council caught up, schemes began a gradual transition to PIN Security Requirements with the latest version (as of this writing) now being version 3.0.

8.3.6.1 General Principles

Card scheme rules make clear distinction between entities validating PINs and those only handling them in transit. For instance, a pure-play acquirer is a non-validating entity unlike an issuer who has to validate online PINs.

All hardware that handles clear-text PIN values must be tamper-resistant. The hardware includes ATMs, HSMs and PIN pads, i.e., either devices that interact with the cardholder during PIN entry or perform PIN translation.

The data flow of an institution's systems must be built in a manner allowing no PIN blocks logging. Store-and-forward schemes are also typically prohibited but can be accepted in the case of additional security provisions made to ensure safe EPBs storage.

The keys must be generated using a random numbers generator satisfying statistical tests of FIPS 140-2 (Federal Information Protection Standard) or its equivalent and the procedures around the key generation should ensure that key compromise is only possible through the collusion of two or more individuals.

Similar requirements are placed on the access to keys and key components. The governing principles are dual control and split knowledge. Dual (or multi-party) control ensures no single person can gain access to a protected item such as a clear-text key, and split knowledge means that no single individual possesses enough information to derive an actual key.

If the key is stored on physical media outside an HSM or is transported, it must at all times remain under the supervision of the authorized individual or locked in a secure tamper-evident container. Usually, all keys are kept in tamper-evident envelopes inside safes that only authorized individuals can open.

The key loading process must be done in a controlled manner ensuring a proper paper trail of actions performed and individuals involved and in a proper seclusion in case clear-text components are used. A proper key loading process also requires dual- or multi-party hardware control. It is also crucial that the keys are validated upon load (in most cases the confirmation of the KCV should suffice).

Besides being compliant with necessary standards keys must be unique and sufficiently long (as mentioned above, at least dual-length at the time of writing) and each must be used for a single purpose (i.e., a ZMK cannot be used for anything but encryption of ZPKs within a well-defined trust zone)

The entire lifecycle of both keys and equipment must be properly logged and documented. At any given moment a paper trail must allow tracing a key or a piece of equipment to its source.

The keys must be securely administered: access to keys must be logged and limited to the chosen few individuals, backup keys must be stored safely, obsolete keys must be properly destroyed. Same requirements apply to the equipment that handles the PINs.

Likewise, access equipment prior to deployment must be logged and decommissioned equipment must undergo the removal of sensitive data and especially the key values. Active equipment must also be protected from physical access where applicable: while ATM, obviously, is accessible to the public, HSMs, when deployed in server rooms, are typically set up in a separate cage with additional locks and extra security cameras.

8.3.6.2 PCI PIN Security Requirements and Testing Procedures v3.0

It is useful to see the principles of PIN security by looking at the PCI PIN Security Requirements and Testing Procedures standard or PTS. The standard has several chapters covering transaction processing in general, symmetric key distribution using asymmetric keys and requirements for key-injection facilities.

Each chapter is divided into several control objectives further translated into specific requirements. The standard provides specific references and outlines testing procedures for audit of compliance to these requirements. Some of the requirements are relatively easy to meet (it suffices to purchase correct equipment or adhere to technical standards), others are hard enough (as they require elaborate processes). Some notes on the way to meet each requirement are found below.

Control Objective 1 of PTS 3.0 is "PINs used in transactions governed by these requirements are processed using equipment and methodologies that ensure they are kept secure". The objective is broken down into several requirements as follows:

Requirement 1 specifies that all cardholder-entered PINs must be processed by secure cryptographic devices and never appear outside of them in plaintext form. It further elaborates on standards to which these devices must comply (ISO 13491, compliance to which is further ensured by certification of either PCI PTS or FIPS). Any standard deployment of a host or terminal management system is to handle the requirement, and compliance to specific standards is handled by a proper vendor choice.

Requirement 2 covers cardholder PIN processing including online and offline PIN validation. The requirement demands written procedures and technical measures which ensure that clerks, merchants or employees will never ask a cardholder for their PIN, that online PIN translation occurs with approved key management methods and that the EPBs are properly enciphered in transit. It further specifies that offline PINs are validated in accordance with the EMV standard. Here, too, procedure manuals are fairly standard, and the offline and online PIN handling is catered for by adhering to proven solutions and complying with EMV.

Requirement 3 defines permitted EPB formats for PIN blocks. EPB formats 0, 1, 3 and 4 are permitted for host-to-host communications while format 2 is used for reader-to-card PIN transmission (the latter conforms to the EMV standard). The requirement further prohibits the conversion of standard EPB formats to non-standard ones along the route of PIN handling. The requirement typically follows from interoperability needs as counterparts demand specific EPB formats to be received from or sent to them.

Requirement 4 prohibits storing EPBs except as part of a store-and-forward transaction and for the minimum time necessary. Furthermore, if the transaction is logged, the EPB must be masked. The requirement is usually supported by major software vendors but must be taken into account during software design and implementation in the case of a new solution.

Requirement 5 defines random or pseudo-random generator requirements for key generation. If keys are generated solely using an HSM, that is catered to by default.

Control Objective 2 of PTS 3.0 is "Cryptographic keys used for PIN encryption/decryption and related key management are created using processes that ensure that it is not possible to predict any key or determine that certain keys are more probable than other keys". The objective is broken down into several requirements as follows:

Requirement 6 mandates that all processes of scheme members must be such that compromise of PIN-handling processes cannot happen without collusion of at least two trusted individuals. The requirement is one of the hardest to comply with as it touches multiple facets of organizations at once. According to the requirement, clear-text components must be split between at least two different individuals, general-purpose computers must not be used to store them, provisions must be made to destroy any used paperwork that contains sensitive materials, storage of clear-text components must be properly secured and printing of PIN materials must happen in closed envelopes only.

Requirement 7 prescribes the existence of documented procedures that are demonstrably in use for all key-generation processes. Compliance with this requirement means that all measures mentioned in Requirement 6 are well-documented and responsible individuals are fully aware of detailed policies and procedures.

Requirement 8 governs transmission of private and public keys. Private keys must be split into several parts and shipped via separate channels or transmitted in encrypted form, while public keys must be shipped in a manner that ensures their authenticity and integrity.

Control Objective 3 of PTS 3.0 is "Keys are conveyed or transmitted in a secure manner". The objective is broken down into several requirements as follows:

Requirement 9 defines the transportation of clear-text components between locations or entities. The keys must be sent in a manner that prevents unauthorized access and allows detecting it if it occured. That is typically achieved by the method and procedure and the use of opaque tamper-evident envelopes.

Requirement 10 mandates that any key encryption keys must be at least as strong as the keys protected by them. That is a technical requirement easy to meet designing a key management process.

Requirement 11 mandates documented and demonstrably used procedures for the above.

Control Objective 4 of PTS 3.0 is "Key-loading to HSMs and POI PIN-acceptance devices is handled in a secure manner". The objective is broken down into several requirements as follows:

Requirement 12 demands that keys are loaded into HSMs and other devices in a secure manner under the principles of dual control and split knowledge. The requirement is one of the key reasons behind the measures described in section 8.3.7.

Requirement 13 mandates that mechanisms or devices used to load keys must be protected from any type of monitoring that may allow unauthorized access.

Requirement 14 demands that any access and authentication means used for key load are stored under principle of dual control. A typical way to comply is to deploy HSMs within an additional secure server cabinet under two different locks keys to which are split between two separate custodians.

Requirement 15 mandates the existence of measures to check that keys after they are loaded are authentic and have not been compromised. That is typically achieved by key check values or other checksums which must be manually validated by custodians.

Requirement 16 prescribes documented procedures demonstrably used as well as a clear paper trail for the above. The requirement results in copious amounts of paperwork produced by each key custodian on every action they perform with keys or key components.

Control Objective 5 of PTS 3.0 is "Keys are used in a manner that prevents or detects their unauthorized usage". The objective is broken down into several requirements as follows:

Requirement 17 demands the use of unique secret keys for any identifiable link between host computers. Compliance with the requirement leads to the introduction of trust zones (see section 8.3.4).

Requirement 18 demands measures to monitor unauthorized substitution of keys. That is achieved electronically by monitoring systems for errors and in the physical world by using tamper-evident seals, bags and envelopes.

Requirement 19 demands that keys are used for a single purpose and are not shared between the test and the production environments. Key purposes are enforced by using some variants or key blocks (see section 8.3.3) while the separation of test and production environments is typically achieved, alongside a complete separation of network and devices, by only ensuring default LMKs are used on all HSMs in the test environment.

Requirement 20 demands that keys used in transaction-originating devices are unique, except by chance. That is achieved by following existing practices of key load and generation.

Control Objective 6 of PTS 3.0 is "Keys are administered in a secure manner". The objective is broken down into several requirements as follows:

Requirement 21 demands that secret keys exist in one of three manners only: either inside a secure device, or in encrypted form (with KEK as strong as the key itself, see Requirement 10), or in clear-text form but separated into several components. A standard key management process takes care of the requirement: usually, KEKs are stored in split, clear-text format inside tamper-evident envelopes in separate key custodian safes, while all the other keys only exist outside of HSMs in enciphered format.

Requirement 22 mandates the existence of key replacement procedures in the case of compromise. The new keys must not be feasibly related to the original keys. That is best achieved by re-generating any compromised keys with a random number generator complying with requirement 5.

Requirement 23 prescribes that any keys generated with a reversible key calculation methods such as key variants must only be used in the original HSMs and only at the same level of key hierarchy (e.g., a KEK variant must not be used to encrypt data or as a master key). See also section 8.3.3 for details.

Requirement 24 prescribes proper destruction of the keys that are no longer in use.

Requirement 25 mandates limit access to secure keys on limited need-to-know basis and in a protected manner so that no other person could obtain or observe the component. That is done by storing all materials in safes accessible by a few key custodians and by instructing custodians accordingly.

Requirement 26 prescribes keeping detailed logs for any key movement in or out of storage and into secure devices. That again contributes to paperwork the key custodians have to carry and maintain.

Requirement 27 covers the backups of keys and key components. The requirement is that, if possible, no backups are kept but if they are,they must be adequately secured and restricted to the absolute necessary minimum.

Requirement 28 prescribes the existence of documented procedures demonstrably used.

Control Objective 7 of PTS 3.0 is "Equipment used to process PINs and keys is managed in a secure manner". The objective is broken down into several requirements as follows:

Requirement 29 prescribes making sure that any device put into production has not been tampered with. That is achieved by instating strict validation procedures of the incoming equipment shipments and by maintaining a clear paper trail of such procedures.

Requirement 30 demands physical and logical protection for devices. That means making sure physical access to devices is restricted and well documented and devices are routinely patched for known vulnerabilities.

Requirement 31 governs procedures for destruction of the devices that are no longer in use and the destruction of key materials in the case of taking a device to repairs.

Requirement 32 demands that any device used to generate and encrypt keys is restricted in use and access. That is achieved by dual physical control as mentioned in Requirement 14 and by making sure the device enters key generation mode under dual access (standard feature of any compliant HSM vendor).

Requirement 33 prescribes the existence of documented procedures demonstrably used.

8.3.7 Key Custodians and Key Ceremony

As mentioned, one of the key principles of proper access management to keys and key components is dual- or multi-party control. In a typical set-up a processing institution nominates at least three *key custodians* or employees trained and qualified for the job but not belonging to the same department or reporting to the same direct manager. It is customary to also nominate backup key custodians who share access to cryptographic materials with the corresponding primary custodians.

Each custodian is allocated a safe box inside which the custodian's cryptographic material is stored. Usually each key component, a cryptographic or physical key, a smartcard or other media is enclosed in addition in a tamper-evident envelope to ensure an additional level of the sensitive data protection.

Key generation processes and access to such hardware as HSMs are arranged in such a manner that the presence of all the three custodians is mandatory. The process of generation of clear-text key components, key recombination and import is called *key ceremony*. During the process sensitive steps are performed by key custodians in seclusion to avoid the possibility of key or key component compromise.

8.3.7.1 Sample Procedure

To illustrate the aforementioned requirements and principles, consider the following sample key management procedure. It is by no means complete but should provide a general idea of how a compliant processing organization should define its guidelines.

Assume that a pure acquiring player supports card-present transactions with online PIN and, therefore, requires PIN translation. HSMs required to support the predicted volume are supposed to be purchased from a certified vendor; the packaging is supposed to be inspected upon receipt for tampering and the storage and handling of HSMs further documented until the moment they are securely deployed in a server farm.

To ensure a proper access control the HSMs are placed in a separate closed cage with dual locks on its front and back (for example, by using a built-in lock and a padlock). The custodians gather at an HSM, inspect it for signs of tampering and initialize the master keys. The keys are stored on at least two smart cards assigned to different custodians. Each custodian assigns an additional PIN code to the smart card in seclusion to avoid others peeking.

The custodians add an entry to the HSM access log, lock up the HSM, seal their smartcards and physical keys in separate tamper-evident envelopes kept with them at all times until their deposit in a safe box.

Each custodian is given a safe box to which only this particular primary or backup custodian has access. The custodian maintains an inventory of the safe box marking new and destroyed items as well as an access log containing the details on each piece of cryptographic material taken out or placed back into the safe box.

When it is time to generate a ZMK the custodians gather again at a facility with HSM access. Custodians 1 and 3 have physical keys allowing them to actually touch the device while custodians 1 and 2 have smart-cards allowing key generation. In the case of such distribution of the access artefacts no two custodians can collude to gain unauthorized access to the HSM or otherwise compromise sensitive materials.

The custodians inspect the HSM exterior, then enable access to it and, if relevant, put it in necessary mode to generate the ZMKs. The custodians approach the HSM console each in turn and generate a key component of the ZMK. Each generated component is to be written down by its custodian on a dedicated form and kept outside of other observers' eyes. The custodians also make sure that no person approaching the HSM after the part of that particular custodian is completed is able to see the clear-text key component (for example, by clearing the screen once the clear-text component is written down).

Then the custodians repeat the ceremony, this time entering the clear-text components into the HSM to form a working ZMK. One of the custodians writes down the value of ZMK under LMK on a form for future use. Then the custodians return HSM to operational mode, if necessary, and lock it up again. They seal the clear-text components in tamper-evident envelopes.

Next, each custodian has to send the respective key component to the other party's counterpart. The best practice to do it is doing that on different dates and using different delivery methods delivery such as mail and courier services. Each custodian must know exactly to whom the component is sent and communicate the tracking numbers and/or package serial numbers to that person. The other party's custodians must confirm the receipt of materials, inspect them for tampering and place them into secure storage. In case an envelope bears some signs of tampering, its contents do not match the manifest or the serial number of the package is wrong, the entire key is considered compromised and the process is restarted.

Chapter 9

Other Payment Methods

CONTENTS

Besides hard cash and "pure" card payments described in the book, several other payment methods have emerged over the years. Some of them function as a complete alternative to payment cards while others mimic payment card technology or complement it. Certainly, cryptographic currencies stand out as an entirely different method of technology practically denominated in a currency of its own.

These methods can be largely divided into the following groups:

- Electronic wallets (staged or pass-through)

- Cash-based

- Telco billing

- Bank transfers

- Invoice

- Digital currencies

Let us take a brief look into these groups in some more details.

9.1 Electronic Wallets

Consider an old-school physical wallet. It is topped up with cash and can also contain payment cards. A consumer goes to a store, takes out some cash from the wallet and pays for goods and services. Once the cash in the wallet runs out, it has to be topped up again. The consumer can also pick a card out of several ones present in the wallet and use it to make a payment.

In general, *electronic* (or *digital*) *wallets* mimic physical wallets. They can be divided into two subgroups: staged and pass-through ones.

A *staged wallet* is a digital wallet used in stages. That is, it is an analogy of cash being placed into and taken out of a wallet: a staged wallet is used in stages, hence the name. The first stage is top-up during which money is placed into the wallet either by a single payment-card transaction or via a bank transfer or via a cash deposit in a kiosk or a supporting store or, finally, via a peer-to-peer transfer from another holder of the same wallet type.

Staged wallets are primarily used for card-not-present purchases. However, brick-and-mortar shops become increasingly more able and willing to accept payments from such wallets.

From the card schemes' perspective a staged wallet has some regulatory and fiscal drawbacks.

From a regulatory point of view it is no longer possible to track each individual transaction originated via a scheme-branded card. Money, once topped up in a staged wallet, can be used for any purpose allowed by the wallet provider, including illegal fund transfers and laundering.

Fiscally, each transaction that bypasses card scheme networks means lower fees for the card-scheme and less interchange for participating banks.

As such, card schemes are imposing additional fees and require extra data on staged wallet transactions.

The examples of staged wallets include WebMoney in Russia, Osaifu-Keitai in Japan or such global providers as Skrill and PayPal.

A *pass-through* wallet is a digital wallet having one or more underlying payment cards that can be used to perform a particular transaction. Each transaction with a pass-through wallet is translated to a transaction with one of the cards tied to it.

Pass-through wallets were brought over to the card-present space with the introduction of Apple Pay. In the case of Apple Pay, one or more payment cards are tied to a person's account with Apple. By leveraging card tokenization a consumer having an iPhone using NFC technology can transmit payment details to a contactless terminal in a store without the need for the store owner to update terminal hardware or software.

Other wallets, such as AliPay or WeChatPay, rely on a QR code scan for a transfer of funds between consumer's and merchant's wallets.

The examples of pass-through wallets include Amazon Payments, PayPal, ApplePay, Samsung Pay, AliPay available globally, and local providers such as BKM Express in Turkey.

Card schemes have also made some forays into the field of pass-through wallets introducing Visa Checkout and MasterPass, to name a few.

The two modes of operation of a digital wallet are not mutually exclusive. For instance, PayPal can be topped up as a staged wallet and used as a pass-through depending on a user preference.

9.2 Cash-based Methods

The payment method is used for online payments in markets with low penetration of payment cards.

A consumer performs a purchase in an e-commerce store choosing cash voucher as the payment method. The consumer gets a printable document with a unique identifier on it. Then the consumer takes the document to a participating service point or an automated kiosk and deposits cash to the full specified amount. Once the voucher is paid in cash, the online store ships the goods or provides the services.

Multiple examples of the method can be found in developing markets. To name a few, Efecty in Colombia, ESAPAY in Malaysia and Brunei, and Fawry in Egypt are cash-based online payment methods.

9.3 Telco Billing

In many markets with low banking access and payment-card penetration, consumers widely use telecom service providers as post-paid or pre-paid customers.

Consequently, many online and brick-and-mortar stores allow consumers to pay for goods or services from their cellular phone balance or by including the payment in their next telecom bill.

The method is widely used in developing markets where mobile access penetration is far greater than the percentage of banked population; examples include Flooz in Togo and Benin and FNB Cell Pay Point in South Africa.

9.4 Bank Transfers

In mature markets with ubiquitous access to banking services such as the United States, United Kingdom or European Union, there are payment methods facilitating fund transfer between a consumer's and a merchant's bank accounts.

Certainly, a consumer could approach a local branch of their bank, instruct a clerk to wire money to the merchant and, upon confirmation, have the merchant ship the goods. The method, however, is not suitable for online purchases and so a plethora of bank transfer payment methods have emerged both simplifying the authorization of the fund transfer online and speeding up the transfer of funds itself.

For example, such methods include ACH in the United States, Faster payments in the UK, Sofort in Germany, iDEAL in Belgium/Netherlands/Luxembourge area, eDankort in Denmark as well as SEPA Direct Debit elsewhere (or everywhere) in the European Union, eNETS in Singapore and so on.

9.5 Invoices

In certain markets there are payment-services providers allowing consumers to pay by invoice.

When such method is used, the merchant usually receives the full payment amount while the consumer is invoiced periodically over a span of several months. The method lays off the illiquidity risks from the merchant to the service provider while, on the other hand, providing financing to the consumer in the form of installment payments over what originally is a lump sum payment.

9.6 Digital Currencies

Digital currencies, especially the pioneering Bitcoin, are an entirely new breed of payment method unrelated to any existing currency or technology.

In the case of a block-chain-based digital currency there is no single authority that issues or controls the payment instrument as that role is distributed between multiple nodes in a low-trust network of "coin miners".

The conversion between a digital and a traditional currency is not a part of digital currency mechanisms (unlike electronic wallets) and is instead performed similarly to foreign currency exchanges by a digital currency broker.

As digital currencies are built in an inherently anonymous and untraceable manner, accepting or acquiring payments with the instrument involves a significant legal risk because it is a comfortable channel for illegal activities and money laundering. Furthermore, the legal framework in most countries is not prepared for that type of financial instrument.

The aforementioned factors contribute to the volatility of digital currencies. However, despite that consumers are increasingly willing to use digital currencies and merchants conversely expect to be able to accept them.

ALGORITHMS AND ENCODINGS

Chapter 10

Validation Algorithms

CONTENTS

10.1   Luhn Algorithm

The Luhn algorithm is specified by the ISO/IEC 7812-1 standard. Validation of an account number is performed according to the following steps:

1. Truncate the check digit from the number that is being validated.

2. Moving right to left, double all digits on odd positions (i.e., the rightmost one and every other digit leftwards from it).

3. If the product of doubling a digit is greater than 9, replace the resulting number with the sum of its digits.

4. Sum up the result and add the check digit to it.

5. The result, modulo 10, should be 0.

Consider the example of account number 491023693576 shown in figure 10.1.

The sum of all digits is $8 + 9 + 2 + 0 + 4 + 3 + 3 + 9 + 6 + 5 + 5 + 6 = 60$ which divides by 10. Hence, 6 is a valid check digit.

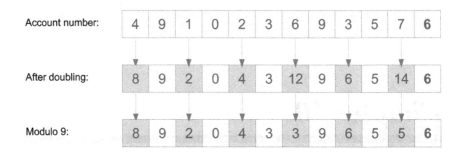

Figure 10.1: Example of Luhn algorithm

To calculate the check digit, follow steps 1 to 4 of the algorithm above, assuming the check digit of 0. If the total amount is already divisible by 10 then 0 is the check digit; exit. Otherwise, replace the check digit with 10 less the sum modulo 10.

As it is quite easy to see, a mistake in any single digit of the account number causes the Luhn checksum to become invalid. The checksum also detects almost any transposition of two adjacent digits, except for 09 becoming 90 or vice versa.

That makes the Luhn checksum an easy and practical method to validate PAN numbers during mail or telephone orders as well as in electronic commerce purchases when the card is punched in or written down by a human and is therefore most prone to these types of mistakes.

10.2   Longitudinal Redundancy Check (LRC)

The Longitudinal Redundancy Check or LRC is used as the trailing value of the data stored on the magnetic stripe. It is a type of redundancy check algorithm easy to implement in binary hardware and particularly good at detecting noise-related errors.

The LRC is best defined as the 8-bit two-complement value of the sum of all bytes modulo 2^8, meaning that the sum of all the values and the LRC yields 0.

To calculate the LRC value XOR all bytes of the byte array in question, then calculate the two-complement value by inverting the result (XOR-ing with 0xFF) adding one and then taking modulo 2^8 again (which can be done by AND-ing the value with 0xFF).

To illustrate, consider the example of FA 13 58 A0 C5.

XOR-ing 0xFA, 0x13, 0x58, 0xA0 and 0xC5 yields the value of 0x8C. To calculate its two-complement we XOR it with 0xFF and obtain 0x73 as the result. Then we add 1 to get 0x74 which is the desired LRC value.

To validate the calculation add the sum of all the values to the calculated LC value. The result is 0x100 which once ANDed with 0xFF yields 0.

10.3 Key Check Value (KCV)

The Key Check Value or KCV is used to confirm the keys validity and is utilized for the validation of encryption keys in the payments industry.

A KCV is typically a 3-byte (6 digits) control value transmitted alongside an enciphered key or with clear-text components. It is obtained by encrypting an input block of zeroes with the appropriate algorithm (see section 12.2 and section 12.3). Of the outcome only the first bytes are kept and the rest are discarded.

It is possible to use a longer or shorter value for the KCV utilizing less or more bytes but the 3-byte value is the defacto standard in the industry.

Chapter 11

Code Tables

CONTENTS

11.1   ANSI/ISO ALPHA Data Format

Table 11.1 contains the ANSI/ISO ALPHA data format used to encode Track 1 values. The data is stored in 7-bit vectors with the least significant bit being the parity (thus, the character of ' ' is stored as 0000001).

11.2   ANSI/ISO BCD Data Format

Table 11.2 contains ANSI/ISO BCD data format used to encode Track 2 and Track 3 values. The data is stored in 5-bit vectors with the least significant bit being the parity (thus, the digit 0 is stored as 00001).

Table 11.1: ANSI/ISO ALPHA data format

Hex value	Char	Hex value	Char	Hex value	Char	Hex value	Char
00	space	10	0	20	@	30	P
01	!	11	1	21	A	31	Q
02	"	12	2	22	B	32	R
03	#	13	3	23	C	33	S
04	$	14	4	24	D	34	T
05	%	15	5	25	E	35	U
06	&	16	6	26	F	36	V
07	'	17	7	27	G	37	W
08	(	18	8	28	H	38	X
09	)	19	9	29	I	39	Y
0A	*	1A	:	2A	J	3A	Z
0B	+	1B	;	2B	K	3B	[
0C	,	1C	<	2C	L	3C	\
0D	-	1D	=	2D	M	3D	]
0E	.	1E	>	2E	N	3E	^
0F	/	1F	?	2F	O	3F	_

Table 11.2: ANSI/ISO BCD data format

Hex value	Char	Hex value	Char	Hex value	Char	Hex value	Char
00	0	04	4	08	8	0C	<
01	1	05	5	09	9	0D	=
02	2	06	6	0A	:	0E	>
03	3	07	7	0B	;	0F	?

11.3 ASCII Character Encoding Table

ASCII, abbreviated from American Standard Code for Information Interchange and also referred to as US-ASCII, is a 7-bit character encoding table that drew inspiration from earlier telegraph codes superseding them as the standard for text encoding in telecommunications. The origins of the code can be traced to a 5-bit code invented by Emile Baudot in 1870, which was the first machine-readable fixed-width binary code[1]. Baudot code evolved into 6-bit ITA2, the International

---

[1]Credit for the first fixed-width binary code ever belongs to Sir Francis Bacon who invented the so-called "Bacon cipher" in 1605 using five-letter sequences of letters A and B to encode the Latin alphabet. However, due to the scarcity of electromechanical devices in the 17th century the code was not machine-readable.

Telegraph Alphabet which, as its predecessor, had shift codes changing the meaning of the symbol codes, modifying registers or alternating between digits and letters.

In 1963, the ASCII table was published. Besides eliminating the need for shift control characters, the table had several other useful features. The key properties of the ASCII encoding table are listed below:

■ ASCII control characters (e.g., "line feed" or "new line") have codes in the range of 0x00 to 0x1F (0 to 31). Also, 0x7F is a control character.

■ ASCII digits are coded starting from 0x30 (48) through to 0x39 (57). In other words, and that comes in handy when analyzing ISO messages, to form an ASCII code for a decimal digit it is sufficient to add 0x30 to it. For example, sequence "3790" is encoded in ASCII as 33 37 39 30.

■ Space is encoded as 0x20 (32).

■ Uppercase letters are encoded in positions 0x41 through 0x5A in alphabetical order and lowercase letters are encoded in positions 0x61 to 0x7A. In other words, turning on and off 6th bit (adding/subtracting 0x20) provides an easy method to convert ASCII-encoded strings between upper and lower case.

In subsequent revisions the ASCII standard was expanded to 8 bits and codes in 0x80-0xFF range were allocated to additional national characters. These code pages have largely been replaced by backward-compatible UTF-8 encoding in wide use.

In the payments industry most applications and certainly all online authorization protocols only use the lower range of ASCII table with national encodings sometimes used in clearing files.

A 7-bit ASCII table is very easy to find on the Internet and is, therefore, not brought here.

11.4   EBCDIC Character Encoding Table

EBCDIC stands for Extended Binary Coded Decimal Interchange Code. It is a proprietary 8-bit character encoding developed and first used by IBM on mainframes and minicomputers. It was devised and announced by IBM in 1963, the same year ASCII encoding came into being.

Although IBM actively participated in the development of the new 7-bit character-encoding standard, the full migration of existing software and peripheral devices to the new standard was considered not feasible, so instead IBM had to maintain backward compatibility and, therefore, EBCDIC was an incremental extension of earlier Binary Coded Decimal Interchange Code (BCDIC) encodings used by peripheral devices that processed or punched punch cards.

Due to the vast popularity of IBM mainframe computers operating since the early 1960s and to this day in financial institutions across the globe the encoding lingered[2].

EBCDIC has several notable properties:

■ While ASCII uses 7 bits to encode Latin characters, EBCDIC uses full 8-bit codes.

■ There are multiple EBCDIC code pages which are not fully compatible.

■ Control (non-printable) characters are encoded in the range 0x00 to 0x3F. 0xFF is also a control character.

■ There are three characters for spaces in EBCDIC: 0x40 (decimal 64, space), 0x41 (decimal 65, required space or no-break space) and 0xE1 (decimal 225, numeric space). The 0x40 character corresponds to ASCII code 0x20 (decimal 32, space).

■ Decimal digits are assigned codes from 0xF0 (240) to 0xF9 (249). Therefore, to encode a digit in EBCDIC format it is sufficient to add 0xF0 to it. For example, sequence 3790 is encoded in EBCDIC as F3 F7 F9 F0.

■ Latin uppercase letters are encoded in ranges 0xC1 to 0xC9 (decimal 193 to 201, letters A to I), 0xD1 to 0xD9 (decimal 209 to 217, letters J to R) and 0xE2 to 0xE9 (decimal 226 to 233, letters S to Z). Lowercase letters occupy parallel code ranges 0x80 to 0x89, 0x90 to 0x99 and 0xA1 to 0xA9.

Online tools for conversion between EBCDIC and ASCII as well as printable tables can be easily found on the Internet and, therefore, the full table is not offered here.

11.5 Base64 Encoding

Base64 encoding represents binary data using 64 alphanumeric and special characters. To convert a binary value into Base64 representation the following steps are performed:

1. The original binary sequence is padded with zero (0x00) octets so that the total length of the sequence is divisible by 3.

2. The sequence is converted into a string of 6-bit values.

---

[2]The EBCDIC encoding is not the only legacy of punched cards in modern payments. Classic punch cards had 80 symbols—hence multiple proprietary 80-byte file formats are still used in the industry.

3. Each 6-bit value is mapped to a character according to the encoding table, except for trailing padding zero values replaced with a special padding character, =.

The encoding table is easy to locate in the public domain.

To illustrate the calculation let us consider the following binary sequence of 5 octets: DE AD BE EF 00. To encode the sequence it should be padded to 6 octets for the total length to be divisible by three. In binary form, the resulting string is represented in figure 11.1

		Value								Padding	
D	E	A	D	B	E	E	F	0	0	0	0
1101	1110	1010	1101	1011	1110	1110	1111	0000	0000	0000	0000

Figure 11.1: Base64 padded input string

The total bit length of the resulting sequence is 48 bits hence, it will be encoded with 8 characters, one per each 6-bit word, as shown in figure 11.2

Binary	110111	101010	110110	111110	111011	110000	000000	000000
Decimal	55	42	54	62	59	48	0	0
Char	3	q	2	+	7	w	A	=

Figure 11.2: Base64 encoded string

The resulting sequence is therefore encoded as 3q2+7wA=. Note that the same binary value of 0 is encoded differently when it is part of the original binary data (in which case, 0 is mapped to A) and when it is a padding byte (and is mapped to =).

11.6 BER-TLV Encoding

BER-TLV stands for Basic Encoding Rules—Tag Length Value and refers to BER encoding of ASN.1.

ASN.1 stands for Abstract Syntax Notation One and is a standard describing a language for the abstract description of arbitrary data structures as well as several sets of rules that allow encoding and transmission of these structures.

BER or Basic Encoding Rules is one of such rule sets and it is used in the payment industry as part of EMV chip and contactless technology. It is sometimes referred to as BER-TLV or TLV (tag/length/value) since each data element is encoded as type identifier followed by element length, followed by data and optionally concluded by an end-of-content marker (the latter is not used in payments and is therefore not covered here).

11.6.1 Tag or Type Identifier

As mentioned above, a BER-encoded data structure always starts with the type identifier or "tag" occupying at least 1 byte and potentially unlimited in length. In practice, tags that are used in EMV applications are either 1 or 2 bytes in length.

The bit pattern of a 1-byte tag, as prescribed by the BER-TLV standard, is shown in figure 11.3.

8	7	6	5	4	3	2	1
Tag class		P/C		Tag number			

Figure 11.3: BER-TLV 1-byte tag

In case the tag number cannot fit into 5 bits, all 5 junior bits of the first byte should be set to 1 and the format of the resulting 2-byte tag is as shown in figure 11.4.

Byte 1									Byte 2							
8	7	6	5	4	3	2	1		8	7	6	5	4	3	2	1
Tag class	P/C	1	1	1	1	1			M		Tag number					

Figure 11.4: BER-TLV 2-byte tag

Here the M or the most senior bit of the second byte is set to 1 if another octet with tag number follows (i.e., total length of the tag is at least 3 bytes). If any additional bytes are required for the tag number, their format is identical to that of byte 2. As mentioned above, in EMV applications no tag id occupies more than two bytes.

The tag class values are defined in table 11.3.

The EMV standard only utilizes the values of 1 and 2 for its tag meaning that all EMV standard tags begin with bit sequence 01 or 10.

The P/C bit indicates whether the element following the tag is primitive (i.e. contains the actual value) or constructed (is composed of multiple tag-length-value sub-elements). The value for constructed ones is 1. The EMV standard contains both primitive and constructed tags.

The remainder of the tag is the actual tag number. For a single-byte tag it can range from 0 to 30. If the value of these bits is set to all ones (i.e., tag number 31), the number is continued in the second byte.

11.6.2 Length

The length can be encoded in either a short or a long form.

In the short form the length in bytes is encoded as a single-byte value with most senior byte set to 0. That allows encoding values of up to 127 bytes length. For example, a value with length of 75 bytes is represented as the bit string of 01001011.

In the long form the leftmost bit of the first byte of the length value is set to 1 while the other 7 bits represent "length of length" or number of bytes that follow and contain the length of the actual binary value. The EMV standard only uses lengths of up to 255 bytes and, consequently, only requires a total of 2 bytes for encoding lengths in the long form. For example, the value of 140 (binary 10001100) is encoded as shown in figure 11.5.

Here, bit 8 of byte 1 indicates the long form of the length value and bits 7 to 1 indicate that only 1 byte is to follow. Byte 2 contains the full-length value in bytes. As mentioned above, the EMV standard does not use longer forms of the length value.

Table 11.3: Tag class values

Value	Description
0	Universal—native for ASN.1
1	Valid for a specific application
2	Context-dependent tag
3	Defined in private specifications

Byte 1							
8	7	6	5	4	3	2	1
1	0	0	0	0	0	0	1

Byte 2							
8	7	6	5	4	3	2	1
1	0	0	0	1	1	0	0

Figure 11.5: Sample double-byte length value

Chapter 12

Cryptography 101

CONTENTS

12.1 Introduction

The purpose of the chapter is to provide basic cryptographic terms and their definitions to the extent relevant for understanding of payment-processing technology.

Payment processing implies passing around sensitive data between parties or data which needs to be protected. Since the full control of all physical access to hosts, devices, network elements and even cables participating in payment processing is not feasible, the industry relies on cryptographic means of messages protection during their exchange between parties.

A raw or undisguised message is called *plaintext* or *cleartext*. To hide its substance is to *encrypt* or *encipher* it, obtaining *ciphertext* as the result. The reverse process is called *decryption* or *deciphering*.

Cryptography has the following major functions:

Confidentiality—ensuring that the message is only seen by its sender and recipient and that a third party that might be eavesdropping on the communication channel is unable to discern its contents. The ability is widely used to keep channels between payment parties secured.

Authentication—allowing the receiver of the message to confirm its origin so that a third party will not be able to masquerade as a sender. For instance, authentication is used to confirm that the chip on the card from which the transaction originated is genuine as issued by the bank.

Integrity—allowing the receiver to verify that the message has not been tampered with in transit. For instance, during a full-grade EMV chip transaction cryptographic methods ensure that its amount has not been modified.

Nonrepudiation—not allowing the sender to deny that the message was indeed sent by it.

A typical cryptographic algorithm accepts two parameters: the data (cleartext to be enciphered or ciphertext to be deciphered) and the *key*. The key can be kept secret while the algorithm may be exposed to independent scrutiny.

Cryptographic algorithms can be classified into *stream ciphers* and *block ciphers*. A stream cipher operates on a byte or a bit of cleartext at a time while a block cipher operates on a fixed-size data vector (typically 8 bytes/64 bit or 16 bytes/128 bit).

Algorithms can be further classified based on their use of keys for encryption and decryption. If the same key is used to both encrypt and decrypt the message, the algorithm is called *symmetric* (see also section 12.2, describing the DES algorithm which is a symmetric block cipher). If different key pairs are used for encryption and decryption, the algorithm is *asymmetric*. Here, in the case of data encryption, the encryption key is usually called the public key and the decryption key is usually called the private key.

Besides algorithms which encrypt and decrypt messages, modern cryptographic systems also use *one-way hash functions*. A one-way hash function converts a variable-length input (a message) into a fixed-length output (the message digest). Such a function differs from an algorithm because it is unfeasible to restore the original message based on its digest. One-way hash functions server as a tool for the generation of MAC (*message authentication code*) where a secret key is added to the message before a one-way hash function is applied to it.

Public/private algorithms are widely used to both encrypt and sign the data sent. To generate a digital signature the sender can produce a one-way hash of the message (appending timestamp to it to avoid replay attacks) and encrypt the message digest with their private key sending both the message and the obtained signature to the other party. Then the receiver generates the same one-way hash, decrypts the signature with the sender's public key and compares the result to the received value. If the hashes match, the signature is valid.

There are several methods to apply a block cipher to a data array whose length is bigger than the cipher's input block size. First and foremost, the data is padded to a length divisible by block cipher input block length. Two most common methods to encrypt the padded data are *ECB (electronic code book)* and *CBC (cipher block chaining)*. In the case of the ECB mode each block is encrypted independently (increasing vulnerability of the overall solution to some attacks, as identical inputs would yield identical outputs). In the case of the CBC mode the data is encrypted sequentially with encrypted value of one block being XOR-ed with plaintext of the subsequent block prior to its encryption. The first block in the chain is XOR-ed with a special value called which needs to be communicated to the recipient of the ciphertext so that they could decipher the message.

12.2   DES and 3-DES Encryption

The DES (Data Encryption Standard) algorithm is a symmetric block cipher developed in the early 1980s by IBM researchers jointly with the NSA and defined as a standard algorithm for symmetric data encryption for US government agencies (Federal Information Processing Standard or FIPS).

The algorithm contains several key steps designed in a manner that both prevents most cryptographic attacks and is suitable for development of specialized hardware that can perform necessary calculations faster than a software counterpart.

The DES algorithm is a block cipher that operates on 64-bit blocks enciphering 8-byte plaintext into 8-byte ciphertext. Over the course of the algorithm the block is permuted and then broken into 32-bit halves and combined with the key repeatedly for 16 rounds. At the end, the halves are recombined and a final permutation is performed.

The key length of the original DES algorithm was 8 bytes or 64 bits. One bit of every byte was unused by the algorithm and was thus utilized as a parity check value. As computational power of generally available hardware grew, the algorithm had to be augmented accordingly and thus 3-DES or T-DES encryption algorithm was designed.

As its name implies, the algorithm utilizes three keys K_1, K_2 and K_3 applied to each data block in succession encrypting with K_1 and K_3 and decrypting with K_2: $C = E_{K_1}(D_{K_2}(E_{K_3}(M)))$, where C is the ciphertext and M is the message. Similarly, the reverse transformation is done by decrypting with K_1 and K_3 and encrypting with K_2: $M = D_{K_1}(E_{K_2}(D_{K_3}(C)))$

As an input the algorithm can receive one, two or three keys and depending on that the variant of the algorithm is sometimes denoted as 1TDES, 2TDES or 3TDES correspondingly. With one key, i.e., when $K_1 = K_2 = K_3$, the algorithm is reduced to the standard DES, and with only two keys K1 is assumed to be equal to K3. These keys are usually transmitted and recorded as a concatenated array of 8, 16 or 24 bytes corresponding to effective key sizes of 56, 112 and 168 bits.

12.3 AES Algorithm

By the end of the 20th century, there had been several concerns with regards to DES and its TDES variation. Progress in hardware made possible specialized devices that can brute-force a single DES encryption in a very short time frame. The algorithm as well as its tripled counterpart were designed for hardware implementation and ran relatively slow when implemented in software. Furthermore, the block size of 64 bits was considered too small.

It was due to the issues that an Advanced Encryption Standard (AES) selection process was initiated by NIST in the United States. Eventually, an algorithm called Rijndael was accepted as the new official standard for symmetric data encryption.

The algorithm works on blocks of 128 bits with keys of 128, 192 or 256 bits in length. The algorithm represents the input 16 bytes as a 4×4 column-major matrix and performs 10, 12 or 14 rounds of encryption for keys of 128, 192 or 256 bits, correspondingly. A round key is derived from the provided encryption key per each round of encryption. Then the algorithm performs the following steps:

- The round key is XORed with the input matrix.

- For 9, 11 or 13 rounds matrix bytes are substituted according to a substation table. Then the algorithm shifts rows of the table, effectively mixing bytes across columns and then multiplies each column by a coefficient matrix obtaining a linear combination of the input bytes. The result is XORed with the round key for the appropriate round.

- In the final-round bytes are substituted and rows are shifted, and then the result is XORed with the final round key.

The algorithm is considered very secure. The EMV standard includes the description on its use in cryptogram generation while the PIN Transaction Security 3.0 standard mandates transition to it for EPB encryption.

12.4 Message Authentication Code

A Message Authentication Code or MAC is a short (relative to the message size) value used to authenticate a message. It is different from a checksum or a hash value as it is typically calculated using a secret key.

In payments the MAC typically in use is a variation called CBC-MAC, whereas a block cipher algorithm is used in CBC mode over the message with an initialization vector of 0. Then only the output of the last enciphering round is sent.

To illustrate, consider the TDES algorithm and a message that is of 24-byte length after padding. CBC encryption with initialization vector of all zeros means that first 8 bytes of the message are to be encrypted as is with the TDES key resulting in value of H1. Then H1 is XOR-ed with the second 8 bytes of the message data. The result is encrypted to obtain H2. H2 is, in turn, XOR-ed with the last 8 bytes of the message data and the result is encrypted to obtain H3 which is the output of the algorithm.

12.5 Asymmetric Encryption

Asymmetric encryption, as the name implies, utilizes two different keys (or a *key pair*) for encryption and decryption. The encryption key (aka "public key", see above) can be used to encrypt data or verify a digital signature. The decryption key (aka "private key") can be used to decrypt data or calculate a digital signature.

Two major scenarios are possible using an asymmetric encryption algorithm: one is message encryption and the other is message non-repudiable signature. To illustrate it consider the scenario when a bank and a scheme each generate a key pair and share the public part of the key pair with the corresponding party. Let us denote the bank's key pair as K_E^{Bank} and K_D^{Bank}, and scheme's key pair as K_E^{Scheme} and K_D^{Scheme}. Then the bank obtains K_E^{Scheme}, and the scheme gets K_E^{Bank}.

Assume that the bank wants to send a secret message to the scheme. For example, the bank has encountered issues with some PANs and would like to securely share them with the scheme support team for further investigation. The bank already has scheme's public key and can thus take the PANs, form a message M_{clear} out of them (possibly by appending expletives to indicate the gravity of bank's situation) and encrypt message M_{clear} with K_E^{Scheme}, obtaining M_{enc}^{Scheme}.

As only the card scheme possesses the relevant private key, it is the card scheme alone that can decipher this message, applying K_D^{Scheme} to M_{enc}^{Scheme} to obtain M_{clear}.

To illustrate the second scenario let us assume that the scheme issues a statement instructing certain banks to limit transactions of a particular type. A forged statement of the sort can cause major disruptions to payment services of multiple banks potentially causing panic and maybe even triggering a bank run. To make sure that will not happen the scheme uses its private key K_D^{Scheme} to sign the notification N_{clear} and publishes the clear-text notification alongside the signature

N_{sign}^{Scheme}. Upon receiving the notification and the signature, the bank verifies it using K_E^{Scheme} in its possession.

The encryption and signature can also be combined in one message. In that case, for example, the bank encrypts message M_{clear} to form M_{enc}^{Scheme} and provides a signature, M_{sign}^{Bank} by using K_E^{Scheme} and K_D^{Bank}, correspondingly. The two values are sent to the card scheme. Then the scheme uses its private K_D^{Scheme} to obtain M_{clear} and the bank's public key K_E^{Bank} to verify M_{sign}^{Bank}.

Chapter 13

PIN Block Formats and Algorithms

CONTENTS

13.1   EPB (Encrypted PIN Block) Formats

EPB or encrypted PIN block formats are described in the ISO 9564 standard. There are several different formats of the PIN block and many of them are very similar. Formats 0, 1, 2 and 3 describe the packaging of a PIN value into a 64-bit PIN block. Format 4 describes a 128-bit PIN block. While formats 0, 1, 2 and 3 are meant for some flavor of DES encryption, Format 4 was defined for use with AES encryption algorithm.

In all cases the values are stored as a packed binary-coded decimal and the blocks share the following common characteristics: the first nibble always specifies the block format (it can be 0, 1, 2 or 3, see below) while the second nibble specifies the PIN length (and can, therefore, vary from 4 to 14, although PINs longer than 6 digits are not often used). Therefore, a generic EPB of formats 1 to 3 has the structure shown in figure 13.1: Here F denotes the format indicator nibble, L denotes the PIN length and the X values are defined by the specific format of the PIN block.

Format 0 is used across hosts when a PIN and a PAN number are available.
A format 0 PIN block is calculated by XOR-ing two vectors. For vector

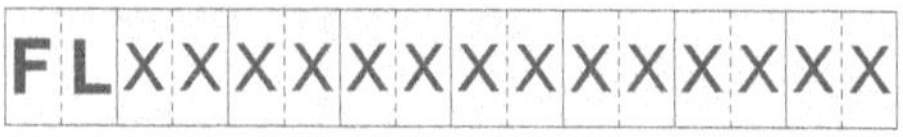

F L X X X X X X X X X X X X X X

Figure 13.1: EPB formats 0, 1, 2 or 3

1 the format indicator, the length and the PIN are packed as nibbles and padded with value of 15 (0xF) to the full length of 16 nibbles. For vector 2 the rightmost 12 positions of the PAN number without the check digit are taken and padded on the left with 4 zeroes. In the case of EMV tokenization (see section 4.6.3) the token number is used instead of the PAN. Then the values are XORed and the result is encrypted.

Format 1 is used when the PAN is not available for some reason. In that case, the format, length and PIN value are packed into the block, and the result is padded to the full 16 digits with a unique transaction identifier or a random number.

Format 2 is used for local communications and is offline only. For instance, in case of an offline PIN validation by the integrated circuit card the EPB is formatted using format 2. The format is similar to vector 1 of format 0: the format indicator (2), length and the PIN value are padded to full block length with value of 15 (0xF). See section 5.3.10.5 for uses of this PIN block format.

Format 3 is also used for inter-host communications. It is similar to format 0, however, rather than using constant filler value of 15 (0xF), a string of random values from the range of 10 to 15 (i.e., hex 0xA to 0xF) is used to pad vector 1 to the full length of the block.

Format 4 is a 128-bit format defined to supplant Formats 0 and 3 in inter-host communications after performing the transition to PIN encryption with AES. The first 8 bytes of the block are padded with 0xF as in Format 0 and the second 8 bytes are filled with random values as in case of Format 3.

Consider the following examples. Let us assume the PAN is 9999990123456788 and the PIN is 4321. Let us also assume that the unique transaction number is 750923 (base 10).

In that case the PIN blocks look as follows:

Format 0 For vector 1 we take the format indicator (0), the PIN length (4) and pack the PIN and pad with 0xF. Vector 1 looks like follows (PIN digits are highlighted in **bold**): 04 **43 21** FF FF FF FF FF.

For vector 2 we take the last 12 digits of the PAN without the check digit and left-pad them with zeroes. The digits are highlighted in bold. 9999**990123456788**. Vector 2 looks like follows: 00 00 99 90 12 34 56 78.

Then the values are XOR-ed (easy to see the first two bytes are not modified by exclusive-OR) to obtain the block value of 04 43 B8 6F ED CB A9 87

Format 1 The beginning of the PIN block (first 6 nibbles) is composed of the format indicator, the length and the PIN value. They should be padded with a unique sequence number with 10 more nibbles. The hexadecimal value of the transaction number is 0xB754B and therefore the full value of the block is 14 43 21 00 00 0B 75 4B.

Format 2 As mentioned above, the PIN block is similar to vector 1 of format 0. The format indicator, the length and the PIN value are simply padded by 0xF: 24 43 21 FF FF FF FF FF

Format 3 For vector 1 we take the format indicator (3), the PIN length (4) and pack the PIN and pad with random values from the range of 0xA to 0xF. Vector 1 looks as follows (PIN digits are highlighted in bold): 34 43 21 AF CE DB BB AC. For vector 2 we take the last 12 digits of the PAN without the check digit and left-pad them with zeroes. The digits are highlighted in bold: 9999**990123456788**. Vector 2 looks like follows: 00 00 99 90 12 34 56 78.

Then the values are XOR-ed: 34 43 B8 3F DC EF ED D4

Format 4 For vector 1 the format indicator (4) and the PIN length (4) are padded to the length of 16 nibbles with value of 0xF. They fill out half of the vector's 16 bytes length. The second half of the vector is filled with random values: 44 43 21 FF FF FF FF FF DE AD BE EF DE AD BE EF

Vector 2 carries the PAN. Since the length allows it, the PAN is packed into the vector fully except for the check digit. The first nibble of the vector indicates how many digits there are in the PAN beyond the first 12.

In other words, after stripping the check digit the first nibble of vector 2 is exactly 0 for a 13-digit card number. For a more common 16-digit PAN the value is 3.

Vector 2 is further padded with zeros. Unlike formats 0 to 3, the values are not simply XORed: Vector 1 is encrypted using AES first, then XOR-ed with vector 2, then the result is encrypted again (i.e., CBC mode with a zero initialization vector is applied).

Index